Struggle and Hope

STUDIES IN COMPARATIVE ECONOMIC SYSTEMS

General Editors: Wladimir Andreff, *Professor of Economics at the University Paris 1 Panthéon Sorbonne and Director of ROSES*; Bruno Dallago, *Associate Professor of Economic Policy and Comparative Economic Systems at the University of Trento and President of EACES*; János Kornai, *Allie S. Freed Professor of Economics at Harvard University and Permanent Fellow at Collegium Budapest, Institute for Advanced Study;* and Hans-Jürgen Wagener, *Professor of Economics and Vice-Rector at the European University Viadrina at Frankfurt/Oder*

Recent developments in different economic systems have presented new challenges to economic theory and policy. Scholars in comparative economic systems have to debate and clarify the nature of the economic system, its place within the economy and the dynamics of its transformation in a comparative perspective.

This new series is designed to contribute to the debate and advance knowledge in the field. It will provide a forum for original comparative research on the economic system and economic performance including important aspects such as economic institutions and their change, economic actors and policy instruments in the transformation process.

The books published in this series will be written by leading international scholars writing in a theoretic or applied way and using either country-specific studies or cross-country comparisons. They will show how economic analysis can contribute to understanding and resolving one of the most important questions facing the world at present and in the future.

Struggle and Hope

Essays on Stabilization and Reform in a Post-Socialist Economy

János Kornai

Allie S. Freed Professor of Economics, Harvard University, US and Permanent Fellow, Institute for Advanced Study, Collegium Budapest, Hungary

STUDIES IN COMPARATIVE ECONOMIC SYSTEMS

Edward Elgar
Cheltenham, UK • Northampton, MA, USA

Published by
Edward Elgar Publishing Limited
8 Lansdown Place
Cheltenham
Glos GL50 2HU
UK

Edward Elgar Publishing, Inc.
6 Market Street
Northampton
Massachusetts 01060
USA

A catalogue record for this book
is available from the British Library

Library of Congress Cataloguing in Publication Data
Kornai, János
    Struggle and hope : essays on stabilization and reform in a
postsocialist economy / János Kornai.
    Studies in comparative economic systems
    Includes bibliographical references and indexes.
    1. Economic stabilization—Hungary.   2. Hungary—Economic
policy—1989–   3. Post-communism—Hungary.   4. Europe, Eastern—
Economic policy—1989–   5. Post-communism—Europe, Eastern.
6. Economic stabilization—Europe, Eastern.   I. Title.
HC300.283.K673   1997
338.9439—dc21   97–25017
                                                                          CIP

ISBN 1 85898 606 0 (cased)

Typeset by Manton Typesetters, 5–7 Eastfield Road, Louth, Lincolnshire LN11 7AJ, UK.
Printed and bound in Great Britain by Bookcraft (Bath) Ltd.

To Julcsi, Zsófi, Anna, Tomi and Miska

Contents

Figures

Tables

Preface

The writings in this volume first appeared between 1994 and 1996.[1] They discuss two subjects, as the subtitle conveys. The first is the equilibrium problems of the post-socialist economy – including the tensions caused by shortage, inflation, internal and external debt, current account and budget deficits – and the stabilization measures designed to surmount them. The second is reform of the welfare sector. The two subjects are closely linked by several strands, historical, political, economic and social, a fact which provides some justification for treating them in the same volume. The analysis of each subject is based on a study of Hungary's economic situation and Hungarian data, but the message extends Hungary's borders, containing ideas relevant to the problems of the whole post-socialist region.

The title of the book may seem dramatic to those who feel economists should remain dispassionate, examining matters solely in the cold light of the figures. I hope the content and tone of these writings, not just the title, will convey that their author has never forgotten that the ultimate subject of his researches is the fate of human beings, clarification of the causes behind their sufferings and successes, and ways of improving their prospects. I share the feelings of all those living in the post-socialist countries, as we struggle to escape from traps laid by decades of history, the sins, or in the best case, blunders, of our leaders and, let us admit, our own failures. How fine it would be if we could fly freely and establish some brave Utopias! For the legacy of the previous system will continue to weigh us down for decades to come. Society still struggles in fetters – and I refer here mainly to the years since 1990 – because the failures in the countries of the region have been compounded, the bold solutions postponed, and the politicians in office reluctant to address unpopular tasks. When the radical measures can no longer be postponed, they have so many painful side-effects that it is hard to watch without anguish and anxiety, even for those who devised them, or who have merely exerted an intellectual influence on their preparation.

I am fond of using similes from medicine and health in my writing. I know from medical friends that it is rare for a true doctor to be indifferent to a patient's suffering. It causes particular distress to order a painful operation or after-treatment, or prescribe bitter medicine that can hardly be swallowed.

[1] For a list of these studies and details of first English publication, see the Appendix.

Conscientious healers of the Hungarian economy's ills feel their tasks are distressing, because they themselves know the drawbacks of whatever remedy they propose. If the balance of payments has to be improved, that is likely to increase inflation. If the budget deficit has to be cut, that will make many people's lives harder, because they will receive fewer state benefits or pay more taxes. Many more examples could be given.

None the less, what eases the conscience of researchers addressing these problems is the knowledge that these sacrifices are not in vain. This is underlined by the second term in the title: hope. Perhaps this preface is the right place to make a personal confession on this matter. For a long time my writings were imbued with pessimism, explicitly or implicitly. I felt for decades that the researcher's task was to unveil the truth, even if that scientific achievement did *not* contribute to resolving the problem revealed. I thought the real, underlying problems of the socialist countries were determined by the socioeconomic *system*. So long as the system remained, the fundamental and deep-rooted problems could not be overcome.

That attitude to life was quite rightly adjusted with the change of system that began in 1989–90. I would not like to join those who fail to see the wood for the trees – who forget, amidst the present-day tribulations, that a fundamental change has taken place in our world. Nowadays it is far from hopeless to expect that some measure of reform will eventually lead to real improvements. In this sense I have changed from a pessimist into an optimist.

My optimism does not apply to the short term. I would like to abstain from any rosy forecasts. I set little store by claims that we still have a year or two's hardship ahead, but that by Year X there will be a perceptible improvement. The pronouncement remains the same, but Year X keeps advancing, so as to stay two or three years ahead.

My optimism rests on the fact that I have been dealing with comparative economics for very many years. I have tried to recognize the advantages and drawbacks of both the socialist and capitalist systems. It is plain from much of my writing that I have no illusions about the capitalist market economy. My expectations of it, even before 1990, were far more modest than those of many Eastern European intellectuals. Without fostering any illusions, or failing to take into consideration the dark side – the existence of troubles, injustices and sufferings – I think that capitalism exhibits superiority over socialism in the long term. It can provide greater productivity, greater welfare and greater freedom. The long term may turn out to be long indeed, and tensions and reverses may repeatedly ensue, but eventually this systemic advantage will make itself felt. It is on this conviction that I base the hope I would like to convey in the title of this book. This hope prompts me to go beyond a positive, explanatory analysis of specific phenomena, and put forward economic-policy proposals and reform concepts. I am confident that these can now play a constructive role, easing the difficulties and hardships of the transition, and preparing for structural changes with a lasting effect.

My ambition to go beyond the bounds of economics in the narrow sense is reflected not only in the title of the book and the style of some of the writing, but in its content. Eastern Europe is now encountering the mainstream of Western economics, in all its professionalism, severity and rigour. Now, as in the past, I am half in and half out of that mainstream. I have half stepped out of it, for one thing because I do not want to limit my works to the confines of a tight discipline. Most of the studies in this book touch on problems that belong to other disciplines, such as history, political science, sociology and psychology. I feel it a duty to discuss, in the case of some subjects, the aspects of political philosophy and ethics behind them. I consider myself a student and practitioner not only of economics in the narrow sense, but of social science. There will be some people for whom this lessens the value of my works. I hope there will also be readers inclined to think it a virtue.

Two years have elapsed since the publication of the earliest piece in this volume and the time of writing this preface, and they have not been just any two years. They were replete with events and changes of great import. I felt it would not be right to bring these writings completely up to date. I vouch for them as they appeared, even with mistakes. So apart from some small adjustments (correcting minor errors and stylistic infelicities, and eliminating some overlaps between them), each of the contributions appears in this book in the form in which it was originally published.

Where I feel I have something important to add, I have done so, but in a way that clearly informs the reader: this is a new footnote, or a new afterword added to the study. I think that intellectual honesty dictates this procedure.

I also feel it a duty to inform the reader if I have altered my earlier opinion on some essential matter. I may now hesitate about whether my earlier view is correct, or I may have realized that my previous opinion was false. Readers will find such self-questioning in several places, either in the form of critical remarks in a later study about an earlier one, or as a new footnote or afterword of the kind I have mentioned, conveying my altered position.

In some places, this procedure may make it harder for readers to keep track. But at least they will sense that they have before them the work of an author who is himself wrestling with the great difficulties of the problems he examines.

Finally, I would like to express my gratitude to those who have cooperated in compiling this book. Let me single out first of all the contribution made by Mária Kovács, whose meticulous, circumspect attention to every detail and many wise suggestions have been of inestimable help, as they have in all my work for many years. I am also thankful for the research assistance of Ágnes Benedict, Mónika Lukács, Miguel Messmacher and Judit Rimler. I am grateful to Brian McLean, who has translated almost all my writings into English for several years, identifying fully with the text, and conveying my message with fidelity, subtlety and force of expression. My thanks go also to András Malatinszky, for his contribution to the translation of Chapter 2, and to Pál Olchváry, who translated Chapter 7. Julianna Parti's precise and reliable editing has been of the greatest assistance. Tibor Szendrei gave valuable help with computerizing the figures. Apart from those mentioned, several institutions and many colleagues of mine have given me great support. I have expressed gratitude to them in the first footnote of each chapter.

I express my thanks to Mr Edward Elgar, for undertaking to publish this book, and to the staff of Edward Elgar Publishing Limited for their conscientious work in editing and publishing it. I am delighted that these writings, most of which had, singly, reached only the relatively small readership of a learned journal, can now appear in volume form, before a wider public of those interested in the post-socialist transition.

János Kornai

1. Eliminating the shortage economy: a general analysis and examination of developments in Hungary[1]

1. INTRODUCTION

One of the most typical features of the classical socialist system is a shortage economy:

> An economic system is a shortage economy if the following conditions coincide: shortage phenomena are (1) general, that is, found in all spheres of the economy (in trade in goods and services for consumers, in means of production, including investment goods, in labour, in exported and imported products, and in international means of payment); (2) frequent, and not only exceptional or sporadic; (3) intensive, making their influence felt very strongly on the behaviour and environment of participants in the economy and the traits and results of the economic processes; and (4) chronic, applying constantly, not just occurring temporarily.[2]

The transfer to a capitalist market economy is accompanied by the elimination of this shortage economy.

This chapter considers the problem on two planes. One is the plane of general analysis, where the specific historical situation, differing from country to country, is disregarded. The other plane uses an examination of developments in Hungary as an illustration of what is said. Although there are occasional references to the situation in other countries, I do not attempt to provide any comprehensive comparative analysis. The chapter alternates between the general and the Hungarian plane.

This research is an integral continuation of my earlier work on the subject of shortage, which began with *Overcentralization in Economic Administration*,

[1] I would like to thank all those who commented on the initial versions of this study, particularly, for their valuable advice, Francis Bator, Zsuzsa Dániel, István R. Gábor, János Gács, János Köllő, Mária Lackó, John Litwack, Gérard Roland, András Simonovits, David Stark, Katalin Szabó and Éva Várhegyi. My researches were supported by the Hungarian National Scientific Research Foundation (OTKA), the European Bank for Reconstruction and Development, and Collegium Budapest, Institute for Advanced Study, to which I would also like to express my thanks here.
[2] See Kornai (1992d), p. 233.

summed up initially in *Economics of Shortage*, and was drawn together
comprehensively in *The Socialist System*. My assumption in writing this
chapter has been that its readers will be conversant with the literature on
shortage economy and familiar with the concepts employed in it.[3]

A wide-ranging debate on the shortage phenomena that appear under the
socialist system has begun in the last 15 years, with argument about the
conceptual apparatus, measurement of the shortages and, above all, their
causes. This chapter does not undertake to provide an intellectual history of
this field, or to clarify the extent to which various views have been confirmed
or denied by subsequent historical developments. My own ideas have undergone many changes since I began to deal with this subject. I have tried to
utilize what I have learnt from others to revise and develop further my own
ideas, and at the same time to produce a synthesis.[4] It was in accordance with
this aim that I formulated, in relation to the socialist economy, the chapters
dealing with shortage in my book *The Socialist System*, and the present study,
concerned with the present and future of the post-socialist economy, has been
conceived in the same spirit.

Numerous authors are studying the elimination of the shortage economy
under the post-socialist system. For most of them this is not the main subject
of their examination, but is one of the questions touched on. Let me mention
in particular the studies of Berg and Sachs (1992), Laski *et al.* (1993), Rosati
(1993) and Zukowski (1993), which have had a thought-provoking effect on
my own work.

Section 2 of this chapter describes the phenomena observed during the
elimination of the shortage economy. The subject of Section 3 is causal
analysis. Section 4 concerns the relations between the elimination of the
shortages and the state of the labour market. Finally, Section 5 assesses the
changes.

---

[3] See Kornai (1959 [1957], Chapter IV, 1980 and 1992d). For a recapitulation of the debates on
shortage, I recommend Kornai (1992d), Chapters 11, 12 and 15, Hare (1989), and van Brabant
(1990).

[4] I had already delved deeply into earlier works when I was writing *Economics of Shortage*.
References to these can be found in Kornai (1980), pp. 29–30 and 133, and Kornai (1992d),
pp. 228–9. Here I would like to mention (for simplicity's sake in alphabetical order) all the
economists who have taken part in analytical clarification in this field since 1980, and from
whose works I have learnt a great deal: the Hungarian researchers Tamás Bauer, Attila Chikán,
Zsuzsa Dániel, János Gács, Zsuzsa Kapitány, Mária Lackó, Béla Martos, András Simon, András
Simonovits, Attila Károly Soós, and Judit Szabó, and the foreign researchers Robert J. Barro,
Jean-Pascal Benassy, John P. Burkett, Wojciech W. Charemza, Christopher Davis, Stephen M.
Goldfeld, Stanislaw Gomulka, Irena Grosfeld, Herschel I. Grossman, Paul Hare, Domenico M.
Nuti, Richard Portes, Richard E. Quandt, Jörgen W. Weibull and David Winter. Those listed
have published several studies, but for brevity's sake the list of references includes only a
single, representative publication for each author not quoted elsewhere in this study.

2. THE PHENOMENA OBSERVED DURING THE CHANGES

This section has a dual purpose. The first aim is to illustrate the ways in which the process of eliminating the shortage economy can be observed and measured.[5] This is all the more important because the chapter will go on to suggest that the process is closely connected with the change of system. So establishing what stage some country has reached in the elimination of the shortage economy also gains us some important information about its progress in relation to the change of system.

The other purpose of the section is to present the specific changes in Hungary, on the level of the phenomena, as they are perceived by the buyers of products and services.

2.1 Producers' Goods

One of the characteristics of the chronic shortage economy is that disturbances, delays and often grave damage in production are frequently caused by shortages of various inputs (materials, semi-finished products, components, equipment or labour). Producers often perform a forced substitution; production may be suspended for longer or shorter periods because some indispensable input happens to be in short supply. Shortage phenomena form the commonest constraint on production growth in the processes of instantaneous and short-term adjustment, rather than any difficulties with sales.

In a mature market economy, this situation is reversed. There may be sporadic problems with obtaining inputs there as well, but far more frequent and abiding constraints are placed on production by a shortage of orders and sales difficulties. With this phenomenon in mind, I have called the former a *resource-constrained* system and the latter a *demand-constrained* system.[6] In some cases it is not the physical resource itself that forms the effective constraint, but the quantity of it that is placed at the user's disposal as a supply. So the pair of concepts of a *supply-constrained* and a *demand-constrained* system can be used more or less synonymously with the previous pair. A pure case of one or the other never arises in real economies; both the supply side and the demand side can act as a constraint on the micro level.

---

[5] The verb 'illustrate' here does not imply that I am promising a full and comprehensive methodology, but merely offering a few illustrations of practicable and effective methods of observation and measurement.

[6] I first published this pair of concepts in my (1979) study. For literary antecedents of this see Kornai (1992d), p. 292.

When comparing the systems, it is enough to clarify which side plays a dominant role in constraining production.[7]

Under reform socialism, and then during the post-socialist transition, the economy moves away and then switches from a resource-constrained (supply-constrained) regime to a demand-constrained regime. This process has already taken place in Hungary, as Table 1.1 shows. The role of the input constraints has been reduced to insignificance, while that of the demand constraints has grown strongly. So production is no longer occurring under the conditions of a shortage economy customary for decades. According to Table 1.1, the change was not a sudden one, but happened gradually.

To illustrate the way many experts on the socialist and post-socialist economy evaluate the change in a similar conceptual framework, let me give a few quotations. In Czechoslovakia, where the switch took place very quickly, Vintrová writes, 'With unexpected speed, the predominantly "supply-limited" (deficit) Czechoslovak economy has turned into one that is entirely "demand-limited", even though a number of structural deficits still survive owing to rigidity and new ones are appearing. But almost overnight the main problem has become the lack of sales.' Rosati establishes that the changing macroeconomic conditions in Poland 'are all symptoms of transforming the Kornai-type, supply-constrained economy into a Keynesian-type, demand-constrained one'. Zukowski, in another article on Poland, states after describing the shifts in supply and demand, 'In this way, a resource-restrained system turns into a demand-restrained one.'[8]

Under a resource-constrained (supply-constrained) system, the producer is uncertain about the acquisition of inputs, and so a hoarding tendency develops. Stocks accumulate primarily on the procurement side of the firm, whereas sales are easy due to the chronic shortage, so that stocks on the sales side are relatively small. The situation under a demand-constrained system is reversed, since procurement is easy, but selling is difficult. According to this train of thought, the ratio between the stocks of inputs and outputs will be a good reflection of which side is dominant in the constraint on production. Table 1.2 gives international figures for comparison and shows the change in Hungary. An essential shift has occurred in the ratio between the two kinds of stocks, although this has yet to reach the ratio typical of a mature market economy.[9]

---

[7] The subject of this dichotomy is the effective constraints on the *instantaneous* growth of production. It is another matter to say what factors determine the allocation of resources and the volume and structure of production *in the long term*, and what role is played in this by the demand and supply sides. This chapter does not deal with the latter topic.

[8] See Vintrová (1993), p. 84, Rosati (1993), p. 251, and Zukowski (1993), p. 1175.

[9] To avoid any misunderstanding, let me stress that I am not examining here the ratio of total stocks to total production, though this is a most important indicator as well, representing the efficiency of production and turnover and of coordination. Here the post-socialist economies of Eastern Europe still make rather a poor showing, but this is another matter. The subject of this

Table 1.1   Impediments to production: Hungarian survey data (in %)

Quarter	Insufficient demand	Shortage of labour	Insufficient supply of raw materials and spare parts			Financing problems
			Domestic origin	Imported		
				Rouble area	Dollar area	
1987:1	26.0	22.2	41.2	42.6		31.2
2	27.4	23.7	42.3	46.7		24.3
3	21.3	24.1	46.6	50.4		22.1
4	24.1	15.8	39.4	41.8		20.4
1988:1	28.0	15.7	50.0	16.6	32.8	32.7
2	28.3	24.7	44.1	17.2	35.3	36.4
3	27.3	23.0	45.3	18.2	64.0	35.0
4	30.7	19.3	38.5	14.9	22.4	40.1
1989:1	38.0	21.5	37.6	14.4	17.9	49.6
2	40.1	22.0	28.7	11.0	11.8	46.1
3	40.4	21.9	27.5	10.3	8.9	46.8
4	51.2	13.4	21.4	8.0	6.3	49.4
1990:1	51.3	12.1	13.8	5.8	3.9	57.8
2	56.1	13.9	13.0	3.4	2.2	45.2
3	51.0	10.3	15.3	4.6	5.2	51.9
4	54.5	4.3	11.3	3.2	3.7	48.7
1991:1	60.6	4.3	9.4	2.3	2.6	53.2
2	70.1	4.0	7.1	1.5	2.4	54.1
3	66.8	3.3	6.2	1.2	2.0	52.7
4	65.9	3.0	7.2	0.5	1.0	47.3
1992:1	65.1	3.3	5.8	0.3	1.0	51.0
2	62.2	7.4	5.9	0.7	1.5	45.9
3	56.1	4.4	10.6	1.7	3.1	47.8
4	54.5	4.8	8.7	0.7	2.3	42.9
1993:1	57.7	2.2	6.1	1.3		45.5
2	66.3	3.0	8.1	3.3		47.2
3	67.9	3.7	7.5	3.1		48.6
4	62.5	4.3	9.4	2.4		47.3

Note: The survey applies the methodology elaborated by the German research institute IFO and used in several other countries. Respondents are asked to cite 'impediments to production'. Each respondent can mention as many impediments as desired. The figures show relative frequencies in percentages. (For example, in the first quarter of 1987, 26% of respondents mentioned insufficient demand, alongside other factors.) There are other impediments mentioned by the respondents but not included in the table. The rouble area refers to the former member countries of Comecon. The survey did not distinguish the rouble area and the dollar area in 1987 or in 1993. The data for these two years refer to all imported raw materials and spare parts.

Source: Kopint-Datorg (1994).

Table 1.2   Ratio of input and output stocks in manufacturing

Country	Input stocks/output stocks						
	1981–85	1986	1987	1988	1989	1990	1991
Capitalist countries							
Austria	1.06	1.13	1.15	1.27	1.32	–	–
Canada	0.92	1.04	–	1.12	1.05	–	–
Finland	1.92	1.60	1.72	1.76	1.75	1.45	–
Japan	1.09	0.71	0.71	0.72	0.74	–	–
Portugal	1.66	1.31	1.53	–	–	–	–
United States	1.02	1.02	1.04	1.05	1.03	0.99	–
Hungary	6.10	–	–	5.16	4.65	3.50	2.67

Source: Compiled by Attila Chikán on the basis of the following sources: United Nations (1992) and Chikán (1994).

Still, this meaningful index again shows that Hungary has moved most of the way towards eliminating the shortage economy apparent in production.

Here again, the change is a gradual one. Worth noting, however, is the way the shift in proportions accelerated at the beginning of the 1990s.

2.2   Consumer Goods

If this study were about the Soviet Union's successor states, or Poland or Romania, it would be necessary to recall and describe numerically the period before the change of system, when there was still a serious shortage of basic foodstuffs, fuel or other indispensable consumer goods. The state of acute shortage then would have to be compared with the present position. In Hungary these most excruciating shortages ceased much earlier, in the 1970s. Steady progress was made in eliminating the shortage economy in consumer goods and services, as in producers' goods. The various phenomena of shortage occurred more rarely or less intensively in the case of more and more products, groups of products or whole sectors. The long queues for goods became shorter, and then ceased altogether. Forced substitution occurred more rarely; it became more common for the buyer to find the originally sought good or service without any difficulty.

chapter is elimination of the shortage economy, in analysing which attention must be on the *internal composition* of stocks, that is the ratio of input stocks to output stocks, not the ratio of stocks to production.

Let me mention as examples three groups of products where the shortage economy survived in rearguard positions in Hungary. One is motor cars. Table 1.3 gives the main figures about queuing for new cars. The table ends with 1992, since when there has been no queuing due to shortages.[10] On the contrary, car dealers have been holding considerable unsold stocks.

Table 1.3   Queuing for new cars in Hungary

Year	Cars sold without queuing (%)	Cars sold after queuing (%)	Waiting period (years)
1982	21.5	78.5	2.6
1983	25.3	74.7	2.4
1984	23.6	76.4	2.1
1985	24.4	75.6	1.9
1986	22.5	77.5	2.0
1987	24.5	75.6	1.9
1988	23.2	76.8	2.3
1989	42.7	57.3	2.9
1990	52.3	47.7	2.3
1991	93.8	6.2	1.2
1992	100.0	0.0	–

Source: Compiled by Zsuzsa Kapitány on the basis of the following sources: 1982–88: Kapitány (1989), pp. 593 and 595; 1989–92: Kapitány (1993), pp. 45–6.

The second group consists of products to do with electronics, information technology and telecommunications. In the 1980s, the range of such products imported by the state foreign-trade companies or manufactured by the state-owned firms was extremely limited. The shortage was severe, and was eased only by semi-legal or absolutely illegal imports. Such imports were swelled at a later stage by what was known as shopping tourism, this being one of the groups of products on which it was concentrated. Since 1992–93, the choice in Hungary has been ample, and sellers are experiencing sales difficulties.

The third example is housing, which is worth mentioning not only because of its exceptional influence on the standard of living, but because there are

---

[10] Even in a mature market economy, it may be necessary to wait several weeks for the delivery of a car if the customer does not buy from stock, but makes special requests for a certain combination of various quality criteria (colour, features, and so on). But the length of this waiting period depends solely on organizational and technical factors, and cannot be considered a phenomenon of shortage. There is a technical-cum-organizational waiting period of this kind in Hungary as well, of course.

several important concepts and relations which can be clarified by taking it as an example.

There are some logically distinguishable phenomena that are frequently confused. One is *housing shortage*. A shortage exists if the potential tenant of a rented flat or the potential buyer of an owner-occupied dwelling is prepared to pay the going price, but the transaction fails to take place at this going price because of a shortage of supply. There is excess demand for housing. The opposite case is where the landlord of the rented accommodation offers the rights of tenancy to a potential tenant, or the owner of a dwelling offers the rights of ownership to a potential buyer, but the tenant/buyer does not have enough money to pay the desired rent or purchase price. The problem the tenant is struggling with is not shortage, but *affordability*. On his or her present and likely future income, he or she cannot afford to spend the specified amount on housing, or, colloquially, cannot obtain housing for *lack of money*. In this case there is excess supply of housing.

We need to describe housing shortage in more detail in order to characterize the state of the housing sector. Reference is made to a 'housing shortage' without qualification (or possibly to a 'general housing shortage') when the shortages in that sector are frequent, intensive and chronic. But there can be shortages in particular geographical areas or in particular types of housing even when a general, intensive and chronic shortage of housing is not characteristic of the sector.

That leads on to a discussion of the next phenomenon: *choice of housing*. Even in economies where there is an excess supply of both rented and owner-occupied housing, the choice may be narrow. Dwellings are among the most varied of goods, whose quality is determined by a very large number of characteristics. The choice will grow as a function of the development of the economy (and within it the housing sector) and of the refinement and adaptiveness of the coordination mechanism. Even when there is excess supply in a group of goods as a whole, the satisfaction of buyers' demands depends on how wide or how narrow, and how efficient is the market in which the transactions take place.

Finally, a distinction must be drawn between what has been discussed so far and the actual *housing situation*, the consumption of housing. Regardless of whether the shortage, the effective constraint, lies in the supply of housing or the purse of the tenant or buyer, the actual tenancy or sale transactions take place in the end. The housing sector contains a finite stock of housing at a certain time which will be allocated one way or another. A high proportion of the dwellings in poorer, more backward countries are cramped and low in quality. Many people live in squalor. This depressing reality may hold equally if there is excess demand in the market, in other words a housing shortage, or if there is excess supply, and households do not have enough money to create for themselves the housing conditions they desire.

A severe, chronic housing shortage developed everywhere under the classical socialist system. This was the case in Hungary as well, but later, in the decades after the 1968 reform, the housing shortage steadily eased.[11] Even today, two phenomena exist side by side. There is still excess demand for state-owned housing that can be rented for bureaucratically prescribed and set rents, much lower than the rents prevailing in the market. But this segment represents a smaller and smaller proportion of the national housing stock, less than one fifth in 1993, though more in the cities, particularly Budapest. Even in this segment the shortage is eased by a 'grey market': an existing tenant can pass the tenancy on to a new tenant in exchange for a sum of money agreed between them. Meanwhile the majority of housing is already in private hands. One of the main changes in the 1990s has been the lifting of certain oppressive, bureaucratic restrictions on the housing market. For instance, the administrative constraint marked by the principle of 'one family, one dwelling' was lifted in 1989, and the rents of privately owned dwellings and sub-tenancies were freed.

Hungary now has an available supply, free of bureaucratic constraints, of all kinds of dwelling, but the choice is meagre, in other words the housing market is fairly narrow. In this sense the housing sector as a whole no longer has a shortage-economy character. Anyone with the money can rent or buy a dwelling. According to the definitions given earlier, this statement is compatible with the assertion that the housing conditions of wide sections of the population are unsatisfactory, and some groups are living in squalor.

2.3 Summary

The Hungarian economy can no longer be called a shortage economy. Although there are sporadic occurrences of shortage in almost every sphere, the same can be said of mature market economies as well. There are certain well-defined sectors operating on a non-market, non-commercial basis (such as health care), in which intensive and chronic shortages appear, but the situation is similar in these very sectors to that of many mature market economies as well. Looking at the economy as a whole, however, it can be said that *in this respect* Hungary has arrived at the state typical of market economies.

The specific feature of development in Hungary has been that this narrowing down of the shortages and subsequent elimination of the shortage economy have taken place gradually, over a very protracted period.[12,13] The process then speeded up in the late 1980s, particularly after the change of political system.

---

[11] See the studies by Dániel (1989) and Buckley, Dániel and Thalwitz (1993).
[12] In this respect the course of China's transformation resembles Hungary's.
[13] *New note:* On the gradual nature of Hungarian development, see Chapter 5.

3. CAUSAL ANALYSIS

Many people attribute the elimination of the shortage economy to a single factor, for instance the freeing of prices or the restrictive monetary policy pursued. Attempts are commonly made to derive the phenomena of the shortage economy from the well-known relations between demand, supply and prices. In this chapter a more complex explanation is advanced. Great significance is attached to the effects of political and institutional changes, as well as economic factors in the narrow sense. Instead of attempting to explain the end of the shortage economy exclusively in terms of macroeconomic or microeconomic factors, I shall employ both approaches.

3.1 Privatization, Decentralization and Deregulation

A broad class of institutional changes will be reviewed here.[14]

3.1.1 Greater freedom of entry and the appearance of new private firms

There is no free enterprise under classical socialism. Large production units established by the party-state – state firms and quasi-state agricultural cooperatives – operate almost exclusively. The creation of every new firm is the result of a sluggish and protracted process of bureaucratic decision-making. The fact that there is a shortage of some product or service will not induce the birth of a new firm.

The capitalist market economy, on the other hand, is marked by freedom of entry.[15] Shortage gives a strong incentive for a new business to enter and meet it, since it offers special opportunities for profits. Even if the firms already operating ignore the shortage signals, the new firms will become capable sooner or later of plugging the gap.

The scope for entry has been steadily widening in the Hungarian economy, with more and more firms being founded (see Tables 5.14 and 5.15). A high proportion of the new entries can be seen to have occurred in fields where there used to be a shortage.

---

[14] The reform of the socialist economy and the subsequent post-socialist transformation brought numerous other institutional changes that likewise contributed to eliminating the shortage economy; these will be mentioned later in the chapter.

[15] Here I ignore for now the existence of administrative constraints in certain segments and the fact that the presence of strong firms already operating in a market impedes the entry of a newcomer entrepreneur.

3.1.2 Import liberalization

Under classical socialism, imports are surrounded by strict administrative constraints. When a shortage in a certain product appears, the decision-makers in the bureaucracy are not automatically persuaded to import it. There will be imports to make up for the shortage if they see fit, but they may equally well refrain from such a measure, obliging the buyer to make a forced substitution, or if this does not happen, they simply acknowledge the persistence of the shortage.

A developed market economy does not normally have any import restrictions of this kind, which might cause a shortage to appear in domestic supplies.[16] Excess demand induces imports, since there are prospects of above-average profits. Liberalized imports are largely capable of eliminating many shortages in tradable goods and services, even where domestic producers are unable or unwilling to satisfy the excess demand.

Hungary has undergone a gradual liberalization of imports in several stages over the last ten or fifteen years, so that by 1992–93 they had become almost free of administrative controls[17] (Table 1.4).

The role of imports in compensating for shortages has been made easier by the change mentioned under 3.1.1, greater freedom of entry. Large numbers of new, private, foreign-trading firms have appeared. There used to be a few dozen large state-owned foreign-trade firms, each largely monopolizing the imports of a certain group of products, but they are now replaced or joined as competitors by a myriad of new foreign-trading undertakings large and small, which try to move quickly into every domestic market left unsatisfied by domestic production.

3.1.3 Elimination of the system of directives

Under classical socialism, state-owned and quasi-state firms are prescribed detailed, obligatory output targets and input quotas. The intricacy and rigidity of this system of commands and the insensitivity of the planners drawing up the directives to the needs of users and consumers contribute to the widespread friction in the coordination processes, to the weakness of the economy's ability to adapt, and so to the occurrence of shortages.

The system of directives came to an end in Hungary after the 1968 reform, and the autonomy of state-owned firms increased. Although their autonomy was still curbed by various kinds of bureaucratic interference, their activity

---

16 Import quotas are imposed for trade-policy reasons in many developed market economies. Restrictions are normally placed for protectionist reasons on products for which domestic producers can fully supply the market. So in these circumstances the import restrictions do not generate a shortage.

17 On the history of import liberalization and its completion during the post-socialist transition, see the studies of Gács (1991b and 1994), and also Chapter 5, note 70.

Struggle and hope

Table 1.4   The proportion of liberalized products in Hungary's imports

Branch/sector	Proportion of liberalized products as a percentage of turnover		Proportion of liberalized products as a percentage of turnover in 1988		
	1989	1990	1991	1992	1993
Mining	0	4	51.6	98.8	98.8
Power generation	–	–	100.0	100.0	100.0
Metallurgy	0	67	92.7	99.6	99.6
Engineering	86	89	98.0	99.7	99.7
Building materials	31	28	100.0	100.0	100.0
Chemicals	2	73	85.9	89.2	89.2
Light industry	6	45	54.4	69.2	69.3
Other industry	0	43	–	–	–
Food industry	60	60	10.9	10.9	10.9
Total industry	*43*	*71*	*71.6*	*77.4*	*77.5*
Agriculture	24	36	–	–	–
Forestry	0	100	–	–	–
Total imports	*42*	*69*	–	–	–

Note: The data for 1990 refer to January–October. The data for the periods 1989–90 and 1991–93 are not directly comparable.

Sources: 1989 and 1990: Gács (1991a), p. 9. 1991–93: Compiled by Zsolt Macskási based on data from the Ministry of International Economic Relations.

became more flexible than before. This contributed to the fact that instances of shortage were less frequent and intensive in the reform socialist economy than they had been before the reform.

3.1.4   Hardening of the budget constraint on firms

The budget constraint on state-owned and quasi-state firms under classical socialism is soft. The state ensures their survival even if they make persistent losses. As a result, they have a weak responsiveness to prices and costs: they do not react strongly to the signals of relative prices, and make no great efforts to reduce their costs. This insensitivity to prices and costs appears on both the supply and the demand sides, blunting the firms' ability to adapt.

The budget constraint on firms in a mature capitalist market economy is hard. Firms maximize their profits. Persistent losses or insolvency lead to bankruptcy and ultimately to liquidation. Business behaviour cannot be based on the assumption that the state will bail a firm out; this only happens exceptionally. So firms are strongly responsive to prices and costs. They strive to react to changes in relative prices on both the supply and the demand sides, and make great efforts to reduce costs. This, under the conditions of a mature market economy, applies both to private firms and state-owned firms, so long as the state sector remains fairly small and the state has not become accustomed to protecting its firms in a paternalist way.

Looking at the economy as a whole, Hungary has undergone a gradual hardening of the budget constraint.[18] There are two main factors involved in this process:

1. The relative size of the private sector has been growing steadily and continues to grow, partly through the privatization of state-owned firms, and partly through the appearance of new private firms. Private firms usually have a hard budget constraint from birth; the vast majority cannot expect financial help from the state.
2. Firms previously and still in state ownership progressively realize that their survival is not guaranteed. From time to time this learning process has speeded up. The political changeover in 1990 acted as a warning that the privileged status of the state sector was coming to an end. The new, post-socialist political authorities made it plain that the future belonged to the private sector; the very prospect of privatization made questionable the automatic guarantee of survival extended in the past. On top of this came the experience of initially occasional, and then proliferating bankruptcies and liquidations. It was finally made plain by the new Bankruptcy Act of 1991 and the subsequent surge of bankruptcies that the age of the soft budget constraint had passed. Although the process is by no means over, as symptoms of a soft budget constraint repeatedly recur, confidence in automatically guaranteed survival has been dispelled. The price- and cost-sensitivity of the firms in temporary and permanent state ownership has accordingly grown.

3.1.5   The freeing of prices and dismantling of price subsidies

With few exceptions, prices under classical socialism are set centrally and remain fixed for a long time. The main role in the allocation of producers' goods is played by planning commands; the effect of prices is weak, due to the circumstance mentioned in 3.1.4, the softness of the budget constraint. However, prices have, of course, the customary effect on demand from households, where the budget constraint is hard. Since a high proportion of consumer goods and services have unrealistically low prices, made possible

---

[18] See Kornai (1993a).

by price subsidies provided by the budget, excess demand for them develops.

A process of gradual freeing of prices already began in Hungary with the 1968 reform. This accelerated in the late 1980s and particularly in the 1990s, after the political changeover (Tables 1.5 and 1.6). The process has still not run its course completely: state price regulation remains not only where it is usual, even in economies that strictly limit state intervention (such as cases of a natural monopoly), but in other spheres as well.[19] It can be stated none the less that the degree of price liberalization in Hungary is quite close to that prevailing in many mature European market economies.

Parallel with the deregulation and liberalization of price-setting, the gradual removal of price subsidies is taking place.[20] As a result, by 1993–94 Hungary

Table 1.5   Changes in proportions of market prices in the production sphere

Branch	Percentage of market-priced goods in domestic sales								
	1968	1975	1980	1985	1988	1990	1991	1992	1993
Mining	21	25	30	20	25	25	50	75	75
Power generation	5	7	7	10	10	10	10	10	10
Metallurgy	2	31	96	96	96	96	100	100	100
Engineering	61	86	100	100	100	100	100	100	100
Building materials	57	75	80	84	100	100	100	100	100
Chemicals	43	49	60	55	56	60·	90	100	100
Light industry	88	91	94	98	100	100	100	100	100
Food industry	78	87	93	92	97	97	100	100	100
Total industry	*58*	*71*	*81*	–	–	–	–	–	–
Construction	45	13	13	35	100	100	100	100	100
Agriculture (procurement)	16	37	37	40	50	82	85	100	100
Transport, telecom	0	10	10	25	35	60	60	60	60
Water management	0	10	10	15	25	25	25	25	25
Trade (mark-up)	0	65	1003	97	97	95	98	98	98
All material branches	–	*57*	*67*	*68*	*78*	*83*	*80*	*90*	*90*

Sources: 1968–90: compiled by Mónika Lukács on the basis of calculations by Jolán Ritter Papp and András Bodócsi, 1991–93: compiled by Eszter Szabó Bakos on the basis of estimates by the Economic Control Department of the Hungarian Ministry of Finance.

[19] From time to time the government, presumably with an eye to political popularity, took measures diametrically opposed to the general trend of liberalizing prices. For example in 1993 there was a freeze on the rents for state-owned accommodation, which, for a time, preserved the shortage phenomena and severe financing problems in this important sector.
[20] Budget spending on consumer price subsidies was equivalent to 5.5 per cent of GDP in 1986 and 0.7 per cent in 1993. See Muraközy (1993), p. 39.

Table 1.6   Changes in the proportion of market prices among consumer-goods prices

Consumer goods	Percentage of market-priced goods (domestic sales = 100)							
	1968	1978	1985	1988	1990	1991	1992	1993
Foodstuffs	13	22	36	73	91	94	100	100
Other comestibles	0	0	29	100	100	100	100	100
Clothing, textiles	25	89	97	100	100	100	100	100
Ironmongery, technical goods	13	85	6	100	100	100	100	100
Furniture	0	0	97	100	100	100	100	100
Vehicles	0	0	22	24	100	100	100	100
Household chemicals	0	0	69	91	100	100	100	100
Cultural articles	0	0	86	91	99	100	100	100
Petroleum products	0	0	30	0	4	100	100	100
Building materials, timber goods	9	0	70	100	100	100	100	100
Fuels	0	0	2	5	2	34	100	100
Medical goods	0	0	5	9	100	100	100	100
Other industrial goods	0	0	91	100	100	100	100	100
Total retail spending	17	50	–	80	84	90	100	100
Power, district heating, other household energy	0	0	0	0	0	11	40	40
Water rates	0	0	0	0	0	0	0	0
Rent, housing investment[a]	0	0	80	82	82	82	–	–
Free-market turnover	0	100	100	100	100	100	100	100
Other services	0	0	–	–	–	79	75	75
Total personal spending	*21*	*45*	*57*	*80*	*85*	*91*	*93*	*93*

Note: [a] In 1993 prices for housing were free and there was an upper limit on rents.

Source: Compiled by Mónika Lukács and Eszter Szabó Bakos based on calculations by Jolán Papp Ritter and the Economic Control Department of the Ministry of Finance, and data from the Central Statistical Office.

had developed a relative price system closely approximating to a market system of prices.[21]

[21] It was mentioned in Section 2.2 that the shortage phenomena have not yet ceased in certain sectors (for example health care). This is connected, among other things, with the fact that the institutional changes described under 3.1.1–3.1.5 have not yet taken place in these sectors.

Here I merely record the situation. This chapter does not set out to decide to what extent it is desirable for these sectors to be privatized, decentralized and deregulated. There are several ethical, social and economic criteria in this connection that need weighing in conjunction with each other (see Chapters 7 and 8). However, the experience during the post-socialist transformation in Hungary confirms that without institutional changes pointing in this direction, the shortage in these sectors will remain, even though the shortage economy may be eliminated from the economic environment as a whole.

3.2   Improving the Adaptiveness of Production

The institutional changes listed will together cause production to adapt more flexibly and readily, and with less friction, to the prevailing market situation on both the supply and the demand sides. Remaining within the immediate subject of this chapter, I shall discuss only excess demand. (The effect of excess supply is opposite in its direction.) The presence of excess demand will evoke reactions that will lead to its decline: (i) price adjustment, more specifically a relative rise in prices, and/or (ii) quantitative adjustment, that is an increase in the supply and a decrease in the demand.

A quantitative adjustment may be induced either by direct perception of excess demand or by a price change. Price changes can now exert a stronger effect because firms as well as households are cost- and price-sensitive. Some of the quantitative adjustment is short-term, achievable on existing production capacity, and some long-term, requiring the creation of new capacity. Even if the desire to invest is present, this takes time. Meanwhile price adjustment and short-term quantitative adjustment will be used to overcome the shortage.

Readers will be able to trace point by point how the adaptive processes described here, well known from market theory, become dominant as quickly and in as wide a sphere as the first five institutional changes described in the previous section. The generators of price and quantitative adjustment are free entry and imports, freeing of producers from the rigidities of planning commands, the hardening of the budget constraint, that is the imperative of profitability, and the free movement of prices.

As a result of the institutional changes, there develops the market situation known since the days of Adam Smith as *sellers' competition*.[22] This replaces the earlier regime, which was marked by *buyers' competition*. The concept of competition was dimmed and drained of blood in the eyes of economists by the pure Walrasian theory of perfect competition, which described an extreme, pure market situation in which atomized buyers and sellers conduct transactions, prices are set by anonymous processes, products are perfectly standardized, and so on. Perhaps people moving from socialism to capitalism may be able to sense more plainly that in the previous situation and in the new, true rivalry has occurred in most areas of the economy, so that not everyone is satisfied: there are winners and losers. Either the seller has an advantage over the buyer or the buyer has an advantage over the seller. The latter situation develops if any of the versions of *imperfect competition* apply in the market,[23] the most widespread form of competition in all modern

---

[22] See Smith (1898) [1776], p. 43.

[23] The pioneers of the theory of imperfect competition were Chamberlin (1962) [1933] and Robinson (1933). Of the present-day literature, I would mention particularly the works by Dixit and Stiglitz (1977), Hart (1985), Krugman (1979) and Kuenne (1967).

market economies, and this is already the situation in Hungary today. Let me summarize the main characteristics of imperfect competition.

The seller[24] offers the buyer a differentiated, not a standardized product. Although there are close substitutes for the product (otherwise he or she would be a monopolist), the offer differs from that of others in quality, packaging, geographical proximity to the buyer, speed of delivery, conditions of payment, and so on.

With perfect competition, the seller is a price-taker, receiving the price from the anonymous processes of the market. With imperfect competition, conversely, the seller is a price-maker. However, attention must be paid in setting the price to the effect the price of the seller's own product will have on the demand. He or she faces a declining demand curve, in which the higher the price goes, the smaller the demand for the product.

It can be shown in both theory and practice that a producer aiming to maximize profits under conditions of imperfect competition will set a price which is higher than the marginal cost; the volume of production, on the other hand, will be lower than the quantity at which the unit cost is at its minimum. Excess capacity will appear at the producer. So the seller is willing to produce more at the price demanded, provided the buyer is willing to purchase more at that price.[25] Although the seller does not reduce the price, he will try to win the buyer over from his competitors by other, non-price means.

That brings us to a statement essential to my subject: the producer under imperfect competition competes for the buyer, tries to learn as much as possible about his demands[26] and adapt to them, advertises to draw attention to his goods, seeks to arouse new demands with new, better products, and in these ways hopes to gain an advantage over his rivals. He is the one who competes for the buyer's favour, reversing the situation in a shortage economy, where the buyer tries to win the seller's favour with flattery or bribes.

In the theory of imperfect competition stress is frequently and rightly laid on the aspects of this form of competition which lead to losses: under-utilization of capacity, lavish advertising expenses and rapid changes of models and designs. Buyers who have just emerged from socialism, however, sense its advantages as well: there is a very strong incentive for the seller to

[24] Here and elsewhere in this chapter, 'seller' means not only a trader, but a producer selling his own products as well.

[25] Using the terminology of disequilibrium theory, this can be expressed by saying that notional excess supply appears. The producer would be willing to sell more at the price demanded than he is actually able to sell.

[26] Let me mention here Hayek's well-known argument: the great advantage of the market over bureaucratic control is the far stronger incentive it provides to obtain and utilize the information that lies scattered about. See Hayek (1935).

make efforts to win the buyer from his rivals.[27] Such incentives may be produced not only by real rivals, but by a sense of danger from a potential rival, through the entry of a new competitor. This idea is explored in the theory of contestable markets.[28] Another aspect of true rivalry appears in Schumpeter's theory of competition.[29] According to his interpretation, the main agent in the process is the entrepreneur, who tries to gain a cost and quality advantage over his competitors by making innovations.

The theories mentioned, which focus on mature capitalism, take as given the kind of behaviour of firms and producer–sellers that is aimed at gaining buyers. In the post-socialist transition, however, this kind of behaviour is only just developing. This is clearly perceptible in Hungary, where sellers' competition and the behaviour demanded by rivalry is spreading. Yet many producer–sellers, not having grasped the implications of the new situation, continue with their accustomed routine for a shortage economy. Sooner or later, however, the seller will be obliged by the new market situation to adopt new behaviour. The acquisition of adaptive behaviour is a learning process that takes a long time.

There is one phenomenon to be mentioned that acts against the improvement of adaptability. Among the five institutional changes discussed in Section 3.1 is hardening of the budget constraint. In the long term this trains firms to adapt, but in the short term it leads to frictions: a firm whose product cannot immediately be replaced may fail, so that a shortage arises. The fewer barriers to free entry and imports are removed, the more this will happen.

3.3   Avoiding Runaway Demand

Another main cause of the replication of the shortage economy, apart from weak adaptability of production, is a situation in which macro demand runs away by comparison with macro supply. This kind of constantly recurrent disproportion must be overcome before the shortage economy can be eliminated for good. Each change discussed in Sections 3.2 and 3.3 constitutes a *necessary condition* for eliminating the shortage economy.

What I term the 'running away' of demand is a phenomenon in which some group of users of the supply do not feel themselves constrained in their purchases by their own financial situation (wealth, income or ability to raise credit), and are prepared to acquire as much as they can of the resource, product or service they desire, or as much as they are permitted to acquire by

---

[27] The features of imperfect competition that induce these efforts are singled out by Scitovsky (1985) and Domar (1989). See also the study by Weitzman (1989), which makes an attempt to model the phenomenon.

[28] See Baumol, Panzar and Willig (1982).

[29] See Schumpeter (1976) [1942].

administrative means. The actual transaction is limited by the physical supply, the selling intention of the producer, or the administrative quota. In other words one of these is the effective constraint, but the demand is not constrained in an effective way.

Of course there are upper constraints on runaway demand as well; no one in their right mind wants to purchase an 'infinite' quantity. But such upper limits have no significance, since they almost never turn into effective constraints; the essential point is that the runaway demand is almost always greater than the supply.

There are four components of macro demand that are liable to run away under classical socialism, and this is because the intrinsic attributes of the system induce them to do so. These intrinsic features are overcome by economic reform and then the post-socialist transition.

3.3.1 The ending of investment hunger

Under classical socialism, there is an expansion drive that affects decision-makers at every level of the bureaucratic hierarchy, and this causes an insatiable investment hunger. There are always ministries, branch leaders or managers willing to invest. The chronic shortage ensures that they will always have a sales market, and the soft budget constraint exempts them from concerns about the profitability of the future production to be created by the investment.

Investment hunger did not cease during the period of reform socialism.[30] The demand for investment was curbed administratively from time to time by those directing the economy, but it really came to an end when the institutional changes reviewed in Section 3.1 took place.

The insatiable investment hunger of the managers of the state-owned firms disappeared without trace when the budget constraint on them hardened and the future sales prospects for products became uncertain. Expectations about privatization had an effect in the same direction.

Insatiable investment hunger never affects private firms, because of their very nature. They are obliged to weigh the likely risk of the investment: whether recent costs will be covered by later earnings, and whether the investment will bring a profit over and above them. Amidst the uncertainties of the transformation, with positive and in certain periods high interest rates prevailing, the investment demand from the private sector is very moderate.

So, looking at the economy as a whole, the investment hunger generated by the intrinsic attributes of the system has ceased; the investment component of macro demand is no longer liable to run away. This can be clearly ob-

---

[30] The chronic excess demand for investment is confirmed in an article by Lackó (1989).

served in the Hungarian economy, where investment's proportion of GDP and even its absolute volume have sharply declined.[31]

3.3.2   The toughening of the export markets

Under the classical socialist system, demand for exportable products is also prone to run away, for several reasons.

The partner countries in *soft-currency* relations are shortage economies themselves, in which excess demand appears for many products. This means they are unexacting about quality and other criteria, and intent on importing as much as possible of the goods they are short of. As far as domestic export behaviour is concerned, the undemanding Eastern market is convenient for both the foreign-trading and the producing firm, and they too push for these exports. So it follows that the effective constraint with very many products is not the demand from the partner, but the supply in the exporting country.

In *hard-currency* relations, of course, there is an effective demand constraint in the partner country. But the demand can still be raised through price concessions made possible by subsidies. Since there is a great hunger for the imports that can be bought for hard currency, and the economic leadership may also be hard pressed to service the country's foreign debt, they follow the principle of 'exporting at any price and any cost', trying to divert as much domestic production as possible into exports. So the intrinsic features of the classical socialist system ultimately cause the development of behaviour that makes the demand for exportable products liable to run away as well.

Hungary's reorientation towards the hard-currency markets began a good while before the change of political system in 1990 and the collapse of the Comecon trading bloc in 1991. However, at that time it was still possible to raise hard-currency exports through unbridled distribution of subsidies, and moreover, at least as a last resort, there was the Comecon market as well.[32] So to that extent the demand constraint was not consistently effective, and the tendency for export demand to run away had not been completely eliminated.

The change in this respect was completed at the end of the 1980s, and above all after the political changeover in 1990 and the collapse of Comecon. After that, the hardening of the budget constraint speeded up, the relative weight of exports by private firms under a compulsion to make profits rose, and the subsidization of exports decreased. It became steadily less possible to apply the 'export-at-any-price-and-cost' principle, and clear that the buying intention on the export market constituted a genuine effective constraint. The

---

[31] See Kornai (1993b), pp. 206–10, and also Table 5.4, this volume.

[32] From time to time, the top economic leaders would place administrative limits on exports to the Soviet Union and other socialist countries, because they were not sure that Hungary would receive an appropriate offset payment. This ran counter to the efforts of leaders at lower levels who would have been glad to continue these convenient exports.

intrinsic attributes of Hungary's domestic system and the curious Comecon relationship between shortage economies were no longer generating a propensity for the demand for export products to run away.[33]

3.3.3 The limiting of state spending
Government spending, the third great component of macro demand, is also liable to run away under the classical socialist system. All state bureaucracies are prone to overspending, and so this is not system-specific, but the classical socialist system differs from a parliamentary democracy in that it lacks a built-in mechanism to curb this desire to overspend. The government is not publicly accountable; there is no parliamentary opposition to criticize the government's spending plans beforehand and check the implementation of the budget afterwards. The state budget is compiled by the top leadership out of the public eye, as it sees fit. Since the central bank is subordinate to the same leadership, a budget deficit of any size can be financed by borrowing from the central bank – in other words by the inflationary means of printing banknotes. In that sense the budget constraint on the state is also soft. The documents put before parliament normally conceal the actual budget deficit, and in any case, parliament automatically gives its seal of legal approval to the plans presented by the leadership of the party-state.

This situation altered only after the change of political system.[34] The bureaucracy's propensity to overspend remained, of course, and for this and other reasons there is always a danger that the state budget will be in deficit, as in fact it has been, as is well known. But this happens before the eyes of parliament, the auditor-general's office, the press and not least the public, and the international financial organizations (the IMF and the World Bank). This control puts a curb on the propensity to spend. In this sense it can no longer be said that there is no built-in mechanism for checking government demand.

3.3.4 An end to the hoarding tendency
A tendency for producers to accumulate stocks can be observed under classical socialism. Supplies of inputs are uncertain, and so all firms try to ensure continuous running of the plant by hoarding as much of their materials,

---

[33] In my view this change cannot be viewed as a standard external shock. The collapse of socialism led separately, in each post-socialist country, to profound internal institutional changes. On an international scale it was the same collapse that led to commotion in the trading relations between these countries and radical changes in the nature of their future relations.

[34] In 1989, the year before the first multi-party elections, the government of Miklós Németh made public the fact that the earlier budgets (and announcements concerning the stock of foreign debt) had been falsified. The budget deficit and the debt had been greater than the figures previously published. This event heralded in a way the still more substantial change in 1990. Thereafter it was plain that the state's financial affairs could no longer be kept so easily hidden from the taxpayers.

semi-finished products and components as possible. This they can do with impunity, because they are insensitive to costs, due to the soft budget constraint.[35] Such conditions all make the intermediate demand for producers' goods – another important component of macro demand – liable to run away.

The propensity to hoard also ceases (see Table 1.2), mainly due to the institutional changes described earlier. As the various factors gradually bring the shortage economy to an end, the urge to hoard subsides.

The components of runaway demand in the socialist economy (3.3.1–3.3.4) combined form a curious kind of potential monetary overhang. Though there are no liquid financial means available to investors, exporting firms, officials with control over government spending or firms accumulating stocks of input to realize their excess demand immediately, they can still expect, given the supply or the administrative permit allowing the transaction to take place, that the money will be found somehow. Their potential ability to pay exercises excess-demand pressure with effects similar to those of repressed inflation. This potential monetary overhang is absorbed as a result of the institutional changes described earlier.

To sum up, the institutional changes gradually remove the mechanisms that generate, due to the intrinsic, internal features of the political and economic system, the tendency for certain main components of macro demand to run away.[36]

At this point the set of institutional changes can be taken to include not only the privatization, decentralization and deregulation considered in Section 3.1, but the other changes mentioned in this section as well: the ending of the special foreign-trade relations with Comecon countries, and the public, primarily parliamentary control of the state budget and state spending. So when institutional changes are mentioned further on in the chapter, this extended set of changes is meant.

3.4 The Role of Personal Income and Consumption

The role played by the biggest component of macro demand, personal consumption, in reproducing the conditions of the shortage economy differs essentially from those of the four other components already discussed. Clas-

---

[35] The connection between softness of the budget constraint, shortage and the hoarding tendency is proved with a mathematical model by Goldfeld and Quandt (1990a and 1990b).

[36] This steady change does not take place in a monotonous, unidirectional way. At the time of the reforms carried out within the socialist system, that is, before the political change, certain tendencies for demand to run away speeded up even further, instead of slowing down. Effective limitation of macro demand can apply far more consistently after the political change has taken place.

sical socialism has no intrinsic mechanism that *necessarily* generates a running away of household incomes, and so of household demand for consumer goods. This is the only one of the main components of macro demand to be very strictly and effectively limited by the bureaucracy. There are effective incentives at every level in the hierarchy to enforce the maintenance of these limits.[37]

Classical socialism is not *necessarily* marked by repressed inflation in the consumer market. There may be a long period in which there is no steady accumulation of unspent household income (unspent because it cannot be spent) and no development of a personal monetary overhang.[38] The planners strive to keep the purchasing power in the hands of the public, and the supply of consumer goods and the set consumer price level reconciled, despite the customary frequency and intensity of the shortage phenomena.

The word 'necessarily' has been emphasized twice. For it is not impossible that the leadership of some classical socialist country may let the reins slip from their grasp, so that there is a real general excess demand for a longer period in the field of personal consumption as well. Forced saving due to shortage – monetary overhang – may accumulate. Since the consumer price level is more or less fixed, repressed inflation will appear in that case.

The situation alters in socialist economies that embark on reform. These countries suffer various combinations of repressed and open inflation, through the combined effect of the following factors.

The level of nominal wages rises, perhaps far more quickly than productivity. Pressure in this direction is exerted by political liberalization, the influence of the workers' movements, and the shortage of labour, which is still characteristic in this period. The weakening party-state is able and willing to stand up to this wage pressure less forcefully than the previous, more repressive regime did. The stronger the forces pushing up wages, the greater the excess consumer demand that can arise.

Either the government manages to withstand the inflationary pressure on prices, in which case the phenomena of repressed inflation are more prominent, or it cannot (or even does not wish to) withstand the inflationary pressure, for instance because it has a declared intention of liberalizing prices. In this case an upward movement of prices will be induced both by the excess demand (on the demand side) and by the abolition of subsidies (on the

---

[37] If the four main components of macro demand (see 3.3.1–3.3.4) are inclined to run away, the sum of them, the aggregate demand, will run away as well. This applies even if the fifth and largest component, consumer demand, has a well defined magnitude strongly controlled by the economic leadership.

[38] The forced saving caused by the excess demand for the products of the state-owned sector can be partly or wholly absorbed by the second economy and the black market. See Nuti (1986).

cost side).[39] The earlier price stability or repressed inflation will give way to open inflation.

Right up until the 1990 turning-point, a curious combination of shortage and repressed and open inflation prevailed in Poland, with open inflation appearing to an increasing extent. This was brought to an end by the drastic stabilization measures introduced on 1 January 1990.

The processes in Hungary were far less extreme, taking place over a much longer period at a much steadier pace (see Table 4.3). There was already appreciable inflation in the 1980s, although it remained in single figures right up until 1987. After that inflation speeded up, and continued to do so for a time after the political changeover in 1990. It reached its highest annual rate in 1991, when it stood at 35 per cent. Since then there has been some success in slowing it down, with the annual rate in the 22–23 per cent bracket for 1992 and 1993.

Attention needs to be drawn here to the logical connection between the statements in the previous paragraph. The assertion is not that the commencement of inflation and then its acceleration were the cause, and the elimination of the shortage economy the consequence. The shortage economy cannot be eliminated simply by setting the economy on an inflationary path, while its other characteristics remain unchanged. The line of argument in this chapter leads to a far more complex explanation than that. Both the elimination of the shortage economy and the inflation are *consequences*, and in fact consequences produced partly by *identical, shared causes*. But once the inflation has commenced and accelerated, it may have an effect on the shortage situation. The faster the inflation, the greater the reduction in the purchasing power of the money in the hands of the buyer (the real-balance effect), so that if there is any monetary overhang it is absorbed.

This brings us back to the subject of the previous section, runaway macro demand. It is a *necessary condition* for eliminating the shortages that there should be no running away of personal incomes, either those of a wage nature or earnings from other sources. If nominal wages and other earnings grow unchecked, particularly at a time when the freeing of prices has not advanced far, the shortages can become extremely intense. (This was the situation in Poland and in the Soviet Union and its successor states before the great financial reform.[40]) This did not occur in Hungary because the price, wage and financial policy was more cautious in this respect to start with.

What factors can stop wages running away? If the budget constraint has hardened enough, for the state-owned as well as the private sector, the wage pressure will be impeded by the firms' interest in surviving and maximizing

---

[39] Even if some excess supply of some products appeared, their price still did not fall, being generally known to be sticky downwards. This asymmetrical behaviour of prices pushes up the general price level even further.
[40] See Lipton and Sachs (1990).

their profits. Also acting in this direction is growing unemployment, an excess supply of labour. But bureaucratic restriction of nominal wages in order to prevent a running away of macro demand seems to be essential until the institutional transformation and the new state of the labour market are established. This occurred in Hungary, for instance, and in Poland, where firms paying wages judged excessive were subject to penal taxation. This bureaucratic restriction is not in itself a necessary condition for eliminating the shortage economy, which may occur without it as well. It is the kind of measure that will sooner or later become incompatible with the autonomy of firms and the efficiency of allocation. It is a typically *transitional* measure that can speed up the change from a sellers' market to a buyers' market.

3.5 The Role of Monetary Policy

Is it necessary to have a restrictive monetary policy for the shortage economy to be eliminated? Before answering that question, let us clarify the concepts entailed. In monetary policy aimed at controlling the money supply, there is a choice between the following types:

Type A: The aim is to *restrict* money supply by comparison with the demand for money. The growth rate in the money supply needs to be smaller than that of the demand for money generated by the expected nominal GDP calculated on the basis of expected inflation and real interest rates. If this is the intention behind the monetary policy, a decision must also be made on the degree to which the restriction is to be applied.
Type B: The aim is *neither to restrict nor to expand* money supply by comparison with the demand for money. The policy is designed to ensure that the growth rate of the money supply will be exactly the same as that of demand for money generated by the expected nominal GDP calculated on the basis of expected inflation and real interest rates. In other words, assuming an unchanged velocity of money, the growth index of the money supply will equal the product of the expected inflation rate and the expected real-growth index.
Type C: The aim is to *expand* money supply by comparison with the demand for money. The growth rate of the money supply needs to be greater than that of the demand for money generated by the expected nominal GDP calculated on the basis of expected inflation and real interest rates. If this is the intention behind the monetary policy, a decision must also be made on the *degree* to which the expansion is to be applied.

The attribute 'restrictive' is applied in Hungarian financial jargon not only to a Type A policy, known in Western parlance as a tight, strongly disinflationary monetary policy, but also to Type B, which actually allows for the planned rate of inflation at any time. This is only restrictive in so far as it ensures that inflation is kept under control. It will not grow faster than planned in the economic policy, especially not on the cost-increase side.[41]

Alternatives A, B and C are three possible *intentions* behind monetary policy. Even if the monetary policy-makers reach a clear decision on their intention, a number of further questions remain open. What means are they able and willing to employ to attain their purposes? And most importantly of all, are they capable of attaining what they intend coherently and consistently?

Hungarian economic researchers have still not undertaken to categorize the monetary policy of the last six to eight years in these terms. The figures available reflect an inconsistency between the various, perhaps mutually conflicting, intentions and the mutually conflicting means. The final result during much of the period has corresponded most closely to the middle case, a Type B, accommodating monetary policy. A Type A, restrictive monetary policy applied in a more or less consistent way at best in various shorter periods. There were several signs, in 1993 and 1992, of a return to an expansionist, Type C monetary policy, although the signs were not entirely plain and the monetary expansion was not great.[42]

To return to the main subject of the chapter, the prime condition for eliminating the shortage economy is the completion of the institutional changes described in Sections 3.1 and 3.3, which has successfully been accomplished in Hungary. But this must be accompanied *secondarily* by an appropriate monetary policy. If the monetary policy is a restrictive one of Type A, it can act as a catalyst, speeding up the elimination of the shortage economy. It erects another barrier in front of the components of macro demand that are liable to run away. Tight restriction on the stock of investment credit helps to overcome the investment hunger. Strict control of the stock of credits available for inventory financing helps to overcome the hoarding tendency. If the remnants of bureaucratic price-setting survive, leaving the possibility of inflation being bureaucratically repressed, a policy of curbing and restricting the growth of macro demand will ease the shortage phenomena that accompany repressed inflation. The restrictive monetary policy will impede pursuit of an income policy that yields to wage pressure, including a permissive wage policy.

All this can also be said to some extent of a Type B monetary policy accommodating the planned inflation. This will at least not impede the elimi-

---

[41] Policy Type B is commonly referred to in economic literature as an *accommodating* monetary policy, since it continuously adjusts to the demand for money of the nominal GDP. This is a far more apposite term than 'restrictive'.

[42] In making these statements I have made use of the studies of Balassa (1993) and Várhegyi (1993).

nation of the shortage economy, even though it may not boost it, so long as the prime condition – completion of the institutional changes listed – is fulfilled.

Based on this train of thought it can be stated that it is a *necessary condition* for eliminating the shortage economy that at least a Type B or even stricter monetary policy should apply.

A Type C monetary policy will expressly work against the elimination of the shortage economy if it is applied when the minimum institutional changes required have yet to be completed. Elimination of the shortage economy in some of the post-socialist countries has become stuck or been slowed precisely because a Type C monetary policy has been applied. But if the elimination of the shortage economy has been accomplished, a Type C, expansionist monetary policy will not cause it to recur, so long as there is no restoration of the earlier institutional system. On the other hand such a policy may help to speed up inflation and undermine the possible earlier achievements in stabilization. This, however, is no longer a shortage-economy phenomenon, but the connection between monetary policy and inflation that normally applies in market economies.

3.6   A Review of a Few Macro Relations

An illustration of what has been said so far is provided by Figures 1.1 and 1.2, which present the basic macro relations in an extremely simplified form, using the method of depiction customary in macroeconomics.

Figure 1.1 illustrates the normal state under classical socialism. Actual macro production is equal to the macro supply S. The system is supply-constrained. Both the supply curve S and the demand curve D are vertical; they do not react to the price level. The vertical line for macro demand is to the right of the vertical line for macro supply; in other words there is macro excess demand. The arrows pointing to the right signify that the curve for macro demand is prone to run away. The precise amount by which D exceeds S is immaterial. The essential point is merely that D is always bigger, because of the propensity of some of its components to run away. Excess macro demand does not simply consist of the demand covered by money already in the buyers' pockets. To it can also be added the buying intention whose cover is not yet in their pockets, but of which the firm or state institution is aware: if it occurs, the state will cover the expense.[43]

Figure 1.2 presents the state after the shortage economy has been eliminated. The most important change in comparison with Figure 1.1 is that the curve for macro demand has turned. This curve (in the comparative, static

---

[43] Attention was drawn to this peculiar monetary overhang in Section 3.3.

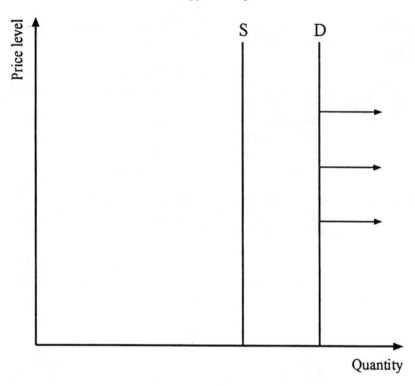

Figure 1.1   The macro state of the shortage economy

realm of the figure, in which it is assumed that all other circumstances are unchanged) slopes downwards. Even if no other factor does so, the so-called real-balance effect will make the owners of money reduce their demand if the purchasing power of their stock of money falls in line with the rise in the price level. The assumption made about the macro supply is that the curve is vertical, in other words independent of the price level.

The turn of the curve for macro demand makes it *possible* for the two curves to intersect, in other words for the macro supply and macro demand to coincide.[44] The institutional changes then initiate the market mechanism that will *effectuate* this coincidence on the macro plane.

[44] Figure 1.2 shows the so-called classical case, with the curve for macro supply vertical. Also known is the Keynesian case in which macro supply is an increasing function of the price level. Although the distinction between the two cases is extremely important both theoretically and in economic policy, it is immaterial at this point in the present analysis which case is presented. The essential fact here is that the two curves intersect because of the turn in the demand curve.

Explanations of the difference between the two cases can be found in general works on macroeconomics – for example Sachs and Larrain (1993), pp. 55–76. The distinction is also

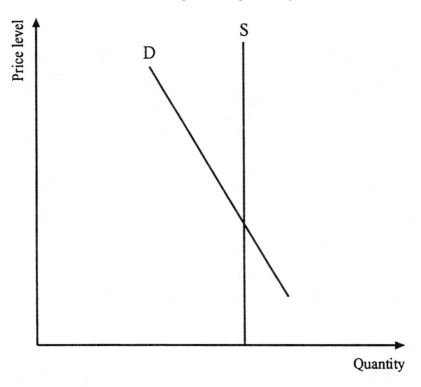

Figure 1.2   The macro state after the elimination of the shortage economy

Some economists would interpret the situation illustrated in Figure 1.2 as follows: the basic market equilibrium of the economy on the market for goods has been restored. For my part I would not dismiss this description, since it holds its own in a *certain sense*. But it must not be forgotten that the point of intersection is seen on a two-dimensional, static figure, which presents supply and demand as a function of a single variable, the price level. It may be that at a certain moment, at the momentary price level, the macro demand in the economy equals the macro supply, but meanwhile, looking at the trend, the price level constantly rises, in other words inflation takes place, while the supply falls, supply and demand fail to coincide on the micro level, and so on. So it would not be correct to say the economy shown in Figure 1.2 is in market equilibrium without further careful qualification.

made in the works of the disequilibrium school – for example Malinvaud (1977), pp. 29–32. Here I would simply like to mention that the difference between the two cases depends ultimately on two different explanations of the behaviour of wages and the labour market.

3.7   The Self-Generation of Shortage

As shown already, there are several concurrent causes of a shortage economy. From the time when this state came into being, people became used to the shortages around them, and this was built into their expectations and behaviour, which further enhanced the shortage. Shortage breeds shortage.

Let me cite two examples, both of which have been mentioned before. One is the tendency to hoard: the fact that input shortages can be expected induces the firms to accumulate stocks, which further increases the disproportion between supply and demand. The other example is investment hunger, which was included among the factors causing shortage. One of the reasons why investors dare to invest in a reckless way is that they need have no fear of being landed with the products. In a chronic shortage economy there is always a buyer.

Expectations of shortage belong to the category of *self-fulfilling* prophecies in economic psychology. That is why shortage is hard to eliminate. Only when economic agents sense over a longer period that the shortage has really ended will they begin to reshape their expectations and learn the new behaviour.

3.8   The Effect of the Political Changeover

The institutional changes described in Sections 3.1 and 3.3 began during the period of reforms, in the political framework of the socialist system. The example of Hungary shows that the first important steps towards eliminating the shortage economy can be made during a protracted process of reform. But acknowledgement of this is compatible with the observation that these changes were ultimately speeded up and consolidated by the change of political system. Before that turning point the situation was ambivalent: no one could be sure that the changes were final. There were historical reasons for this anxiety, above all the suppression of the Prague Spring of 1968, or the partial withdrawal of the Hungarian economic reform in 1972–73. So long as the communist party maintained political monopoly, the private sector could not become dominant and there were no legal guarantees for the safety of private property. State-owned firms still felt that their privileges had been curtailed, but they had fundamentally survived.

In Hungary the political changeover came in 1989–90. The communist party lost its political monopoly. There were parliamentary elections, after which not only the parties forming the government, but also those in opposition could declare in a credible way their adherence to the goal of a market economy based on private ownership. From then on, instead of veiled allusions being made to capitalism, the transformation of the economy from a socialist into a capitalist system became official government policy. This swift, radical change in power structure and officially proclaimed ideology gave impetus to the processes of institutional transformation outlined in Sections 3.1–3.3, which led ultimately to the elimination of shortage.

3.9 Summary of the Causal Analysis

Figure 1.3 sums up the relations between the factors affecting the elimination of shortage. For clarity's sake only the *main direction* of the effects has been shown. In addition, all these factors affect each other, and of course there are reactive effects as well. So moving from left to right, in the main direction of the causal chain, the factors nearer the right-hand side react on the factors to the left of them.

The fundamental causal connection may seem self-evident to many: once the socialist system comes to an end, the shortage economy ends with it.[45] But there are numerous intervening factors between the ultimate cause (the change of system) and the ultimate effect (elimination of the shortage economy). A particular kind of hierarchy in the chain of cause-and-effect relationships has been expounded so far in this chapter and appears in schematic form in the figure. According to this, the political structure has a decisive effect on the institutions. These shape the behaviour of the economic actors, and this behaviour generates, eventually, the state of equilibrium typical of the system.

Elimination of the shortage economy requires both the right macro-level government policy, above all monetary, fiscal and income policies suitable for the purpose, and a micro-level transformation that brings into being economic actors whose behaviour is in conformity with the market.

The fundamental idea in this chapter is the one also suggested by my earlier works: the chronic shortage economy is a *system-specific* formation characteristic of the classical socialist system. The first moves towards eliminating it could be taken before the political changeover, but these are ambivalent changes that are not yet well rooted or robust. The elimination of the shortage economy becomes final when the transformation of the political and economic system has itself advanced to the required extent.[46]

---

[45] The following riddle was widespread in the period of the shortage economy: *Question*: What would happen if the communist party came to power in the Sahara Desert? *Answer*: Sand would become an article in short supply.

[46] One question that arises is whether China can eliminate its shortage economy before the political monopoly of the communist party ends. China has certainly progressed a long way through the processes of transformation described earlier. It must be added that the Chinese Communist Party itself is undergoing transformation to some extent, having departed in many respects in its principles and practice from the behaviour typical of communist parties.

How far must the transformation of the political structure go in order thoroughly to eliminate the shortage economy? China's experience will be very important to the process of arriving at a

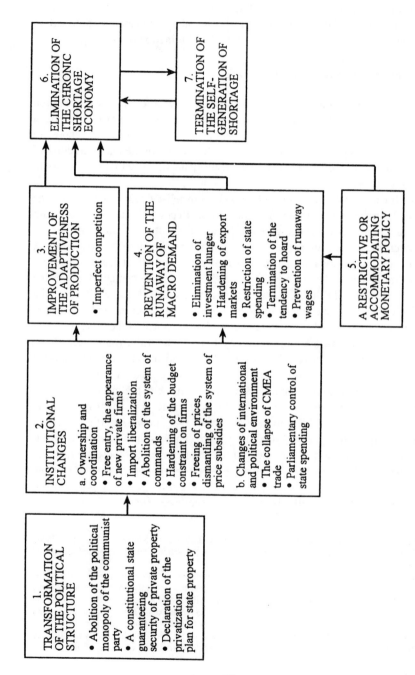

Figure 1.3 The causal chain for the elimination of shortage

It is not a necessary condition for the elimination of the chronic shortage economy that the general change of system, including the specific institutional changes emphasized in this chapter, should take place '100 per cent', with complete consistency. It is sufficient for these to have reached a certain threshold. Let me give a few examples to make this idea clear:

1. It is not necessary (or possible) to have perfectly free market entry. But there must be enough freedom so that a shortage can induce a relatively swift entry.
2. The privatization of state property need not be complete. But there is a need for a private sector large enough to make up for the shortages left by the state sector relatively quickly. This is a criterion I should like to emphasize particularly. There is no need to wait for the private sector to become predominant before taking the financial measures necessary for eliminating shortage. But not until the private sector has attained a minimum size will even the most radical financial stabilization bring lasting results.
3. It is not necessary that imports be entirely liberalized. But there must be sufficient freedom to ensure that the shortages left by domestic production can be filled by imports quickly.
4. Even if the budget constraint has not hardened finally and to a great extent, it must reach the degree of hardness at which state-owned firms can no longer feel their survival is guaranteed. They must sense the need to fight for survival in the market.[47]
5. To continue the previous idea, the change in the economic environment must be sufficient to quell investment hunger.
6. Even if some prices remain fixed, there must be a sufficiently high proportion of free prices to bring about a substantial movement in the price level, so that supply and demand can at least become equal on the macro level.

Hungary began a steady approach to these thresholds in 1968. The first couple of years after the political changeover sufficed to reach the necessary thresholds at all main points. From about 1992 onwards, the Hungarian economy could no longer be called a chronic shortage economy.

---

full, scientifically convincing answer to this question, but such an answer will have to wait until the course of China's political and economic reform has been closely observed over a long period.

[47] This was felt by Hungarian state-owned firms after the collapse of the Comecon markets, inducing them to make a swift transfer in their exports and imports. This occurred before the passage of the Bankruptcy Act and the wave of bankruptcies, that is, before a more drastic hardening of the budget constraint.

The Polish experience after the introduction of the January 1990 measures was similar to this one.

The elimination of the shortage economy took place in Poland over a much shorter period, in a condensed form, as a sudden shock. This was possible because there had begun in the final years of the socialist system a modest, but real, process of reform: there already existed a substantial private sector. It was possible also because the act of stabilization was performed after the change of political system in 1988–89. This provided the sense of irrevocability in such fundamental questions as abolition of the privileged status of state ownership, free entry, protection and encouragement of private property, and so on.

Several successor states of the Soviet Union, on the other hand, implemented radical stabilization measures before the kind of minimum package just outlined had been assembled. The private sector, for instance, was still so rudimentary, and the state sector so protected, that free entry, competition and adjustment to demand could not develop sufficiently. Understandably, shortage and inflation came to coexist in these countries.[48]

It follows from what has been said that elimination of the shortage economy can take place gradually, over a lengthy period, or, through a sudden alteration of the proportions between supply and demand, can be condensed into a short period. But the latter line of development will only lead to the permanent abolition of shortage if the transformation of the political and economic system has previously reached at least a critical minimum level.

Elimination of the chronic shortage economy is a result of the change of system. This statement can be reversed: observing how far a country has gone in eliminating the shortage economy and the extent to which the elimination has proved durable is a concurrent indication of how far it has gone in its change of system.

This is not the only series of milestones for measuring progress in changing the system, but it is one of the most important gauges. The phrase 'transition to a market economy' is often used in politics and public life. Now an economy can be called a market economy if it is not typified by chronic, general and all-pervading shortages. So clarification of where a certain country stands in relation to eliminating the shortage economy will yield simple, tangible, easily quantifiable indices for deciding where it stands in relation to establishing a market economy.

By this measure Hungary has already gone quite a long way. Based on the previous train of thought it can be said that the Hungarian economy has become a market economy. The market mechanism still operates with a great deal of friction – it is not yet mature – but it has already become the characteristic mechanism of coordination.

---

[48] This phenomenon was aptly named 'shortageflation' (by analogy with 'stagflation') by Kolodko and McMahon (1987) on the basis of experience in Poland before 1990.

4. THE SHORTAGE ECONOMY AND THE LABOUR MARKET

The main subject of this study is the market for products (and services). Let us now make a short diversion to draw an examination of the labour market into the analysis as well.

In the classical socialist system, the chronic shortage in the market for products has coincided for a long time with the presence of excess supply on the labour market. Open unemployment or latent underemployment are characteristic primarily of the backward agriculture. But this surplus of labour and other elements of the reserve of labour are sooner or later absorbed by the forced growth characteristic of socialism, assuming that history provides enough time for the process to run its course.

Absorption of the labour surpluses took place in the Soviet Union and the Eastern European socialist countries. The description in the economic jargon of the time was that the extensive stage of growth (the stage based on progressively drawing in new resources) was over, and it was now time for the intensive phase, in which growth would have to be achieved through the more efficient utilization of resources and through rising factor productivity.

From the point at which the socialist economy embarks on the intensive phase, growth slows down, and the economy in several socialist countries begins to stagnate. The economy is not capable of raising the efficiency with which it uses the resources drawn into production, showing a weak performance in raising factor productivity. Every development and growth routine has primarily been tailored to extensive growth. From this it follows that every decision-maker in production, under the influence of the expansion drive, would like to have access not only to more investment (investment hunger) but to more manpower as well. The shortage of labour becomes chronic in socialist economies past the extensive stage; a sellers' market develops for labour as well.

It is generally known that the utilization of labour within the firm is low: there is unemployment on the job. With a soft budget constraint, there is not enough incentive to reduce costs, or to economize on labour. This is aggravated still further by the hoarding of labour, an analogous tendency to the hoarding of input stocks. Since the labour shortage has become permanent, it is worth having labour in reserve, lest there be a hold-up in production because some worker or other is unexpectedly absent, or jobs cannot be filled in the future. So surplus labour is not dismissed. Apart from these economic considerations, there are the political and ethical criteria of guaranteeing employment and job security.

When the Soviet and Eastern European socialist system collapsed, practically every country showed a chronic shortage of labour.[49] This formed an integral part of the shortage-economy syndrome.

During the post-socialist transition, the elimination of the chronic shortage of products and services is accompanied in parallel by the elimination of the labour shortage: the excess demand turns into an excess supply. Unemployment appears and grows. The number of vacancies still exceeded the number of job-seekers in Hungary until May 1990. After that, the number of unemployed rose steadily, reaching a peak unemployment rate of 13.6 per cent in February 1993. Since then it has fallen slightly, the rate in April 1994 being 11.8 per cent. A similar change has taken place in all other post-socialist economies.[50]

The phrase used just now was that the two events occurred *in parallel*. But this does not mean they take place independently of each other. Basically *the same causes* that end the shortage of products lead to the elimination of the excess demand for labour as well, and then as the process continues, to an excess supply of labour and a sizeable growth in that excess supply.[51] Let me mention a few factors, without aiming at completeness:

1. The brake on the running away of macro demand, the stagnation and recession of macro demand, and the elimination of investment hunger bring an end to the hunger for labour as well. Far fewer *new* jobs are created than when the forced growth reached its culmination.
2. Meanwhile more and more *old* jobs are ending. The hardening of the budget constraint on state-owned firms makes production cost-sensitive. Whereas state-owned firms used to turn a blind eye to unemployment on the job before the change of system, they are now less and less able to afford it. Meanwhile the change in the political environment and the official abandonment of the pledge to ensure full employment and job security enables state-owned firms to carry out dismissals. It can be added that the new private firms will not want in any case to employ more labour than absolutely necessary.
3. This change from labour shortage to unemployment is accelerated by the recession accompanying the transformation. A curious triple connection

[49] On the measurement and trend of the labour shortage in Hungary, see the article by Fazekas and Köllő (1985).
[50] In certain post-socialist countries, such as Russia, unemployment rises very slowly. There are several signs that this is precisely because the transformation does not take place in a consistent way. The budget constraint remains soft, numerous firms that are doomed to fail remain alive and capable of retaining labour that in fact has become superfluous.
[51] To avoid any misunderstanding, let me add that I am not saying that the end of the shortage of goods causes the end of the labour shortage and then the development of unemployment. In my view the end of the shortage of goods and the end of the shortage of labour can largely be attributed to *common* causes.

arises between (i) the changes promoting the elimination of shortage, (ii) the fall in production,[52] and (iii) the emergence and then growth of unemployment. The curb on macro demand (among other factors, the income and monetary policy for this purpose) takes the macro supply with it, as a consequence of the well-known multiplier effect. The demand for labour also falls as a result of the recession. Consumer demand falls further because of the rising unemployment, which reduces the macro demand even more. As a result of the recession there appears not only an excess supply of labour, but excess supply in the product market as well. Or even if there is no obvious excess supply in the form of rising stocks of outputs, the amount of unused production capacity will grow, and along with it the notional excess supply.[53] The actual production is substantially smaller than the potential output. So the previous economy of excess demand has visibly become the opposite, one of excess supply.

The remarks above have only touched briefly on the mechanism and motive forces of the transition, the tipping over from shortage to surplus. It would go beyond the scope of this chapter to clear up the question of why the unemployment becomes persistent. There are some well-known partial explanations. Without aiming at a complete list, I mention just a few:

1.   The compositions of labour demand and labour supply are not in accord with each other, due to the constant restructuring of production. The greater the depth and speed of the restructuring (and they will stay very great for a long time in a post-socialist economy), the greater the frictional unemployment.
2.   It may be in the employer's interest to combine a lower staffing level with paying higher wages, because the fear of unemployment will then induce workers to perform better (the *efficiency-wage* theory).
3.   Those actually in employment will tend to work for better wages for themselves, even if the higher wage level narrows employment (the *insider–outsider* theory).
4.   If employment rises too far, approaching too close to full employment, it will induce wage rises and inflationary pressure, so that the economy is warned off this high employment rate again (the *natural-rate* hypothesis).
5.   There is a connection between imperfect competition on the one hand and Keynesian-type underemployment in the economy on the other.[54]

[52] There are several reasons behind the fall in production; the process outlined in this chapter is only one element in this complex relation of cause and effect. See Kornai (1993b).
[53] For the concept of notional excess supply, see note 25.
[54] This connection has been proved for a special model of imperfect competition by Hart (1982).

I have merely listed the names of the best-known theories here. A synthesis of the theories listed (and a few others not mentioned) is emerging.[55] The question is whether these theories taken together suggest that chronic unemployment is an intrinsic characteristic of capitalism.

Numerous difficult theoretical questions arise at this point. In the case of *socialism*, I dare to state firmly, having gone through a great deal of theoretical examination, practical experience and debate, that the chronic shortage economy is a *system-specific* feature. A concomitant of the chronic shortage of products (at a certain level of economic development) is a chronic shortage of labour as well.

My guess is that a similarly system-specific feature of *capitalism* is constituted by frequent occurrences of real and notional excess supply, the excess capacity accompanying imperfect competition, and chronic unemployment. If a shortage economy is typical of the socialist system, the capitalist system can be described as an economy of surplus.

The micro markets of market economies are normally much closer to a state of Walrasian equilibrium (where supply equals demand) than those of socialist economies. But departures from Walrasian equilibrium can also be observed, of course, in market economies, the relative frequencies of positive and negative deviations being the reverse of those in socialist economies. Under the socialist system, cases of excess demand (real and nominal) were a good deal more frequent, substantial and lasting than those of excess supply, whereas under the capitalist system, cases of excess supply (real and nominal) are a good deal more frequent, substantial and lasting than those of excess demand.

I say 'guess', and dare not make a more dogmatic statement than that. It is hard to discern how many of these phenomena are cyclical in character, how many can be ascribed to inevitable frictions of adaptation, and which derive from the system itself.

Whereas the business cycle and unemployment are the subject of a vast literature marked by divided opinions and sharp debates, there has been very little discussion about what is system-specific in the problems of the modern capitalist world. For most Western economists, the system of the capitalist market economy is simply there, and the question itself appears odd.[56] An examination of the system-specific nature requires on the one hand a histori-

[55] The most significant advance in the field of synthesis has been Phelps's book *Structural Slumps* (1994). Disregarding some essential differences of expression and terminology, the messages of that book and this chapter are compatible with each other. Phelps's line of argument seems to provide support for the comparison of the labour markets of the socialist and capitalist economies put forward here.

[56] Putting questions of this kind is largely the preserve of the opponents of the capitalist system, the Marxists and extreme left-wingers. Yet this is a clearly comprehensible question to those who believe in the system as well. I shall return to this point in the final section.

cal vantage point, and on the other a comparison of capitalism with differing systems. The post-socialist transformation offers a unique chance for just such a historical comparative view.

5.   ASSESSMENT

Finally, let us turn to an assessment of the changes. In what ways can elimination of the shortage economy be rated a favourable or an unfavourable development? Rather than aim for a single result, I shall try to break down the effects into their elements.

5.1   Consumer Welfare

In a chronic shortage economy, the welfare of a consumer is determined not only by what is actually consumed, but by the events before and after the purchase.

In a buyers' market, the seller is mainly the one who has to take the trouble associated with the transaction, the information and search, but in a sellers' market the situation is reversed. Every family has to devote hours of spare time to queuing and searching.[57]

If a purchase eventually takes place, forced substitution is common. In the language of utility theory, this means the buyer must be content with a smaller utility. The same happens in a temporal context when the buyer has to postpone a purchase due to a shortage. A still greater loss of consumer welfare occurs when the buyer abandons a purchasing intention altogether.

Buyers are made to feel worse by their defencelessness. They experience rudeness from sellers; they must be humble to them, flatter them, or even try to bribe them. All these various losses to the consumer cease with the elimination of the shortage economy.

Such changes cannot be represented by means of synthetic index numbers. The customary statistics show only the quantity and content of consumption, without expressing the sense of loss incurred by the effort and disappointment entailed in consumption.

The most misleading practice is to use the indices for real wages in the midst of dramatic changes in the market situation. What does a price increase signify in the case of a good that was cheap according to the official

---

[57] Competition among sellers does not wholly exempt buyers from the effort of searching and acquiring information, of course. Particularly under conditions of imperfect competition, choosing between substitutes by weighing a large number of qualitative parameters and relative prices can be a complex task. The more developed the economy and the wider the choice, the harder selection becomes.

state price list, but could never be obtained, and is now expensive, but available on the free market?[58] This change, other things being equal, reduces the index of real wages, while undoubtedly enhancing the welfare of the individual, the utility enjoyed by the buyer, provided the feelings of loss caused by shortage are included among the factors of economic psychology determining welfare.

Although it is statistically difficult or even impossible to detect this favourable effect of the elimination of shortage, the question is what value is put on it by the individuals concerned, who experience the change. They probably put a far lower value subsequently on the elimination of the shortage than they put on the losses caused by it before the change. Hungarian buyers today have grown used to the elimination of shortage, take it for granted and do not feel overjoyed by it. In the language of utility theory, I would say the utility of the abolition of an unfavourable circumstance (the shortage-economy conditions as felt by buyers) does not equal (here is less than) the disutility of the existence of the *same* circumstance.[59] A politician directing the change may be angry about this and brand people as ungrateful, but that will not change human nature. The housewife who used to stand patiently in line at the butcher's and be delighted if some piece of meat or other was thrust at her without any choice being offered now views the great selection not even with indifference, but with irritation and dismay at the high price of meat. She will be particularly ungrateful about the end of the meat shortage if her means are slim and she cannot afford to buy the meat she would like.

This example sheds light not only on the forgetfulness of people when comparing systems, but on the fact that the change of market regime has *distributive* consequences. Let us say for simplicity's sake that exactly the same quantity and assortment of goods is given to the buyers under each regime, but this set of products fails to fulfil all the potential buyers' needs. Both regimes will make use of specific selection criteria to decide who will get the goods and who is left out. In a shortage economy, there are various different principles mixed up in the selection process: merit, loyalty to the authorities and position in the hierarchy, need, connections and bribery, time of joining the queue, and plain chance. The specific mixture of these criteria

[58] This problem is convincingly presented in an article by Berg and Sachs (1992).

[59] This asymmetry is not expressed in the customary utility functions describing consumer behaviour. The modelling of the asymmetry would entail great technical difficulties and require a profound theoretical revision.

Like classical physics, economics builds into its theories an implicit assumption of reversibility. Significant strides were made in certain branches of physics when account was taken of irreversibility in time. A revision of economic theory in this direction has hardly begun. Outside the mainstream of economics, some noteworthy works have appeared that have already built the idea of irreversibility into the theory. See the works of representatives of the evolutionist school: Arthur (1984), Marshall (1961) [1890], and Nelson and Winter (1982).

varies from country to country, period to period and market to market. Several kinds of criterion apply in a market economy as well, but there is clearly a close positive correlation between income situation (that is again determined by various factors) and fulfilment of buying intentions. Here 'money talks' first of all.

5.2 The Sense of Security

The same features of the socialist system that produce the shortage economy generate at the same time a particular stability in prices, wages, employment and welfare provisions. Having been analysed earlier, these features are considered here purely from the point of view of the effect they have on people's sense of security. The elimination of the shortage economy is combined with impairment of this sense of security.

The rigidity of prices and wages, which are strictly regulated centrally and laid down for a long time, makes it harder for the economy to adapt and seriously damages its efficiency. At the same time, it increases the household's sense of security in predicting its future financial situation. The fluctuations of prices, wages, exchange rates and interest rates in the market are far less predictable.

The socialist system through state redistribution provides welfare services according to quite clear rules, although to a low standard. Since these are free or almost free, a chronic shortage of almost all of them develops. To the extent that these services are transferred into the market sphere, the phenomena of shortage come to an end, but as a function of this, the provisions guaranteed by the state are confined to a narrower band.

As discussed in detail in Section 4, the labour and goods markets tip over from a sellers' market to a buyers' market. Everything that was considered in the last section as a gain for *consumers* in the market for goods (less search for supply, greater choice, no need for humility *vis-à-vis* the seller) constitutes a loss for *employees* in the labour market. They now have to search for work; they cannot pick and choose between jobs; they may find themselves in demeaning situations. It may be that the same individual is concurrently a winner as a consumer and a loser as an employee. Guaranteed employment and job security come to an end with the shortage economy.

5.3 The Dependence of Citizens: Relations between the Bureaucracy and the Economy

No one 'planned' beforehand that the socialist system should operate as a shortage economy. But having developed, the shortage economy gave good service to the autocracy of the party-state and the power of the bureaucratic hierarchy.[60] The shortage seriously curtailed individual freedom of choice. It was one of the main guarantees that individuals would live in a state of dependence on the state-owned production firm and the bureaucracy of the party-state.[61] This was felt in their daily experiences by consumers and by the manager of a firm as well. The public were also defenceless collectively against the political decisions of the top leadership, which had a sovereign right to decide on matters of supply, demand, prices, wages, and the scale and distribution of shortage.

Elimination of the shortage economy brings defencelessness *of this kind* to an end. I do not wish to idealize the buyers' market; I do not consider it to be the embodiment of unlimited consumer sovereignty. The tastes of consumers are influenced to a large extent by the producers, not infrequently in a manipulative way. But they can only do such things within certain bounds. The market is a mechanism that adjusts production to consumer preferences to quite a large extent, even though there are frictions. Or consumers must at least give their consent, through their purchasing choices, if producers try out something new; they cannot use force on buyers for any length of time.

The parliament and government of the day, even if operating within a democratic form of state, can influence and restrict the desires of consumers to a certain extent. But it must be added that the more democratic the system, the less it can dictate to consumers.

So in the last resort, the elimination of the shortage economy enhances rights and freedoms as well.[62]

There is yet another phenomenon worth mentioning when discussing the relationship between the bureaucracy and the actors in the economy: corruption. Corruption already existed in the shortage economy; *buyers* would seek access to the good or service they desired in this way, by bribing the seller or the allocating bureaucrat. With the elimination of the shortage economy and the swift expansion of private enterprise, there is a change of direction, with the *seller* now wanting to obtain state orders through corruption. In addition, corruption appears wherever the success of private entrepreneurs depends partly on specific actions by state officials charged with deciding who, and on what terms, acquires state-owned assets up for privatization, gains a tenancy of a state-owned building or site, receives a permit to pursue a state-regulated

---

[60] Of the causes for the emergence of shortage, this one is emphasized in the study by Shleifer and Vishny (1992).

[61] As the book by Fehér, Heller and Márkus (1983) put it graphically, there was a dictatorship over needs.

[62] More precisely, it enhances what are known in ethics as negative freedoms, whereby people are freed from something (for example, state repression or interference in their lives). The spread of positive freedom (when people are free *to do* something) depends in this context on what resources and goods people have at their disposal, in other words, on the general well-being and the distribution of incomes.

activity, and so on. Many more rich business people can now afford to spend large sums on corruption. With the elimination of the socialist system, the repression also lessens. The great achievement of spreading rights and freedoms has the unfortunate side-effect of loosening the controls. Corruption becomes broader in scale and more conspicuous, particularly in the still insufficiently consolidated period of the transition.

5.4 Growth, Qualitative Development and Technical Advance

All that has been said so far about the advantages and drawbacks of the change derives from a static comparison of the two constant states. To this must be added the effects that exercise an influence on the dynamics of the system's operation.

The change seems initially to have a negative effect on the quantitative growth of the economy, which can be measured, for instance, by the indices for aggregate output. The main driving force behind the initial fast growth under the socialist system was investment hunger, which derived, among other factors, from the expectation that the shortage would persist, so that almost any output could be sold – growth was never impeded by a limited size of demand. This old driving force ceases in the post-socialist transition, while the new forces deriving from the profit motive are initially still weak. Also contributing here are other recessive effects accompanying the change.

Meanwhile the change of market regime forces improvements in the efficiency of production. Some of this effect appears quickly, making itself felt in the daily activity of the firm. The previous uncertainty surrounding the acquisition of inputs is reduced, there are fewer problems with obtaining materials, semi-finished products and components. The labour shortage ends, and with it the unemployment on the job. All these changes assist in achieving more effective utilization of the factors of production, which sooner or later contributes to faster growth of the economy.

More important still is the long-term effect. The gravest damage the shortage economy does is to join with other factors in retarding technical progress. It deprives economic activity of the driving force generated by rivalry. Socialism lost out in the competition between the two systems above all because it lagged behind in the long term in raising labour productivity.

From comparing political and economic systems, I have come to the conclusion that this situation will be changed by the switch from the sellers' market to the buyers' market. I believe that, sooner or later, the spread of innovations made elsewhere will speed up in the post-socialist region as well, and truly original, pioneering innovations will also appear. Here I can only express my own confidence. We still have to wait for the facts to confirm or deny this forecast.

5.5   Summary of the Assessment

The transformation, and within it the elimination of the shortage economy, is a combination of favourable and detrimental, welcome and painful changes. I have tried to present both the favourable and the unfavourable effects in an objective way. The economy switches from one normal path to the other. The attribute 'normal' also conveys that these are not idealized, pure theoretical models with extreme characteristics, but actual historical formations containing a mixture of good and bad. Both paths are marked by a combination of features whose assessment depends on the value system espoused by the individual or group delivering the verdict.

I have no desire to conceal my own verdict: according to my system of values, the advantages outweigh the drawbacks. I see the elimination of the shortage economy as an achievement of the post-socialist transformation, although I am aware that there are heavy costs to be paid for it.

It can be assumed that a sizeable proportion of people, on the basis of other systems of values, will form a less favourable value judgement.[63] There are a great many reasons for this. With some people it is the historical forgetfulness mentioned earlier, washing away the memory of the suffering and losses caused by the shortage. With others it is the fact that they are on the losing, not the winning side in the redistribution resulting from the switch to a buyers' market. Finally, there is one other circumstance explaining the public attitude. The decisive criterion for a theoretical researcher comparing systems is the long-term effect, above all the way the elimination of the shortage economy will affect the long-term trend in labour productivity. But the majority of people, understandably, pay little attention to this, and wait impatiently for a directly perceptible turn for the better.

All this explains why a large number of people do not attach particular importance to the elimination of the shortage economy, even though this is one of the post-socialist transition's most notable, tangible and in the long term significant developments.

---

[63] In a 1991 survey, 59 per cent of the respondents considered that prices should be kept low even if that meant there would be a shortage of certain products. See Lázár (1993), p. 43.

2. Lasting growth as top priority: macroeconomic tensions and government economic policy in Hungary[1]

This chapter looks at the problems of five macroeconomic tensions: inflation, unemployment, the budget deficit, the balance-of-payments deficit and the decline in production. Despite its length, it still does not offer a full picture, since it does not address a number of important issues (among others, the question of monetary policy).

Analysing these five macroeconomic tensions provides an opportunity for me to comment on the government's economic policy.[2] Wherever an economist goes at this time of writing (summer of 1994), whether in private company or to a professional discussion, the question is levelled: does he or she agree with the new government's economic-policy package? I cannot reply to this question with a categorical yes or no. Readers will be able to identify during the detailed analysis where I consider the announced economic policy correct, and where I have reservations, concerns or objections.

---

[1] This essay was published in the Hungarian daily newspaper *Népszabadság*, somewhat abbreviated because of lack of space. Since it was written for a daily newspaper, it does not contain acknowledgements, references, precise descriptions of sources or detailed statistical support for my observations.

[2] *New note*: After the first free, multi-party elections in 1990, Hungary was governed by a coalition of parties with a Christian democratic orientation, led by Prime Minister József Antall and, following his death, by Péter Boross. In the 1994 elections, the former governing parties were defeated and a new coalition took over. The senior member is the Hungarian Socialist Party, which grew out of the reform wing of the communist party that ruled the country for decades. The core of the junior party of the coalition, the Alliance of Free Democrats, was formed by the former anti-communist dissident movement.

The new coalition had been in power for about two months when this essay was published. It appraises the economic policy of the new cabinet. The editorial introduction to the series was given the title, 'Kornai's critique of the Government'.

1.   INFLATION, UNEMPLOYMENT AND WAGES

There is a well-known close connection between the rate of inflation and the extent of unemployment. Assuming other factors (including inflationary expectations) to be constant, inflation can be slowed at the cost of increasing unemployment, and conversely there are means of reducing unemployment at the cost of accelerating inflation. Unfortunately the Hungarian economy has both these significant indicators stuck in a bad position. Inflation has slowed since its peak of 38.6 per cent annual rate in June 1991, but become stuck in the 17–25 per cent band of moderate inflation (see Table 4.3). The unemployment rate rose steadily from 1990 until February 1993. Although it has fallen slightly since then, it still stood at 11 per cent in June 1994 (Table 2.1).

The emphasis here is not just on the regrettably high values of the two indicators, but on the fact they are *stuck* at these high levels. There is a danger these high values may become habitual, shaping the behaviour of the actors in the economy.

Let us consider inflation first. We became affected by this unfortunate process for a great many reasons which I will not attempt to analyse here. Nor will I examine comprehensively all the conditions for curbing and slowing inflation, but concentrate instead on a single, though very important problem.

The type of inflation we are dealing with in Hungary can be described as *inertial*, since it is propelled by the inertia of the trend in wages and prices. Practically speaking, wages are indexed: earlier inflation is projected forward into the future and full, or almost full compensation is made for it in advance. In fact there was a case of overcompensation, in the first half of 1994, when the year-on increase in consumer prices in May 1994 was 18 per cent, while nominal average earnings had risen by almost 21 per cent in the same period, and nominal earnings net of tax had increased even more. The increase in wages is exerting upward pressure on prices, turning on the wage–price spiral, and making inflationary expectations self-fulfilling.

Connected with this are the devaluations of the Hungarian currency. If they are not radical enough, the Hungarian forint will appreciate in real terms (with harmful effects considered later). If there is a real devaluation, on the other hand, and this spills over into wage increases to compensate for price increases, it becomes an impetus behind inflation again. The spiral of mutually induced inflation and repeated devaluations continues.

It must be said categorically that the key to the situation lies in the trend in wages, where two separate questions, nominal wages and real wages need to be distinguished. (Unfortunately, these have been confused both in official statements and in the ensuing debates.)

Taking nominal wages first, let us imagine an ideal case in which all sides concerned agree there will be no price and wage increases at all for six

Table 2.1   Vacancies and unemployment, 1990–94

Year and month	No. of vacancies	No. of registered unemployed	Unemployment rate (%)
1990			
March	34 048	33 682	0.7
June	37 859	43 506	0.9
September	26 969	56 113	1.2
December	16 815	79 521	1.7
1991			
March	13 583	144 840	3.0
June	14 860	185 554	3.9
September	15 351	292 756	6.1
December	11 529	406 124	8.5
1992			
March	15 124	477 987	8.9
June	25 346	546 676	10.1
September	25 634	616 782	11.4
December	24 097	663 027	12.3
1993			
March	26 471	693 983	13.3
June	30 771	657 331	12.6
September	35 784	669 761	12.9
December	28 089	632 050	12.1
1994			
March	33 341	610 994	12.2
June	38 141	549 882	11.0
August	39 500	550 800	11.0

Source: Reports from Hungary's National Labour Centre, 1990–94.

months from a set point in time, say 1 January 1995. Let us assume in this mental experiment that there is no delayed effect from earlier price and wage measures and that other economic factors remain the same. In that case, if everybody trusted each other, believing all the other actors in the economy would keep their sides of the bargain and keeping theirs themselves, inflation would duly halt without any fall in real wages or real consumption. But a word of caution: the most critical item in this mental experiment is not the existence of zero change, the freeze in wages and prices, but the *credibility* of the sides taking part in the bargain. If one or other group tries to take advantage of the good faith of the rest, the agreement will collapse, and everything will be as before.

I do not believe any such far-reaching agreement is possible in the present situation. But the closer we get to such a point of agreement, the more we shall manage to slow down inflation.

Unfortunately, under Hungarian conditions, the problem of *nominal wages* is linked to another phenomenon: the fact that *real wages* and ultimately *real consumption* are higher than is justified from an economic point of view. I realize this remark may elicit resistance or even outrage in many people's minds: how dare anyone, in a Hungary racked by poverty, call real wages and real consumption too high? None the less, I must put up with the outcry and stick by my statement.

Consider the following simple, fundamental economic relation. GDP can be used for two main purposes: consumption or investment. (Exports and imports ultimately serve to raise consumption and investment as well.) In Hungary the share of investment, and that of fixed capital formation as part of it, has shrunk. It is much smaller than in countries that have enjoyed fast and persistent growth. (This statement is backed by the international comparison in Figure 2.1. See furthermore Table 5.4.) While the share of investment in rapidly developing Asian countries is persistently high, it is falling steadily in Hungary. Unless we want to rely solely on foreign resources (I shall return to the problems of this later), the ratio of investment to consumption must be altered in favour of investment and to the detriment of consumption.

The government's economic policy-makers are certainly aware of all this. I respect the courage with which they have approached the question of wages and presented a significant part of the problem to the public. But I am afraid they must go further than that. This is not simply a case of earnings running away in the short term and needing short-term, one-off corrective measures. It must be stated plainly that the growth of the economy is being jeopardized by the proportions of investment and consumption which have applied for so long and have become deeply imprinted in the behaviour of the economic actors and the mechanisms coordinating them. These proportions must be changed consistently and permanently, and the downward trend of the share of investment reversed.

In debates frequent mention is made of the crowding-out effect, whereby public spending deprives productive investment of resources. Without belittling this problem, I would like to emphasize that its importance is only secondary. Even conceptually, the distinction between the following three items should not be blurred: (i) investment by the state (fixed capital formation and increase of inventories), (ii) transfers through the budget, including wages and salaries paid out of the state budget and (iii) the material costs of public administration and the armed forces. In this context item (i) must be

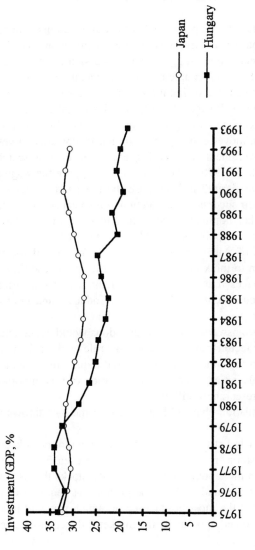

Sources: International Financial Statistics, IMF; issues of *Magyar statisztikai évkönyv* (Hungarian statistical yearbook), *Magyar statisztikai zsebkönyv* (Hungarian statistical pocket book) and *Magyarország nemzeti számlái* (Hungary's national accounts) by the Central Statistical Office; and annual reports by the National Bank of Hungary.

Figure 2.1   The share of investment in Japan and Hungary

added to the other types of investment and item (ii) to the rest of household consumption, while item (iii), though substantial, is not very significant by comparison with the much greater problem of the ratio of investment to consumption. Investment is crowded out primarily by consumption, and only to a secondary extent by material expenditure of the state bureaucracy and the armed forces.

It is not easy to see why the present situation has arisen in connection with both nominal and real wages. Every economics textbook and all the experience of the market economies suggest that a recession as severe as the one which took place in Hungary, coupled with mass unemployment, should push wages down; in the presence of inflation, it should curb the rise in nominal wages and push down real wages. So why has this trivial connection merely had a dampening effect on real wages in some years, no effect at all in others, and actually let them move in the opposite direction, upwards, in yet others? Is it because the government, still the biggest employer, was scared by the taxi-drivers' blockade of 1990 and did not dare to oppose the wage pressure for fear of losing popularity? Is it because the trade unions gained exceptional power after their success in the elections for social security boards and pushed for ever higher nominal wages rather than for the compromise required from the economic point of view? Is it because many private entrepreneurs and managers of state-owned firms come from the old socialist élite and have yet to learn to think in a 'capitalist' way, or because they thought, why not increase wages if it is easy to offset this by raising prices? Is it because the budget constraint is still too soft to induce managers to impose strict wage discipline?

I think that positive answers to all these questions would contain part of the truth (although other factors may also have had a role to play). To explain this unusual phenomenon of economic history would require thorough economic and sociological analysis; an impartial investigation of this important problem is a debt which researchers still owe.

How could the situation change? Experience in the past throws up three main possibilities.

The *first possibility* is a still deeper recession. Unemployment keeps growing in a rampant fashion, reaching a rate of 20 or even 30 per cent. This untenable situation in the labour market eventually blocks the rise in wages, breaks the wage pressure, and restores the proportions required for production to recover. This is the most brutal version, which it would be better to avoid, but it may be forced upon us by the market if the economic actors fail to act more wisely.

The *second possibility* is for the rise in wages to be curbed by administrative means. This was always the practice under the socialist system, and it went on for a while after the political change of 1990, although rather more loosely, in the form of punitive taxes on excessive wage increases. Later, state controls over wages were abolished completely, and in this respect Hungary went further than quite a few capitalist countries, where from time to time administrative wage controls are also applied to curb inflation, for instance during the 1985 stabilization in Israel. So although it is not unthinkable to use administrative means in today's Hungarian economy, there are several considerations that speak against it.[3] We live in an economy that is only just starting to recover from the crippling effects of bureaucratic control; business and politicians would presumably object to administrative curbs as a sign of regression.

But if neither the first nor the second course looks attractive, that only leaves the *third possibility*: voluntary restraint. There have been many examples of this in economic history: the self-restraining wage policy of the trade unions in post-war West Germany, the oft-cited example of post-Franco Spain, and the case of Mexico in the early 1980s.

It is not my purpose in this study to analyse to what extent Hungary's current possession of a socialist majority in parliament and government is an advantage and to what extent it is a drawback from the point of view of post-socialist transformation. It would certainly seem, however, to have advantages in terms of wage and income policy. A government that has been elected to a large extent by workers and employees, and with the help of the unions, can expect more political support and can muster more moral capital for embarking on such restrictive measures. Much of the 'government–employer–employee' conflict must be resolved 'in house', within the socialist party leadership and among socialist MPs.

The wage question will be a test of maturity for Hungarian society in the coming period. Will the government have the stamina to stand by its declared policy? What role will the unions play? Will they understand and be fully aware of their governmental responsibilities and recognize the imperative of economic circumstances, or will they come up with irresponsible demands?

The opposition parties will be put to the test, too. The economic advisers of the Federation of Young Democrats (Fidesz) were arguing before the elections in a similar way to the line taken above. Will the party remain true to these principles under the new political constellation? And as far as the former government parties are concerned, having missed the chance to face the tide when they were in power, will they be strong enough to refrain from

---

[3] *New note:* When a radical programme aimed at adjustment and stabilization finally began in March 1995, the government was indeed forced to apply administrative measures to halt the rise in nominal wages. More precisely, it did so in the sphere under its direct control, freezing wages and salaries paid in the budgetary sphere and by companies in majority state ownership. Wages in the private sector more or less followed the wage policy pursued in the public sector, without government intervention.

going for cheap popularity at least now that it is not their responsibility to
carry out unpopular measures?

In the long term, the trend in wages will ultimately depend most of all, of
course, on the growth of production and productivity. Lasting growth is a
fundamental requirement for *any* economic process to occur in a healthy
manner. This idea, to use musical terminology, will reappear as a leitmotiv
throughout this chapter in connection with each macroeconomic problem
considered. This is the point at which to sound this leitmotiv for the first time:
the tough self-restraint that holds back an improvement in living standards
can only end once production and labour productivity are growing steadily,
so that the expansion of real wages and real consumption can be paid for out
of this with a clear conscience. (To avoid any misunderstanding, let me add
that a restraint on the growth of nominal wages in order to slow the inflation
and the wage–price spiral may also be required even in circumstances of
growth.) Alteration of the investment–consumption ratio can be borne much
more easily if consumption also rises, but more slowly than investment.

Let us now consider unemployment. There are several reasons for it, but
macroeconomics definitely teaches that one of the most important factors is the
wage level. Wages (and as will be explained later, taxes linked to wages)
greatly influence the level of costs and so the profits of firms. There is a critical
threshold for profitability, and unless this can be reached at the prevailing level
of costs, it ceases to be worth a firm's while to produce, regardless of who owns
that firm, and it will lay off its employees instead. Wages and taxes linked to
wages significantly affect the competitiveness of Hungarian production in domestic and international markets. They affect exports as well, and hence the
expansion of the economy. To some extent there is a conflict of interest between the employed and the unemployed. The higher the wages extracted for
the employed, the more people risk losing their jobs.

Here the leitmotiv needs playing again: the main question is growth. So
long as the economy continues to stagnate in terms of its aggregate production figures, the insider–outsider conflict, the job-destroying effect of relatively too high wages, will intensify. The reassuring solution is the creation of
more and more jobs at a high and steady rate, faster than existing jobs are
being eliminated by transformation of the economic structure.

2.　THE BUDGET DEFICIT

While I agree wholeheartedly with the plans of the financial administrators
for a wage policy, I consider the announced fiscal policy only partially
correct. It has aspects I find acceptable and welcome, but I think it certainly
has doubtful, debatable parts as well.

I fully endorse the government's efforts to cut expenditure. I recognize the moral importance of this, as a demonstration that the state is starting its campaign of savings with itself. But the question after all is not one of moral lessons, but of acute economic problems to be solved, and from this point of view, cuts in expenditure, however commendable, will not in themselves relieve the major strains in the budget.

It is obvious from macroeconomic theory and from plain common sense that there is a strong, almost arithmetical relation between the budgetary balance and GDP. Most of the *expenditure* is not dependent on GDP, while part is, but with a negative sign in front of it. The more GDP contracts, the more must be allocated from the budget or financially related funds for unemployment and other welfare benefits. On the other hand, the vast majority of *revenue* is related almost directly to GDP, and with a positive sign in front of it. The more GDP grows, the higher the revenue (even at unchanged tax rates) from personal income tax, general value-added tax, excise duties, corporation tax, social security contributions, customs duties and so on. In the opposite case, if GDP decreases, these revenues will inevitably decline. So it can be said that in the short run, the budgetary balance is a function of the increase or decrease in GDP, and other factors have only a secondary effect.

As long as GDP contracts, the budget deficit will inevitably be reproduced. It is worth recalling the seldom-mentioned fact that the real value of budgetary expenditure in Hungary has been falling steadily since 1989, so that by 1993 it was about 20 per cent lower than it had been four years earlier, and yet the deficit has continued to grow steadily. Here let me repeat the leitmotiv in my train of thought: the budget deficit can only be eliminated permanently in an expanding economy. Growth is a necessary, though not a sufficient condition for overcoming this tension. Unfortunately the government programme lost sight of this important connection.

The same reasoning can be applied in understanding government debt. It is impossible to decide whether the burden of debt on the budget, in terms of its absolute size, is great or small *per se*, in relation to a static moment in time. Like any debt, it represents a characteristically dynamic problem. If GDP increases and the main budget totals grow along with it, the same absolute amount of debt servicing will absorb a shrinking proportion of budgetary revenue. But if GDP is contracting and budgetary revenues shrink along with it, the same absolute amount of debt servicing will require an ever-increasing proportion of budgetary revenue. So the main question is not whether the debt is high or low, but what the loans are being used for. If they promote GDP growth efficiently, they create their own resources for repayment and may even contribute to additional growth beyond that. But if they are used unwisely, they form an ever-heavier burden for the taxpayers to carry.

The stock of debt will be self-proliferating while the real interest rate paid on government securities remains higher than the growth rate of the economy. In this case the increasing debt servicing alone continually generates budgetary deficit, the financing requirement for which increases the demand for credit and so drives up interest rates, which in turn curb investment and, along with it, growth. This line of reasoning explains the strong mutual relations between budget deficit, government debt, rates of interest and growth, and the fiscal whirlpool that can pull the economy down deeper and deeper. Of course efforts must be made to curb the growth of government debt and decrease the interest burden but, ultimately, only an acceleration of growth can reverse the direction of spin, so that the economy escapes from the whirlpool instead of sinking deeper into it.

The relation between GDP and budget revenue applies almost automatically. But it is supplemented by a far from automatic relationship: the consistency and rigour with which taxes are collected. The government programme, very correctly, addresses this issue, promising to be more rigorous. Public opinion, let us face it, is ambivalent.

There are many ways to evade tax. A common case is where firms, including major businesses, are seriously in arrears on their tax, customs-duty and social-security payments. It is justified to call for strict enforcement, but it must be realized that this will have unwanted side-effects. It encourages price increases, because the firm wants to earn the money it owes or, if this is not possible, it may cause the firm to go bankrupt or into liquidation. This in turn causes jobs and production to be lost. These consequences are not welcome to those who call for speedy collection of taxes and other fiscal obligations.

The other common case is where small or medium-sized businesses increase their income by various ruses such as failing to give receipts or register employees. The gain from the state may then be shared between the entrepreneur and the customer or unregistered employee. So strict and consistent tax collection takes extra income not only from entrepreneurs who cheat on their taxes, but from hundreds of thousands of others who become accomplices by being customers in the grey economy and not demanding a receipt, or by working illegally and not insisting on registering their employment. The majority of those concerned are not among the poorest, at the bottom of the income scale, but much more commonly in the middle or even higher. The previous government did not set about forceful action to deter such behaviour in these broad strata in society. Will the present government have the strength and the resolve to do so?

While on the subject of the budget, I would like to address two more issues. The first is the highly controversial one of the income received by roughly a million people employed by the state (about a quarter of total employment). There are several factors to consider here, not least the stipulations of the law and the welfare position of those affected. Looking at the employer's side, the problem is understandably tied up with the budget deficit, since it forms one of the largest items of public spending. But it is also worth considering that the issue from a macroeconomic point of view boils down to two decisions. First and foremost there is the question of how GDP should be divided between consumption and investment, for, after all, the wages of employees paid out of the central budget are also sources of consumer spending. If the intended ratio has been attained in this respect, the second question, that of *redistribution*, presents itself. How much of total consumption should be allocated to employees paid out of the central budget, and how much should the rest receive? The only way any group in society can obtain more from a given total of consumption is for others to receive less. So those who demand higher wages for employees of the state are not arguing with the finance minister about the budget, but with the rest of the population about distribution of total consumption.

The other main set of budget-related problems is usually referred to in Hungarian parlance as 'reform of the major distributive systems'. It is easily understood by any seasoned political analyst why all politicians talk about this issue in general or veiled terms, as if their style were being cramped by the censors. For this is one of the painful points in Hungarian society, where there is nothing like a real consensus. For my part, I have no ambition to enter parliament or serve as a minister: I am not after votes, and so I can speak freely.

Nobody, not even an economist with rather strong *laissez-faire* principles, would go so far as to propose that the state abandon all its welfare functions. However, there are two pure models worth comparing.

In one, the state tries to assist only those in need out of taxpayers' money. Although this condition cannot be applied with full consistency, the principle of need could be a guiding criterion when formulating the institutions of welfare, making laws and decrees, and allocating public expenditure. The principle is an attempt to carry into effect society's solidarity with the poor, the weak and the needy. The drawback is that means tests have to be applied in some way, which in many cases is humiliating. Of course the state assists other sections of society in helping themselves. It takes an active part in building up and in endowing with initial capital a broad network of decentralized insurance companies, health associations and pension funds (operating for the most part as non-profit institutions or as market-type businesses). The state retains responsibility for creating the legal framework within which these institutions operate and for arranging for their supervision. The division of the costs of welfare and social insurance spending between employers and employees still awaits legislative resolution.

The other pure model goes much further than this, and according to various other entitlement criteria, uses taxpayers' money on welfare benefits for citizens who are not dependent on them. Such entitlement criteria may include motherhood, multiple parenthood, a desire to study at a university, sickness, or simply the status of a Hungarian citizen.

Current Hungarian practice is very close to the second model, in which the state plays an extremely paternalistic role, allocating taxpayers' money to welfare according to much broader and more comprehensive entitlement criteria than those of most other countries in the world. I used a phrase in an earlier paper of mine, which I would like to repeat here. Hungary under the Kádár regime (1956–89) became a 'premature welfare state'. Although this country was much less developed than the Scandinavian countries, the welfare commitments made by the state before the change of system were equal to and in some respects greater than theirs (Figure 2.2 and see Tables 5.7 and 5.8). This trend the first freely elected Antall–Boross government did not change, and indeed it assumed further welfare commitments. So far from approaching the first model, Hungary has even been moving in the opposite direction. A hitherto unprecedented degree of centralization took place in the pension and health-care systems, whereas almost no movement occurred towards decentralization and privatization. Extra-budgetary, but centralized funds were created that are run by their own self-governing body which is under strong trade-union control. However, any deficits in them must be automatically covered by the state out of taxpayers' money. This system is unique in the world: nowhere else has so institutionalized and grandiose a 'soft budget constraint'.

The present situation offends many people's moral standards: why should taxpayers support those not dependent on such assistance? But the really serious loss concerns economic development, not ethics. This is the main reason why tax rates are high, especially rates of taxes and levies related and proportional to wages and other income; they are perhaps the highest in the world! This grave barrier to production growth, investment and job creation gives entrepreneurs a strong motive for keeping employment secret even at the risk of detection.

I read with agreement the references in the government programme to its wish to apply the principle of need more consistently. Fair enough, but these are still only faint allusions, rather than clear plans of action. To what extent does the government wish to make the change? How far does the government want to depart from the second model and how near does it want to approach the first?

Of course the advocates of the first model, among whom I belong, do not believe it could be introduced all at once. It will take a long time to organize, and consideration must also be given to the ability of various groups in society to adjust. To give just one example, a different response to pensions can be expected from a young person at the beginning of a career, who can

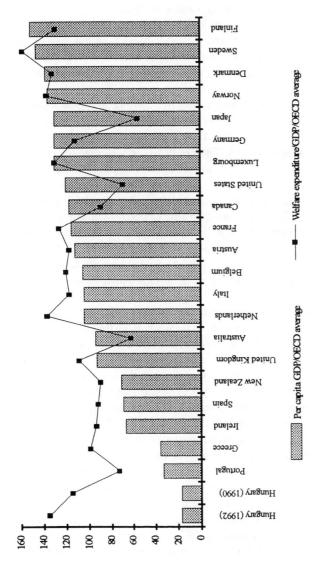

Note: The calculations are based on figures for 1990, except in the first column, where 1992 figures are given for Hungary alone. The increasing height of the bars reflects economic development, Hungary being the least developed country on the chart. In its proportion of welfare spending, however, it is only exceeded substantially by Sweden, while Norway and the Netherlands are on about the same level. The comparison between the first and second columns shows how the gap opened further between 1990 and 1992.

Source: Tóth (1994), p. 322. The author's data are based on figures from the OECD and Hungary's Central Statistical Office.

Figure 2.2 Per capita GDP and the proportion of GDP spent on welfare by OECD countries and Hungary as a proportion of the OECD average (1990)

choose between various pension schemes, and from an older person who has no choice but to rely on the pension provided by the state. The reforms should certainly be carried out with patience, humanity and tact. Far be it from me to press for undue haste, but I must ask the new government none the less: at what pace does it intend to proceed with changes?

What I said earlier in connection with wage policy applies to this sphere of problems as well. The current political scenario offers a unique chance of resolving within the governing party the conflicts of interest over discontinuing the premature welfare state and the excesses of the second model, and of settling the political battles internally.

It would be a mistake, however, to consider this conflict simply as a power struggle between different trends. An approach to the first model, with more consistent application of the principle of need, conflicts with the short-term interests of broad sections of society. The needy would welcome the change. The really rich, I believe, would not protest against it, because relative to their income the loss would be negligible. The problem would arise primarily in the middle-ranking families which cannot be called needy, but would suffer appreciable harm from the loss of a few hundred or a few thousand forints. Will the new government be brave enough to make the change none the less? Will it begin, if not quickly, then gradually and tactfully, to move resolutely and consistently in this direction? And what will the former governing parties have to say? Will they become more socialist than the Socialists?

Here again, reference must be made to the leitmotiv, the role of growth. There is the closest interaction between the reduction of the state's welfare expenditure and the growth of the economy. In one direction, excessive welfare levies and contributions act as a curb on enterprise. Like runaway wages, excessive welfare levies make it hard to reach the critical profitability threshold for viability, and still more for expansion and job creation. So ultimately they postpone and curb growth. The more welfare spending financed through taxes can be reduced, the greater the fall in employment-related production costs, and consequently, the greater the stimulus to job creation, the expansion of production and, in the end, the acceleration of growth. But the force in the opposite direction is no less important: only growth can enable change to occur with less vehement opposition. As the standard of living increases, it becomes easier to do without certain hand-outs from the state and to switch, at least partially, to voluntary insurance. While the standard of living of the middle strata is sinking due to stagnation or recession, they will understandably cling to their acquired rights to the bitter end.

Also worth mentioning here is yet another macroeconomic relation. Much has been said about how savings in Hungary do not cover investment and need encouraging more intensively. Most expert observers emphasize the role of higher deposit rates here. I would like to mention an additional factor: the very strong incentive to save that would come from partial decentralization, marketization and privatization of health care, pensions and other social benefits. People would understand that it was they themselves, to a large extent, who had to set reserves aside for sickness, old age or unforeseen expenses. Some formation of reserves of this kind takes place through the accumulation of money in bank accounts or liquid securities. The rest is done through intermediaries. Citizens buy insurance and join decentralized pension funds and medical insurance schemes, so that these institutions perform the saving and investment functions at their behest. In a mature market economy, the demand and need to form security reserves is one of the main incentives for saving. Unfortunately, this type of saving was curbed by the paternalistic practices of the past.

Returning to the budget, the main opportunity for cuts on the expenditure side is the switch from the *paternalistic model* to consistent application of the *principle of need*. However, this is not likely to contribute to easing the budget deficit. This it cannot do in the short run, as I have mentioned, since the change will certainly take a long time, and it cannot do so in the long run because one of its aims is precisely to allow lower tax rates by reducing the welfare spending that they fund. Those who refer to 'reform of the major distributive systems' as a means of eliminating the deficit are only clouding the issues for a responsible assessment of the fiscal problems.

3.   THE BALANCE-OF-PAYMENTS DEFICIT

There were unsettling signs in the balance of trade and the balance of payments in 1993 and in the first half of 1994. Domestic consumption grew faster than production. The growth of exports ceased, while imports positively jumped. The result was a substantial increase in the current-account deficit, and a consequent rise in Hungary's net debt after a decreasing trend lasting several years.

A responsible government cannot pretend nothing has happened. It certainly has to react to such signs, which the last government unfortunately neglected to do. To reiterate what I said in connection with wages, the courage with which the new government has faced up to the situation is commendable. Its vigour and speed of action are impressive. Nevertheless, I am not sure it is taking the right course in every respect.

It will be noticed that I express myself carefully here, not for any tactical reasons, but because I am not quite sure of my assessment of the situation and the immediate tasks it sets. (When it comes to longer-term tasks I shall risk a more decided opinion.) One problem I see is precisely that there has been no thorough analysis of the causes behind the disquieting phenomena and no full exploration and debate on the alternative paths to a solution. The old reflex reaction has occurred instead: trouble with the balance of payments means it is time for some tight restriction. (Here let me add that 'restriction' is the term that has gained currency in Hungarian professional parlance, but this is not just a case of restraint, but of a decisive *reduction* in several economic processes, for instance in macro demand, production and investment, and a *contraction* in economic activity. For the sake of emphasis I prefer the latter term here.) As an emergency measure, the contraction will probably work, since drastic repression of domestic consumption will reduce imports and probably force domestic producers to export. But there is a high price to pay for this, and it is not certain that such drastic means alone can achieve the purpose.

Before attempting to assess the radical cure being applied, let us return to a diagnosis of the problems. Without claiming that the list is exhaustive, I offer some reasons for the deterioration in the balance of payments, not in order of importance, but in an order that makes it easiest to see the problems.

1. A part has been played by factors beyond Hungary's control, of which I shall mention just two. One is the fall in import demand in Western Europe, particularly Germany, and the other is the loss of agricultural export supply due to the weather. Mentioning factors like these serves as a reminder: it is not worth blaming fiscal and monetary policy measures for the part of the export losses explained by external conditions.
2. Many export activities used to be sustained by state subsidies. Abolition of these, along with stricter enforcement of profitability and bankruptcy and liquidation proceedings, has eliminated several firms or sharply cut back their production. While this has had a healthy effect of natural selection in the long term, in the short term it has contributed to the fall in exports.
3. Mounting damage was caused by the incorrect exchange rate. A large part was played in the deterioration of Hungary's trade performance in 1993 and early 1994 by the fact that the exchange-rate policy had been mistaken earlier on; the effects always appear after a considerable lag. It took time before exports, imports and production adjusted themselves to the exchange rate, in this case adjusting in a harmful way to a faulty one.

So I fully support the devaluation of the forint, and along with some other economists, I have been calling for this for a long time. It was negligent of the previous government not to make up its mind to devalue. It was high time it happened. It will stimulate exports, help to curb imports, make Hungarian goods more competitive at home and abroad, and so presumably help to improve the trade balance and balance of payments. Of course, the benefits will not be immediate, for as I mentioned just now, international experience suggests that several months will elapse before the effects filter through. Apart from endorsing the government's move, I would like to make some additional remarks:[4]

a. Devaluation is bound to push up the price level. If this is followed automatically by full compensation in the wage level, the benefits of the move will be eroded. This brings us back to the same questions discussed in connection with inflation. Hence the question that crosses every economist's mind is how wages will react to the devaluation. If it is followed by full indexation, we shall fall into the same devaluation whirlpool as a number of developing countries, with a destructive cycle of successive devaluations, waves of price increases, wage indexing and restrictions.

b. Devaluation is an important means of raising competitiveness, but not the only one. I think we should be making greater use than hitherto, with careful, objective selectiveness, of the system of tariffs and subsidies, in order to promote exports and protect domestic production. This is not what I was saying in 1989, when there was a great need for a forceful campaign of trade liberalization. That helped the Hungarian economy to build up a system of relative prices which is in conformity with world market prices, and contributed substantially to ending the shortage economy. It coerced the Hungarian economy into competing with its foreign rivals and winding up its least viable production activities. Today, however, we do not have to follow such an extreme free-trade policy in this respect. There is no need to strive officiously to exceed the mature market economies in eliminating all kinds of tariffs and subsidies. Care must be taken, of course, that new subsidies and tariffs do not breach GATT rules, the association agreement with the European Union or other agreements. The question is whether the government has a concept in this respect, and if so, how it wants to prevent a scenario in which *ad hoc* tariffs and subsidies softening the budget constraint are determined by the struggle of lobbies and political clients, instead of economic rationalism.

Again, the deterioration in trade performance due to the faulty exchange rate and some overshooting in liberalization cannot be blamed on the expansion of production or consumption.

---

[4] *New note*: At the time this study was published, I was convinced that the devaluation already carried out should be followed by a further significant devaluation. I informed the financial administration of my opinion, but I refrained from making it public, for fear it might contribute to the already mounting expectations of devaluation, which were having harmful effects.

4. The balance of payments has presumably been worsened because many firms have built up vast inventories. Unfortunately the statistics on this are not reliable enough, and the figures may be exaggerated. But even allowing for this, it would seem that a large accumulation of inventories has taken place.

   What induced firms to do this? After all, the shortage economy, with its associated fears of problems with supplies of raw materials and semi-finished products, has been on the whole eliminated. The main reason, in my view, has been expectations of devaluation. If producers are sure the forint is going to be devalued sooner or later, they plainly have an interest in buying more and more imports at a lower forint price while they can. This attacked the stability of the balance of payments at its most sensitive point, stimulating imports without increasing production.

   Ultimately this occurred because firms were wiser than the government, realizing the forint would have to be devalued sharply in the end. The lesson to draw, as with points 1 and 2, is that this negative event was not the result of expansion of production. To avoid such an occurrence in the future, care must be taken not to leave the economy with expectations of devaluation, but to adjust the exchange rate *continually*, even daily if need be.

5. Pharmaceutical imports have surged, not because the income of consumers of medicines has increased, but for reasons outside the economic sphere, which it would not be appropriate to analyse here.

6. It is questionable whether the export and import figures are correct. Lying behind the widening gap between exports and imports, is there not the phenomenon known rather loosely as capital flight, or at least a more moderate version of this, with partial withdrawal of capital operating in Hungary?

   This occurrence cannot be detected by ordinary statistical means. Nothing could be simpler for a Hungarian firm with relations abroad or a foreign partner (individual or corporate) than to submit to the authorities undervalued invoices on the export side and/or overvalued invoices on the import side, so that some of the capital of the firm functioning in Hungary is immediately transferred abroad, without the movement of capital officially going through the banking system or coming before the foreign-exchange authorities. The firm need not completely cease its operations in Hungary. It may simply reduce them, and gain some liquid capital abroad in exchange. This kind of relocation of capital can be performed by any economic unit from a self-employed entrepreneur or a small private company to a vast multinational corporation. My guess is that this may have had an important impact on the deterioration in the balance of trade. There is indirect evidence for this also in the fact that this deterioration appears to have coincided with some slowing of the spectacular growth of foreign direct investment, apart from a few conspicuous and significant moves in privatization. The economic motivation is presumably the same. Entrepreneurs, investors or proprietors, Hungarian or foreign (or the managers appointed by them) ask themselves where it is better to invest their capital: in Hungary or some other country? Let me stress that in spite of all administrative controls, Hungarian entrepreneurs, as well as foreign ones, will also find a way of investing their capital abroad if their interests so dictate.

Many economists, including some experts working in the government apparatus or the banking system, share the concern that this withdrawal of capital (or in a worse case, capital flight) has an appreciably unfavourable effect on the trends in foreign trade, payments and lending. If so, this cannot be altered by simple restriction, which may even exacerbate the problem instead. Nor does an attempt to hinder the capital transfers administratively look promising. The only thing that can help is to regain the *confidence* of capital, so that entrepreneurs are inclined to keep their capital here, and bring more in as well. I shall return to the question of what this confidence and propensity to invest depends on.

7. Finally, the balance of payments has been adversely affected, apart from the previous six factors, by the following: (i) the rise in investment and production in certain sectors of the economy, creating extra demand for imports, and (ii) the surge in consumption (discussed earlier), which also stimulated imports, and crowded out exports. I would certainly not like to omit these relations from my analysis. One problem is that no one knows exactly how much of the trouble is explained by points 1–6, which are unrelated to expansion, and how much by point 7, which is certainly related to it. Nor is it accurately known how much of point 7 is explained by (i) above, the effect of production and investment growth, and how much by (ii), the effect of consumption growth. Yet that is exactly what needs to be known in order to decide on suitable proportions between the measures to improve the balance of payments.

All I have been able to do is to provide a list of the main causes of the deterioration in the balance of payments, and thereby take issue with the misleading simplification that the problem has been generated by a single cause, namely 'artificial' growth. A single research economist cannot be expected to provide a full quantitative diagnosis to determine how much of the payments deficit is explained by each factor (or possibly, what other, unmentioned factors may have contributed). To draw up a convincing diagnosis would require an apparatus, the involvement of numerous experts, and thorough professional debates.

I made it clear earlier that I understand and endorse the measures taken by the government to prevent consumption running away and reduce the bureau-cratic expenses of government. But I cannot support a policy that, deliber-ately or not, will lead not only to the restriction but to an absolute decline of production, and especially investment, so causing the economy to shrink and contract once again.

The hardest theoretical and practical problems come when we try to clarify the relationship between the growth of the economy on the one hand and the balance-of-payments deficit and foreign debt on the other. (Here I must ask readers to excuse me for touching on the same question twice: once now in relation to the balance of payments, and again later in connection with growth.)

Some people think that to borrow, to contract a debt, must be an evil, reprehensible thing. They applaud the advice of Polonius to Laertes in Ham-let:

> Neither a borrower nor a lender be;
> For loan oft loses both itself and friend,
> And borrowing dulls the edge of husbandry.

Such views are quite common in people's thinking not only about personal debt, but about corporate or national debt as well. They find it frightening that Hungary, having accumulated such big debts in the past, should now go on to increase its debt even more. This, they say, is a process that must be stopped *at all costs*.

In my opinion, such a stance is quite indefensible from an economic point of view. Let us embark on refuting it by considering a well-known macro relation: total investment in the economy (investment in fixed assets plus increment in inventories) minus total new savings generated in the economy equals the inflow of net external real resources, in the case when investment is greater than savings. (In the opposite case, when investment is less than savings, the difference equals the sum of domestic real resources flowing abroad. This case we shall disregard for now.) I use here the generic term 'external resources' to include credit raised abroad and direct investment by foreigners in this country, and also non-repayable aid. Let me draw attention to the fact that this relationship is known in professional parlance as 'iden-tity'. It is not a matter of decision or economic behaviour whether this equilibrium relation applies, for it does so all the same.

If, as in this case, investment exceeds savings, economic policy-makers can try to influence the economic processes in three ways, by encouraging: (i) a reduction of investment, (ii) an increase of savings, or (iii) an inflow of foreign resources. These do not preclude each other, of course. Within option (i), it is certainly worth encouraging a growth of fixed assets rather than inventories, as I have already said. I shall deal with option (ii), increasing savings, later on. So now let us look at the relation of options (i) and (iii): the relation between investment and the inflow of foreign resources.

The most important issue is to compare *medium and long-term* benefits and costs. This reintroduces the leitmotiv, the problem of lasting growth. On the one hand it must be clarified what additional production will be possible in future years and decades due to the inflow of foreign resources now, and on the other hand, what processes of resource outflow will be started by the repayment obligation in the same period. If the former is larger, it speaks for implementation; otherwise it speaks against. There are thousands of examples of both cases in economic history. The fast-growing economies of South-East Asia, the states of post-war Europe and the experience of many developing countries prove that success is quite possible, though not certain. But there is certainly no justification for saying in advance that there is no hope of using foreign resources well! (To illustrate this, I give a single example in Figure 2.3, the history of Japan's current-account balance.)

Here let us return to the situation in 1993–94. Investment seems to have received a boost in the past ten or twelve months. According to the Department of Economic Analysis and Modelling at the Finance Ministry, the value of investment at current prices in the first quarter of 1994 was 59 per cent up on the same period of the previous year, so that the volume of investment has grown substantially, even if price increases are taken into account. This acceleration of investment is also indicated indirectly by a rise of 34 per cent in the real volume of construction between the same two periods. It is remarkable that according to the report of the National Bank of Hungary, the proportion of machinery and equipment within imports rose very substantially, from 20.7 per cent to 26.6 per cent in 1993, which also shows that investment activity was livening up, and that imports are increasingly for investment purposes.

I have yet to see a study analysing investment projects individually and closely. I cannot state that all such projects are necessarily efficient. But I have no grounds for assuming the opposite, in other words that all or the majority of them are *inefficient*. For only in the latter case would the curious situation arise in which the part of the foreign resources drawn into the economy for investment purposes was doomed from the start. Since no careful analysis of the investment projects has been carried out, my doubts remain: maybe the contraction about to hit the economy will set back investment processes that were promising to be useful.

Another thought-provoking approach is closer analysis of production figures. For my part I consider it welcome that according to the Finance Ministry report just quoted, the growth of industrial production now apparent for some time is taking place mainly in firms with fewer than 50 employees. It is

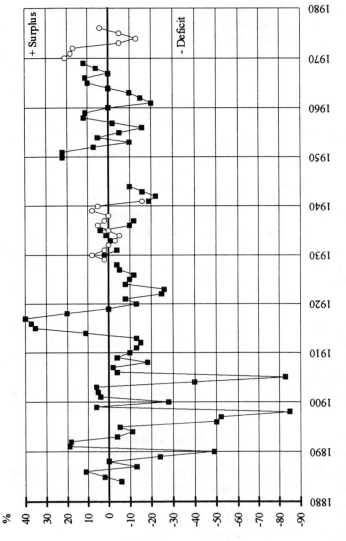

Note: o = Difference arising from the use of different bases of computation.

Source: Ehrlich (1984), p. 188.

Figure 2.3   The trend in the surplus or deficit on Japan's current account as a percentage of exports, 1885–1976

to be feared that this will be the very sector, having revived since the change of political system, which will decline due to contraction.

A further important question closely connected with the long-term cost–benefit calculation mentioned just now is to know in what form and on what terms the foreign resources are drawn into the economy. This will clearly have an effect on the additional commitments that are opposed to the additional production arising out of the investment. Here again, care must be taken to avoid any excessively simplified formula. The idea has become implanted in the public mind that further credits are 'bad', but foreign direct investments are 'good'. In fact both of these represent an inflow of foreign resources, which must be compensated for sooner or later by an outflow abroad of domestic resources. Neither is good or bad as such; the advantages and drawbacks depend on the specific payment terms, their allocation in time, and in the case of foreign direct investment, tax and other concessions granted, restrictions on the repatriation of profits and many other conditions.

From this point of view too it is desirable, if foreign resources are drawn into the economy, that as many such transactions as possible be carried out by banks and firms (Hungarian and foreign) on their own responsibility and at their own risk, without guarantees from the government or the National Bank of Hungary. If the transaction proves profitable in the long term, it will then be primarily the firm that raised the loan and the creditor or the foreign investor who see the profit, while the economy as a whole does well out of it too. If it fails, they are mainly the ones who pay. This strong incentive encourages participants to consider their decisions very carefully. Since the change of political system, there has been a favourable shift within the total inflow of foreign resources towards direct borrowing by Hungarian banks and companies and foreign direct investment, that is an increase in the portion of the debt for which responsibility is borne by the business sector rather than the government or the central bank. It would be very harmful for the economy if a general contraction set back the process of truly *decentralized* borrowing and capital inflow as well.

I give priority to medium- and long-term considerations, but, of course, one cannot ignore the *short-term* effects. Clearly the solvency of the National Bank of Hungary and the commercial banking system must be considered. I am convinced there is no threat of insurmountable short-term financing difficulties, and my conviction has been confirmed by studying the figures for debt servicing and foreign-exchange reserves, and by consultations with experts. Given a resolute government policy, Hungary can maintain and even improve its creditworthiness and reputation for reliability.

To sum up, a well-considered strategy and its thorough implementation are required to promote the growth of exports, curb the rise in imports, and improve the trade balance and the balance of payments. This is one of the key economic-policy requirements. It must be made certain that these proportions undergo a lasting improvement, or else the heightened tensions of today will reproduce themselves. Emergency measures and the most drastic of them – improving the balance of payments by decreasing production – will solve none of Hungary's long-term problems and may even exacerbate them.

Here I would like to return to a problem left open earlier: *domestic savings*. It is clear from the identity presented earlier that the higher domestic savings are at a given level of investment, the smaller the inflow of foreign resources. One of the serious mistakes in recent economic policy was to cut interest rates drastically when domestic savings started to rise. This presumably contributed greatly to the spectacular fall in household savings. The figures show that in 1993, for instance, it was not a case of the income of households running away, but of a jump in the proportion of income spent on consumption and a dive in the savings rate.

Correction of the mistake has begun. The figures for recent months indicate that there may again be an increase in the propensity of households to save. I would like to make a few comments on that.

It is time we changed the situation in which interest rates fluctuate spasmodically. A reasonable monetary policy uses its influence over interest rates very cautiously; this leads to changes of half a percentage point from time to time. In the Hungarian economy, interest rates jump wildly about (Table 2.2), which makes savers feel insecure.

Propensity to save is weakened not only by the unpredictable interest-rate policy but by the other uncertainties prevailing in the economy. The more confidence the households have in the future of the Hungarian economy, the more they are ready to keep their money there. (This has already been mentioned in connection with withdrawal of capital, and will be returned to at the end of this chapter in discussion of the macroeconomic role of confidence.)

It can be said in general that although interest rates have a profound influence on the trend in savings, they are not the only influence. Another important factor already mentioned is the strength of the motive to build up a reserve. Let me now add another: the transparency of the market for financial investments and securities, particularly state securities. Unfortunately the market for state securities is still in a very rudimentary state. Much of the population has no access to such securities at all, particularly not to the ones that are really lucrative, which remain with the financial intermediaries instead. I am convinced that a high proportion of households would be happy to invest in government bonds that provided a defence against inflation, even if the real positive rate of interest was tiny, so long as the bonds were easily accessible without the hustle and bustle of standing in lines. If they did buy them, the problems of public finance would be greatly alleviated, and so indirectly would the pressure on the balance of payments.

Table 2.2　Nominal and real interest rates (%)

Year and month		Nominal interest rates	Inflation	Real interest rates
1991	January	23.3	34.1	−8.7
	February	23.3	33.2	−8.0
	March	24.5	34.3	−7.9
	April	25.7	35.4	−7.7
	May	23.6	36.9	−10.9
	June	23.2	38.6	−12.5
	July	23.2	38.2	−12.2
	August	23.5	34.2	−8.7
	September	26.2	34.0	−6.2
	October	25.7	33.9	−6.5
	November	26.0	32.8	−5.3
	December	25.9	32.2	−5.0
1992	January	24.8	28.2	−2.7
	February	26.1	25.8	0.2
	March	22.5	24.7	−1.8
	April	23.8	23.3	0.4
	May	21.1	22.6	−1.2
	June	20.7	20.6	0.1
	July	17.8	20.1	2.0
	August	14.3	20.7	−5.5
	September	13.4	21.7	−7.3
	October	13.1	23.4	−9.1
	November	13.7	22.7	−7.9
	December	11.5	21.6	−9.1
1993	January	12.4	25.9	−12.0
	February	12.6	24.7	−10.7
	March	11.4	23.4	−10.8
	April	10.3	22.8	−11.3
	May	12.1	21.3	−8.2
	June	12.4	20.9	−7.6
	July	12.1	21.3	−8.2
	August	12.8	22.3	−8.4
	September	13.3	23.0	−8.6
	October	14.1	22.0	−7.0
	November	16.0	21.0	−4.3
	December	16.0	21.1	−4.3
1994	January	17.1	17.0	0.1
	February	15.3	16.6	−1.1
	March	17.0	16.8	0.2

Note:　The second column indicates the price indices concurrent with the nominal interest rate. This reflects the assumption that the saver expects inflation experienced earlier to continue when making a savings decision.

Sources:　*Havi Jelentések* (Monthly Reports), National Bank of Hungary.

4.   STAGNATION AND DECLINE IN PRODUCTION

I am convinced (as the main title of this chapter suggests) that the most important task in economic policy is to promote the lasting growth of the economy. This is not a self-evident requirement. The situation would be different, for instance, if there were overheating in the economy, and a dampening of growth had to be considered. There was a time, in fact, when this was one of the fundamental problems in the socialist economy.

Unfortunately, growth in Hungary has virtually stopped since 1977. For the ten years between 1977 and 1986, the average annual growth rate was a mere 1.6 per cent. Since 1987–88, the situation has become even worse: stagnation, decline, and then stagnation again at an even lower level! According to the latest report from the Central Statistical Office, revising earlier estimates, the downward trend has continued. A 4.3 per cent fall in GDP in 1992 was followed in 1993 by another fall of 2.3 per cent (Figure 2.4; see also Tables 5.1 and 5.2).

It arouses especially bitter feelings to compare Hungary's stagnation and contraction of production with the performance in so many other countries. Hungary's GDP in 1993 was back at its level in 1976–77, or more precisely, slightly above the 1976 level and slightly below the 1977 level. So there has been zero average annual growth for a period of 17 years, while many Asian countries have had annual average growth rates of 4–9 per cent, so that their production has increased by two to three-and-a-half times. There has also been growth to a lesser extent in some small European countries, less developed than those in the forefront and in that respect similar to Hungary (Table 2.3).

Not one of the country's major social problems can be solved if the economy is stagnating or declining. The widespread misery in society, the poverty of certain regions or the severe backwardness of some neglected sectors cannot be cured by shuffling resources from one area to the other. The bargaining over redistribution, inevitable but fruitless under conditions of economic stagnation, has been going on for 15 years. In my view, those who preach social sensitivity while neglecting the main problem – growth – are ducking the issue.

Clearly, the political parties and leading economic politicians in government are quite aware of the importance of growth as well. Yet I sense on various issues essential differences between official statements and the views I expressed earlier and still hold today.

The first difference concerns *the order of priority* given to the tasks of economic policy. Official statements convey the impression that there are two equally important sets of tasks, one being to stabilize the economy and the other to create conditions for growth. I do not believe these two sets of tasks have equal importance: under Hungary's circumstances, there is just *one*

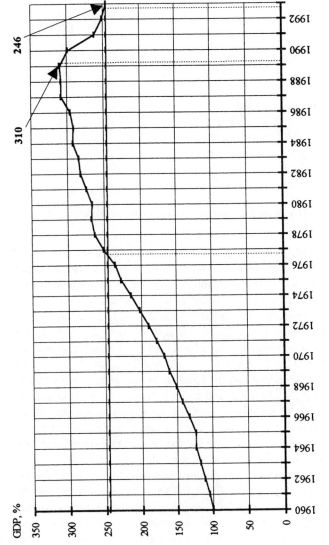

Source: Central Statistical Office (1994f), p. 2.

Figure 2.4   Index of the volume of GDP in Hungary (1960=100)

71

Table 2.3   Growth in GDP, 1977–92: an international comparison

Country	1992 GDP as a proportion of 1977 GDP (%)	Annual average growth rate (%)
Asian countries		
South Korea	354.3	8.8
Thailand	283.5	8.3
Malaysia	283.9	7.2
Japan	190.4	4.7
European countries		
Turkey	178.8	4.6
Portugal	163.8	3.3
Greece	139.6	2.2

Note: Data for Thailand and Turkey were available only up to 1990.

Sources: *World Tables*, World Bank, and *International Financial Statistics*, IMF.

main task, to establish lasting growth, to which the requirements of economic stability must be subordinated. Economists conversant with the language of mathematical models will understand if I say that maximization of the long-term growth rate is the objective-function, while the constraints concerning the balance of payments, the budget, price and wage levels and other economic variables must be observed. Of course, there are various stability requirements that must not be jeopardized for fear of harming growth as well. But a distinction must be drawn in thought and the logic of decision-making between the true objective and the constraints that must be observed for the sake of attaining the objective, and more generally, the normal operation of the economy. (From an ethical point of view, production growth is self-evidently not an end in itself either. The ultimate end of economic policy is to improve people's lives, to which an increase and improvement in its products and services are the main contribution the economy can make.)

The other difference concerns the *time sequence* for the tasks. The government programme employs the following formula: *first* create stability and thereby the conditions for growth, *and then* the economy can start to grow. For the latter, specific dates on the calendar are even mentioned in some statements: growth will ensue in 1996 or 1997 (or put negatively, will not ensue for two or, according to some statements, three years).

In my view this formulation of the time sequence is wrong. In order to subject it to criticism, we must first clarify what growth means.

Various indices are used to measure growth, of which the commonest is GDP. This is an *aggregate* indicator of the output of millions and millions of producers in the economy, some of which, at any given moment, are keeping their production steady, some raising it, and some reducing or ceasing it. The growth or decline in GDP is the result of these many positive and negative changes of various sizes.

One expression that has gained currency in the debates in Hungary in recent years is the 'start-up' of growth. People say 'It is time', or contrariwise, 'it is not yet time to start up growth.' The government programme adopts the same formula: growth should only be 'started up' later, not now, when the conditions are not yet ripe.

But the government is not in a position to start up growth. The sum of the producers does not constitute a disciplined army awaiting its marching orders. It was not like that even under classical socialism, and far less under reform socialism. As for now, after a radical decentralization in the coordination of the economy, starting up growth is out of the question. Economic units will decide for themselves whether to increase or reduce their production. The government can exert some influence over these decisions, either by encouraging and promoting growth, creating the macroeconomic, institutional and legal conditions that favour the growth of output, or by the opposite, talking firms out of expanding and erecting barriers to impede them doing so. So the government does not start up growth, it only influences whether or not growth starts of its own accord. Far from being a quibble, this distinction represents an essential difference of concept about the function of government.

The promotion of growth does not suddenly come on to the agenda when the conditions of economic stability become more favourable than they are now. It should come on to the agenda right now, and it should, in fact, have been put on the agenda much earlier. I would like here to recall an anecdote about Jean Monnet, a former French finance minister and one of the leading lights in European reconstruction after the Second World War. He was talking to his gardener one afternoon, and asked him how long it took for a certain type of tree, of which he was very fond, to reach maturity. 'About a hundred years,' was the reply, and Monnet's reaction: 'Then it was a mistake not to have set about planting it this morning.'

So the sequence of *first* stability, *then* growth, is not correct. These are two *parallel* tasks. Effort must be made at every moment to ensure that whatever economic entity is willing and able to grow should do so as much as possible. And care must be taken at every moment to respect the constraints of stability. Yet another reason for not allowing two years for the creation of stability is that the task is not one which is ever over and done with. It can reasonably be expected that as soon as one macroeconomic tension has been overcome, the same or another tension will emerge. This is not a war in which there can be victory once and for all. At best only minor battles can be won before the struggle begins again, perhaps on a different front. Problems with inflation, unemployment, budget and current-account deficits are recurrent. If we want to postpone growth until all these have been resolved, we shall be waiting for ever.

Even now, the government is performing two sets of action *simultaneously*. One set is directly aimed at growth and the other at equilibrium adjustments. Let us look more specifically, in the light of the earlier discussion, at the aspects of the programme and the measures taken so far that I think pose problems, taking these two sets of action one by one.

4.1 Promoting Growth

Several clever ideas can be found in the government programme and the first contingency plans to be published. Here I would single out the important stimulating role that tax concessions may play in investment projects.

But there are plans that work in the opposite direction and should not be allowed to become reality if growth is to be the prime objective of official economic policy. An illustration of this is the fact that the intended resolute cut in public spending aims to curb infrastructural investment as well. The desirable policy would be to cut other, non-investment spending, but to continue the state development projects at least at the planned rate, if not faster.

So far the programme has not been sufficiently rich in designing actions that can help to accelerate growth. Several measures belong here: changes in export incentives, alterations in tax regulations, further development of the banking system, for example, creating (up to now almost totally absent) institutions for long-term lending, a legal, institutional, credit and taxation system designed to promote housing construction, and so on. It is desirable that considerations of growth should be given greater attention in future plans for privatization. Much greater emphasis should be placed on what obligations the prospective owner undertakes in terms of job creation, expansion and modernization. I do not feel it is my job here to draw up a detailed plan of action. Constructive suggestions are made at countless professional discussions. Perhaps the government or parliament could commission a panel of experts to collect, elaborate and organize them all, and then publish them in a comprehensive report.

An additional reason for gathering in a single, effective document a plan for the changes to encourage growth is that they are scattered about in various reports and statements. In this respect the government's policy does not constitute a 'concept', does not offer a 'vision' of a growing, modernizing, prospering Hungary that has moved out of its rut. Yet precisely such a vision would lend confidence and hope, and engender a new propensity to invest and bring capital into the country.

4.2 Improving Stability

Having discussed the various imbalances individually in previous parts of this chapter, I would like now to make some comments summing up my views.

I fully support the efforts to reduce the budget deficit and the trade and current-account deficits, and to resist the acceleration of inflation. I agree that a major shift is needed in the ratio of investment to consumption, in the former's favour. I also agree that a major shift is needed in the ratio of exports to domestic consumption, in the former's favour. But I must add emphatically to this endorsement that it is desirable to achieve all this at the prevailing level of macro demand, or in the future with a steadily rising level of macro demand, not at the price of a fall in macro demand. A curb on real consumption is unavoidable, but it should be applied only to an extent that is matched by the increment in investment and exports. In other words, the total demand for production, and so total production, should not be allowed to fall during the course of the adjustment.

I do not recommend an irresponsible, amateurish 'dynamizing' of the economy. But it is one thing to refrain from that and another to initiate a further recession.

I do not recommend using a so-called fiscal stimulus in the present situation of the economy, that is macro demand to be raised at the cost of increasing fiscal deficit. At the same time I would like to warn those managing the economy against making a mistake in the opposite direction: they should not risk a fall in production for the sake of a cut in the budget deficit. This was the big mistake made by financial authorities in several countries during the Great Depression of the 1930s, mindlessly cutting macro demand further when the economy was already in a deep slump.

I have no illusions about how accurately the desirable proportions can be calibrated. The results of fine-tuning are rather dubious, and might differ from the intentions of the government. It is almost certain that the changes in proportion mentioned cannot be made without friction. You cannot cut consumption exactly as much as exports and investment can be increased. My objection is to the actual *intention*. The government starts out by planning a fall in GDP because it wants to reduce macro demand in absolute terms. Although the contraction in production it wants is fairly small, the actual production figure could end up much lower than expected. Not only may real consumption fall but investment as well, although it has hardly started to increase. For eight or ten months it seemed as if the economy, mainly in terms of investment and industrial production, was starting to climb out of its trough. The risk is that a reduction in macro demand will push it back again, not simply into stagnation but into a further contraction of production following the output decline of 1993.

Unfortunately, it is not just a case of a single fall in GDP of 1–2 per cent, and then it is over; production can grow again. Macroeconomics clearly shows that both increases and decreases in macro demand have so-called multiplier effects. Decreases in production cause lay-offs. Less is spent by those who have lost their jobs and by the owners and employees of firms that are cutting production, which reduces macro demand yet again, and that effect repeats itself like a series of ripples. Just think for a moment: the spiral of restrictions and recession has been repeated over and over again in Hungary in the last 15–18 years. There is a danger that the spiral will continue and the economy sink deeper and deeper.

My impression is that leading economic policy-makers and their expert advisers feel some kind of panic in relation to growth. The bogey with which they are scaring themselves is the ill-fated dynamization of the mid-1980s, which failed to lift the country out of stagnation and took it further into debt instead. It must be realized, however, that today's Hungarian economy is not identical with the one of ten years ago. The ownership relations have changed: state ownership was dominant then, whereas more than half of the production comes from the private sector now. The excessive, distorted concentration of the economy has ceased; tens of thousands of small and medium-sized firms have appeared alongside the large ones, and so have several hundred thousand self-employed workers. The budget constraint on firms has hardened. There are realistic market prices and the market mechanism works, even if it creaks a little. There has been a fundamental change in the structure of the economy, so that the share of the service sector, for instance, has increased substantially. The hard-currency market is now the main area in which Hungarian exports are sold. What happened after the dynamization programme carried out in 1984 has absolutely no relevance to what effect growth would have these days.

It is most unfortunate that serious difficulties should have arisen with the balance of payments in 1993 and the first half of 1994. However, as I have tried to make clear earlier in this chapter, a substantial proportion of the measures planned, notably the ones aimed at repairing the balance of payments by bringing about a contraction in the economy, are based on an analysis of the imbalance that is incorrect in many respects. The policy-makers have not seen sufficiently clearly what the real causes of the troubles are, and so the correction they are making to the course of the economy will not eliminate them. As I have already emphasized, it would be a mistake simply to blame the deterioration in the balance of payments on growth, which has hardly begun anyway, and use it as a further argument for contraction. Although the increase in the propensity to invest has placed a burden on the balance of payments, it is a burden that I think is worth bearing. The trouble was that personal incomes ran away at the same time, and there was also a number of other unfavourable circumstances and errors deteriorating the export–import ratio.

I would very much like to ask those who shrink from promoting growth what they think is the relation between growth and the current account. Is there a curse on our country, so that time and again in the future, when we go for growth, there will be big trouble with the balance of payments, so that we will never, ever emerge from the spiral of recession and restriction that is dragging us deeper and deeper into the mire of stagnation?

Let me point out that I oppose a contraction of the economy and a reduction in economic activity not because of the burdens it places on today's generation. As I explained in the section on wages (Section 1), this burden, unfortunately, seems to be inescapable. What I would warn against is any call for sacrifices that then fail to have an effect, because the economic policy pursued fails to convert today's belt-tightening into tomorrow's growth. In other words, I am not protesting because some of the government's measures will force us to tighten our belts. I object because the package as a whole may deepen the recession still more, making the prospects of recovery still more remote and uncertain.

Under no circumstances can I accept a defensive, defeatist point of view. Irrational fears of damage to the balance of payments can only cripple action. Instead there are two problems we should reconsider in an impartial, unprejudiced way.

The first is how to encourage the kind of structural changes that allow GDP growth in the future without any damage, or with the least damage, to the balance of payments. Experience of other open, highly trade-oriented countries suggests that growth always places a burden on the balance of payments. The rising demand for imports usually comes sooner than export success. But this is not some kind of automatic, arithmetically determined rule. Matters can be improved by a wise government policy (on prices, exchange rates, export promotion, tariffs and so on). Such a policy can promote the country's export drive and curb its demand for imports, without drastically halting or slowing growth itself.

The second problem is how to draw foreign resources into Hungary in the most practical way that places the least burden on the country. We must not shudder at the idea that we need the inflow of foreign resources. Most countries less developed than the leading industrial ones used foreign resources in the period of shifting from recession or stagnation to growth. I could put this more strongly: I do not know if there has ever been a case of a country accomplishing this shift entirely through its own resources.

What must be avoided is a course of events in which the fact that there was an inflow of foreign resources emerges *after* it has occurred, as an unpleasant surprise. It is far better to consider what to do in advance. This chapter does not set out to make specific recommendations on this. There are many forms of capital inflow which are not mutually exclusive, so that they can be used in various combinations. My impression is that Hungary so far has only used some in the range of possible instruments. Having consulted Hungarian and foreign experts on the subject, we should reconsider the tasks entailed in attracting and utilizing foreign resources.

5.   OPTIMISM AND THE SPIRIT OF THE DEBATES

Success in growth and macro stabilization have a common prerequisite, and that is a *mood of optimism*. The poll of economic activity taken by the research institute Kopint-Datorg in the first quarter of 1994 indicated that the majority of firms were more optimistic than for many years. Many more said at the time of polling, that is before becoming acquainted with the new measures, that they expected both export and domestic sales' prospects to improve. I am afraid that this mood of hopefulness will now be dampened by a cold shower.

In my opinion it is incorrect to defend measures to stabilize the economy or impose wage discipline by saying that the economy is in a disastrous state. It is incorrect, first of all, because it is untrue. The Hungarian economy is robust; there are hundreds of thousands of businesses actually doing business. Luckily the Hungarian economy is already a highly decentralized system, which has a healthy self-propelling motion even if some government or minister should make a mistake. Governments and ministers come and go, but the market and production fuelled by the interests of private owners remain and keep the economy alive.

The crisis management should cease, in my opinion. Everyone is fed up with it. Back in the time of the 1989 negotiations for the change of political system, the tasks of crisis management were already being debated, and the discussion has gone on ever since. This only dilutes the meaning of the word 'crisis'. Not that I want to remove it from the economic dictionary. If the National Bank of Hungary became insolvent in the international financial market tomorrow, there would be a real crisis. If the currently moderate rate of inflation suddenly speeded up into multi-digit hyperinflation, we would indeed have a crisis. If life in the country were crippled by mass strikes, crisis would be the word. Real crises must certainly be avoided, but it is impossible still to be living in a state of permanent crisis management after so many years.

Roosevelt, when he wanted to raise the United States and the world economy out of the Great Depression, said, 'The only thing we have to fear is fear itself.' To whip up a mood of disaster is not only unjustified, but harmful, because it is self-fulfilling. The more the government talks about it, the more it will be believed in, by entrepreneurs, by investors, and by Hungarian and foreign capital and business. And then there really will be a crisis.

For lasting growth, optimism is an essential requirement of economic psychology. Capital will stay here and flow into the country voluntarily and contentedly so long as the perception is of a healthy, steadily growing economy with an expanding market. Just like pessimism, optimism can be a self-fulfilling phenomenon. I sincerely hope that optimism will prevail among the economic policy-makers and economic actors.

While on the subject of these mood conditions for growth, I would like to make a few more remarks about how I expect what I have written here to be received, assuming, of course, that attention is given to it in professional and political public life.

Some of my suggestions are connected with choices between values and, along with these, political decisions. Let me mention three examples of this. One is the wage and income policy. No matter what a government or opposition politician thinks about these issues, he or she must ultimately decide what sort of distribution of economic wealth and burdens there should be between the various groups of households and between succeeding generations. The second issue is tax collection: there is some conflict of interest here between the ethical requirement of fair sharing of burdens and the short-term material interests of the different classes and social groups. Finally, the third issue is the conflict between the principle of need and the paternalistic role of the state. Clearly there are fundamental conflicts of values here.

As a researcher who likes to separate political decisions and value choices clearly from the strict rationality criteria of efficiency, I wish parties and politicians would take sides in these issues clearly and without empty rhetoric, and at last reach beyond general statements that commit them to nothing. I am not sure this wish of mine will come true very soon.

There is clearly a political dimension to the question of whether the situation is really disastrous. There are also political overtones in the question of whether the economy's reaction to being boosted will be the same as it was ten years ago, because 'nothing has changed' since. Or if anything has changed, it has been for the worse.

Several statements in this chapter have suggested that I do not agree with the one-sidedly negative view taken of recent years. As a student of political economy, I am unsurprised, of course, to find a political group intent on gaining power trying to criticize for electoral reasons the policies of its rivals, who are already in power. It is also clear that when they take over government, they have good reason to present their starting position in as negative a light as possible, because that means even modest results in the future will seem greater. If the country is in a serious crisis, even mere survival assumes the proportions of a big success.

It would be important to assess the new government's starting position objectively, without political partiality. As I have said, the current situation has several very alarming features (such as the budget and current-account deficits). Moreover, there are many long-term trends dating back to when the communist party had a monopoly of power, and perpetuated or exacerbated under the Antall–Boross government (for example, the excessive commitments of the premature welfare state, leniency in the face of wage pressure, and gradual accumulation of additional foreign debt). But there has also been some substantial and healthy development, partly as a spontaneous result of the democratic transformation, and partly as a result of correct measures taken by the government and parliament (for example, the formation of a market economy, the spread of the private sector, the establishment of a constitutional state, and so on). These are precisely the achievements that we can build upon when the issue on the agenda is *not* to continue the policies of the 1980s or of the Németh government (1989–90), but to create an economic policy in line with the starting position in 1994.

There is, however, a part of my message, the main idea of growth, that is not really a political issue or a choice between values. Decisions in connection with this must rest on clarification of a host of problems in which the final words must be said on the basis of data, logical reasoning and professional analyses. Let me give a few examples, each of which has been discussed in detail earlier on. Why did the balance of payments deteriorate in 1993 and the first part of 1994? What forms and magnitude of external resources can be accepted without risking a solvency crisis? What factors caused domestic savings to fall, and what will make them grow in the short and long term? These are not issues that should arouse political passions.

Some of the arguments are not, in fact, between politicians, but between their economic advisers. Although this chapter was written for a wider audience, let me say a few words at this point on the theoretical background to the debates.

Those today who favour restriction (or contraction, to use my more decisive expression) do so on the basis of so-called monetarist theory, or under the indirect influence of this theory. Or to be even more precise, their thinking is strongly influenced by a rather simplified and extreme version of monetarist theory,[5] which especially in its dogmatic, doctrinaire version, is far from enjoying a monopoly in the international world of economists. It has many critics, and its reputation has declined particularly in the last five or ten years. The vast majority of economists in the world are trying to arrive at an integration of the former, extremist theories, extracting what is valid from them. Moreover, any theory, according to well-trained and careful appliers of it, is valid only *under certain circumstances*! What may have been true in the first two years of Margaret Thatcher's reign is not necessarily applicable to Britain ten years later. It is worth mentioning that many of the ideas of Keynes are being rehabilitated, without regaining their earlier position of dominance. Various trends of neo-Keynesianism are gaining ground. Here again it can be said that Keynes's ideas are only valid in practice *under certain circumstances*. What may have been a good recipe in America in 1932 may not be useful in 1994 there, let alone in Ukraine or Albania. Yet this should not make us forget the ideas of Keynes that remain valid.

I consider myself neither a Keynesian nor a monetarist, nor a one-sided advocate of any other school. This essay does not promote the teachings of any particular stream. Instead it tries to draw from several sources concurrently.

What is really needed is a synthesizing, integrating utilization of the well-known theories, and beyond that, theoretical innovation as well. In today's Eastern Europe, and specifically in today's Hungary, the situation is quite novel, and therefore no ready-made solution is available. The 1985 Israeli stabilization, which I mentioned before, was marvellous because its designers had the courage to combine the standard scheme with a drastic non-market intervention in wages and prices. My proposal is not to copy this, but to copy its mistrust of ready-made schemes, its theoretical courage in rethinking the problems.

Nor is it a solution to cite successful foreign experiences, and to propose following the Polish or the Czech example. At the beginning of the post-socialist transition, there were drastic declines in real wages in Poland and Czechoslovakia, which did not occur in Hungary (Figure 2.5). This was certainly a factor behind the rise in production after the great recession first in Poland and then in the Czech Republic, preceding the Hungarian economy in this respect.

In 1989 I proposed a very similar macroeconomic strategy for Hungary to the one employed by the Poles and the Czechs. Few people supported it. Not

---

[5] *New note*: Here my essay, I am sorry to say, has taken over the mistaken Hungarian usage whereby the restrictive–contractive economic policy is labelled 'monetarist'. In fact the statements of monetary theory and their economic-policy implications do *not* necessarily include the prescriptions of a restrictive–contractive monetary and fiscal policy. In terms of the history of economic thought, therefore, there is no justification for applying the attribute 'monetarist' to this policy.

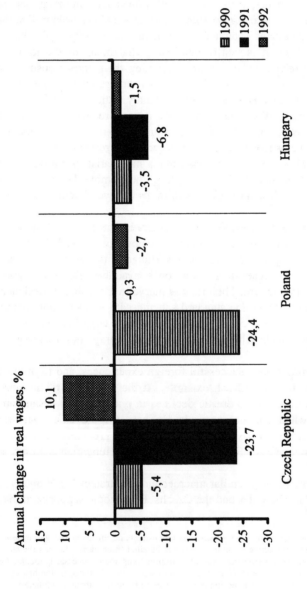

Annual change in real wages, %

▦	1990	
■	1991	
▨	1992	

Czech Republic   Poland   Hungary

New note: This figure was revised during the compilation of this book.

Source: See Table 5.6.

Figure 2.5   Real wages in three post-socialist countries

only did the government that gained power at the time not heed it, but the opposition and several major figures in the economists' community were against it as well. Let me say this: I would not recommend the country *today* to do what it failed to do in 1990, not because I have revised my opinion about the situation then, but because the situation has changed in the meantime. Then we were before a recession, whereas now we are after a major recession (and possibly facing a further one). Then we had no unemployment, while now it has stabilized at a high level. Then inflation was starting to rise, and it might still have been possible to avoid inertial inflation at a high level, while now this has already happened. So we need now an economic policy that corresponds to the current situation.

Let me reiterate that my standpoint with respect to growth is based on professional considerations. I realize that a sizeable proportion of Hungarian economists do not share my views, and as far as I can tell, these are the ones who have the greatest influence on today's economic decision-makers. But I am not alone in my views. Based on a similar, or slightly different train of thought, several fellow economists have expressed closely related views on growth. Political decisions are taken by vote, but economic theories are not usually voted upon. It is not the number of exponents of policies of contraction or the number of opponents proposing a more growth-oriented policy that counts. The question of who was in the right will be decided by research, data, models, computations, scientific arguments and ultimately by the experience in Hungary and internationally over many years to come.

Yet I am not an academic Don Quixote, and I do not want to shut my eyes to the fact that at the time of writing there is indeed going to be a vote in parliament on a supplementary budget for 1994 and the annual budget for 1995, and on other issues of economic policy discussed here. Parties and politicians will argue about economic-policy issues. What can be expected?

Whenever I talk to American or British colleagues on these questions, I am always at a loss. They have become used in recent decades to the fact that conservative politicians listen more to monetarist advisers, and social democrats or liberal politicians tend to follow Keynesian advice. With a degree of simplification, Reagan was close to Friedman, while Clinton tends to follow the advice of Tobin or Solow or their disciples, to mention American names. This formula does not apply in Hungary.

The ideas I have been voicing in the past few years were most prominently represented in the political arena by the politically liberal Federation of Young Democrats (Fidesz). Slightly similar ideas were stated by some economic politicians of the more conservative Hungarian Democratic Forum (MDF) and Christian Democratic People's Party (KDNP), probably under the influence of their own staff, rather than my advice. On the other hand, monetarist doctrines have had a great influence on the economic advisers of both the Hungarian Socialist Party (MSZP) and the liberal Free Democrats (SZDSZ), which are now the two coalition parties. If I mention this abroad, people say it is an enigma.

And it is an enigma to some extent. There may be many correct or incorrect ideas in what I have said about growth here, but there is nothing incompatible with modern social democracy, say, or with political liberalism. On the other hand, there is nothing in it related to the MDF's popular–national notions or the Christian democratic tradition espoused by the KDNP. Why has this strange correspondence evolved between the 'colours' of the Hungarian political spectrum and the alternative strategic ideas in connection with growth?

There is an easy, maybe too easy an explanation: the dialectics of political polemics generates the debate in this sphere. To caricature this line of thinking, one could say: 'If my foe, my political rival, says one thing, I must say the diametrically opposite.' This can be seen to apply in several cases.

Maybe the formation of views today is also influenced by the traditions of contemporary Hungarian economics. Many of the MSZP's and SZDSZ's advisers, that is the experts of the present governing coalition, come from the ranks of the former reform economists. They were rightly angered then by the vain attempts of the Kádár regime to boost the economy. Monetarism then was a major ideological discovery for them, whose macroeconomic theory related closely to a radical reduction in the role of the state and emphasis on the advantages of the market, that is to a number of ideas that came as a revelation to reformers battling against bureaucratic socialism. Apparently many of these economists have been unable to leave behind the views they acquired in their early professionally impressionable years, so that these have become prejudices and their counsels are now having a distorting effect on economic-policy decisions.

Other factors may also play a role in this peculiar development in political and professional opinions, but whatever the reason for it, this is the reality.

In writing and publishing this essay, I must expect that my arguments will be used by some people with whom I disagree on important political issues. My ideas may be used to discredit elements of the announced government policy that I find correct. It is also possible that those who agree with my ideas about growth will connect them up with xenophobic, nationalistic ideas aimed at stemming the inflow of foreign capital, even though these ideas are quite far from my own.

I must also expect that once my views drift into the political arena, they will share the fate of those expressed in the intense debates there. I have tried to formulate my statements accurately, but I must reckon with the possibility that those who do not agree with me will take my words out of context, as they did in earlier debates. My words of criticism or suggestion may be used in ways contrary to their original meaning, so as to make them easier to refute.

Having assessed these dangers, I have decided, struggling against some doubts and worries, to publish the essay. Ultimately I believe that a researcher cannot suppress his or her ideas due to considerations of day-to-day political fighting. Whoever speaks for me or against me, I must adhere as a researcher to the criterion of my conviction of the truthfulness of my statements and the usefulness of my proposals. Since I am so convinced, I publish them.

AFTERWORD TO CHAPTER 2: LOOKING BACK TWENTY MONTHS LATER

On 12 March 1995, eight months after this essay appeared, a programme of adjustment and stabilization was announced by the Hungarian government and the National Bank of Hungary. As I write these lines in April 1996, the implementation of the programme has been in progress for more than 12 months.[6] I feel I must add at least a short note explaining to readers how I view the validity of this study *today*.

First of all it can be established that the underlying ideas in the essay appear in the programme. The question of how much influence my writing had on those devising the programme can be left open. In what follows, I sum up very briefly the places where there are overlaps of ideas. I mention four problems on which there was debate before 12 March 1995, and on which the programme eventually espoused the position I supported (in most cases not alone, but in company with others). I also mention how far the events since then have confirmed the proposals at that time.

1. The most important message in my study was that the task of stimulating growth must not be subordinated to the task of short-term stabilization.[7] It is not permissible, in time sequence or in emphasis, to bring forward one or relegate the other. This contrasted with the view of those who proposed a one-sided policy of restriction and contraction. Lajos Bokros, the new finance minister, from the moment the programme was announced, espoused the idea of 'growth and equilibrium', and this remained the guideline of economic policy even after his resignation.

   My study warned against the contraction of production, drawing attention to the dangers of a new wave of recession. It recommended a shift in

[6] The main data on implementation of the stabilization programme appear in Table 6.1.

[7] Chapter 4, written after the stabilization programme was announced, returns to the question of my position on economic-policy priorities when I wrote this study and the extent to which it later changed.

the absorption of GDP, at the expense of consumption and in favour of exports and investment and, on the supply side, at the expense of imports and in favour of domestic production. All this was to be done in such a way that production did not fall, while the impetus of investment activity should remain, if possible.

This recommendation was reflected not only in the programme, but in practice during the first 12 months of stabilization. The Hungarian action stands out in the varied history of stabilization programmes because the drastic correction occurred without any fall in production to this day. The macroeconomic proportions have shifted in precisely the direction the study recommended.

2. There was debate about the methods of stabilization. My study, right at the beginning of its line of argument, espoused the unpopular idea that wage policy was one of the keys to adjustment, and a squeeze on consumption was inevitable. It drew particular attention to the fact that there is an economic gain in devaluation only if nominal wages do not fully compensate for the price rises caused by the devaluation.

    This is what has happened. The productivity of labour rose while real wages fell. 'The question of wages will be the matriculation examination for Hungarian society in the period before us,' I wrote at the time. The drastic fall in real wages exacted a grave sacrifice from Hungarian employees, and this painful sacrifice was undoubtedly one of the main sources of the success obtained so far in the stabilization.

3. Debate was going on about the method of reducing the budget deficit. Here my study again undertook an open defence of an unpopular idea: that reform of the welfare sector was inescapable, including a reduction in some universal entitlements. One of the leading ideas behind the reform was the principle of need.

    These ideas came to form one of the cardinal points of the stabilization programme. It is too early to talk of radical changes in this respect. However, the taboo of welfare entitlements has been broken, and it is now possible to argue the question on its merits.

4. When it came to the balance of payments, I drew attention to the complexity of the situation, from the shortcomings of exchange-rate policy, through the special problems of imports, to the issue of capital flight. The programme displayed invention and circumspect care in the way it used a broad range of means to produce a swift correction in the trade and current-account balances. An appreciable improvement took place in the first 12 months, and it can be hoped that this will continue.

5. There is one important message in my study in which I see problems with present-day eyes. I spoke out against a mood of impending catastrophe, which had scared public opinion for some months. I said the prob-

lems were grave, but the country was not on the brink of collapse. That is why I did not push into the foreground of my proposals the measures whose direct purpose was to prevent a sudden loss of creditworthiness and an acute debt crisis.

My critics at the time had already commented, in writing and in personal discussions, that in an article in a widely read newspaper, I should have lent my support to those who were trying to spur a hesitant political leadership to action to improve the equilibrium. History cannot be replayed in a way different from what actually happened. It cannot be confirmed or denied that if I had done this, it would have helped to curtail the long period of hesitation. So for want of proof, I cannot reject this criticism, but I cannot truly endorse it either.

I still consider that to have aroused 'panic' and a mood of impending catastrophe then, in the summer of 1994, would not have been justified. For one thing, such incitement can act as a self-fulfilling prophecy. The more we say we are on the brink of a crisis, the more we lose the confidence of investors, domestic and foreign alike, and the more capital flight begins and accelerates. It would be a dubious undertaking to try to persuade leading politicians to avert a crisis on the same public pages where reassurance needs to be given.

I published my study in the summer of 1994. Looking back after two years, I see that it was still several months before the Mexican crisis. There was still plenty of time for considered, energetic, deliberate action. The shortage at that time was not of dramatic notes of public warning, but of political courage, and willingness to take unpopular action.

Unfortunately, we were in the midst of a period when the lost months, weeks, and eventually days came to count, and the postponement of the painful 'belt-tightening' measures steadily increased the dangers. Confidence in the country's creditworthiness weakened at an accelerating rate in the second half of 1994 and early 1995. When the Mexican crisis ensued at the beginning of 1995, there began to be a direct threat of a debt crisis. Even then the hesitation continued for several months, until finally the government was forced, by the ever more frequent and alarming signs, to introduce the drastic March stabilization programme as a preventive measure of crisis aversion.

Something that economic historians and political economists studying crises and stabilization programmes have noted on similar occasions proved true yet again: politicians can usually bring themselves to take unpleasant, unpopular measures only when faced with catastrophe. On this occasion Hungary fared better than some countries, because the measures of aversion were taken at the last minute *but one*, before the catastrophe could occur.

3. A steep road: an interview by László Zsolt Szabó on the stabilization programme[1]

Professor, apparently the government's announcement on 12 March 1995 caught even some members of the government by surprise. Did you play any part in drawing up the government's economic measures?
I am an independent researcher and an independent teacher. This means I have not been an adviser to this government or to the last. Nor am I an adviser to any political party, and so in this sense I did not take part in preparing the government programme. I consider my main way of contributing to be my writing. When it comes to public thinking and politicians, I seek to influence them by putting my ideas in writing. They may have been so influenced, but you would have to ask them about that.

In general terms, how did you receive this package of measures?
I have some critical comments to make; there are some things I miss in them – but these are secondary. I would like to emphasize that I agree with the ideas underlying the government programme now put forward, and I look on them as necessary, correct and inescapable. I must add straight away that these measures will be accompanied by many trials and sorrows: many people will suffer. I am fully aware of this and I sympathize with those who are placed in a difficult situation. I do not consider the government programme as a piece of good news, but as the beginning of a course of therapy that is essential for the country's good.

What in your view is the reason why we have come to this?
The problems have a long history. We have to go back to the 1970s and 1980s, when Hungary's economic policy was typically one of living for the moment. The Western press at the time, with a measure of admiration and irony, called Hungary the land of 'goulash communism'. We in Hungary often called it 'frigidaire socialism', because there began to be some rise in the standard of living – everybody was pleased about that, everybody saw only the advantages

[1] Text of a conversation broadcast by Duna Television on 9 April 1995.

of that. But even at that time we were running up debt to accomplish it. By debt I mean here primarily foreign debt, but to this must be added the debt built up by postponing action, putting off tasks of investment and conservation of social wealth. So as we lived for the moment, we were rolling before us a body of debt that would place greater and greater burdens on later generations. No government had the courage to set about dealing with that body of debt or even to face up to it at all. That was typical of the 1980s. Then came a great, and in a way unrepeatable occasion: 1990, the first freely elected parliament, the first democratically elected government. But the new government too missed a great historical opportunity of setting about resolving this complex of problems. It would have been unpopular at any time to do so, and the government preferred to keep postponing the unpopular measures. Then there came another chance, although not such a great one as in 1990. But as everyone knows, the best time to take tough measures is the beginning of every term of governmental office, during the honeymoon with the public – the first hundred days. Once again, the opportunity was not seized. So the present package of measures has come at last after successive postponements.

You mentioned in a paper in 1993[2] not just postponement, but a kind of transformational recession as well. What is this transformational recession?
Several factors are combined here. The change of system itself causes economic difficulties. Prices are freed, with new prices replacing the old, compulsory ones set by the state, which means that the economy, production and consumption need realignment. And the conditions are not immediately ripe for such restructuring, so that a great deal of capacity goes unutilized. There are macroeconomic changes: the shortage economy gives way to an economy of surplus. The queues vanish, but at the same time the general proportions between supply and demand alter. This also leads to recession. Moreover, it takes time to set up new mechanisms and new legal regulations, and a coordination vacuum appears for a while. So there are a great many factors whose joint result tends to be, as every post-socialist economy shows, that production falls to a greater or lesser extent, normally to quite a large extent. And this has compounded our problems. It is the habit of living only for the moment and putting problems off until the future, combined with the presence of transformational recession, that has placed the country in a very tough economic predicament.

Yet you wrote down very precisely, in 1989, in 1993 and in 1994[3], what tasks had to be accomplished at all costs in order to bring about a recovery from

[2] See Kornai (1993b).
[3] See Kornai (1990 [1989], 1993b) and Chapter 2, this volume.

this recession. Could you sum up the essential points in these writings of yours?
You are asking too much of me; I would like to side-step that to some extent. I wrote a short book on the economic transformation in 1989, and thereafter a succession of studies. It would be hard to sum them all up in a couple of sentences. Perhaps I could mention just as an example the question of the budget. I had already put very strongly in my 1989 book the proposal or demand for radical settlement of the budget deficit. Then in 1992 I published a study that centred on the budget problem.[4] There I referred to fiscal traps; in other words, I put forward the idea that the transition causes very grave and almost inescapable fiscal difficulties. The old, simple method of collecting state revenues – the national bank simply deducting tax payments due from the accounts of a few thousand state-owned enterprises – has come to an end. Now, suddenly, there appear a hundred thousand new participants in the economy, in the sphere of company taxation, and several million individuals paying personal income tax. Some of the actors in the economy move into the grey and black spheres not covered by the tax authorities, which causes grave difficulties on the revenue side. Meanwhile on the expenditure side there remain the great welfare commitments made earlier, plus some new welfare tasks such as the payment of unemployment benefit, which did not have to be faced before. This occasions severe fiscal problems. So several of the problems that have come so much to the fore today were raised a good while earlier in the economic writings of others and of myself.

If the problems were so obvious, why is it, do you think, that these measures are being taken now, or rather only now?
I am fond of using metaphors from medicine and health care in my writings – let me resort to one now. Take the case of a heart patient. As we know, heart patients are quite likely to suffer a heart attack, which is either fatal or at least causes severe damage. It depends on the patient when he starts doing something about his heart disease. There are some who start protecting themselves very early on, turning to a healthy way of life, giving up smoking, drinking only in moderation, not eating too much, and so on. But there are some who do not do this, not even when the doctor presents them with worse and worse ECG results. Then, perhaps when a neighbour has a heart attack, they bring themselves to do it after all. But there are some who do not draw the right conclusions even then, only when they themselves experience an attack. I think what has happened in Hungary is that the 'doctors' – at home and abroad – have been putting more and more baneful results before the patient. And there have been cases of heart attack here and there in the world, which

4 See Kornai (1992b).

have served as a warning that we could suffer one too. The forecasts of a catastrophe, the early warnings of really big economic trouble serve to stress the urgency of the situation and those who have to make the decision start to feel that action cannot be postponed any longer.

No doubt certain economic indices have contributed as well. Which are the main indications that the situation has become untenable?
I think the most serious of the short-term stabilization problems is the question of the external balance, which appears directly in the disturbance to the balance of payments. Hungary's balance-of-payments deficit is mainly linked with problems with the balance of trade – the proportions between exports and imports. I feel this to be the most dangerous area. Clear signs have appeared that the situation is untenable. In 1993, Hungary already had a strongly negative balance of trade – it imported substantially more than it exported. It still might have crossed our minds in 1993 that this could be a temporary occurrence and that better proportions would return. The situation became really serious when 1994 brought the second very strongly negative balance of payments. The figures are well known: the deficit is equivalent to 9–10 per cent of GDP, which is intolerably high. When a country produces a balance-of-payments deficit and accompanying trade deficit like this two years running, something has to be done. There is no longer a sensible economist in the world, I think, who would say it can just be ignored.

It is interesting to hear you say this, because in 1993[5] you were more lenient about the balance-of-payments deficit, although even then you wrote that we must not allow it to precipitate any kind of crisis.
My view all along has been that a sensible and acceptable level of deficit in the balance of payments can be borne under certain conditions. I would go further and say I consider it quite normal and healthy, at a medium level of development, in the throes of a great transformation, to draw upon foreign resources for internal development purposes. When matters improve a bit, we can readily do so. That is one case. The other is when a situation develops, cumulatively, through the steady building up of problems, in which the threat is precisely that the normal flow of foreign resources into the country will dry up. We cannot afford a situation in which not only does the capital stop arriving, but investors start taking it out or fleeing with it, in panic. At that point there has to be a change. Measures must then be taken to bolster the country's creditworthiness, reliability and attraction for investors.

[5] See Kornai (1993b).

Perhaps we could return for a moment to the stock of debt, which you mentioned earlier in connection with the balance of payments. What connection is there between the balance-of-payments deficit, the stock of debt, and economic growth, the growth in gross domestic product?

What is desirable for Hungary at present is a change in the structure of the utilization of GDP. And there is a danger now, in the midst of stabilization measures, that the idea of this structural change becomes lost in the debate. The desirable change in the structure will allow Hungary to export more and invest more. And a substantial proportion of our investment should be designed to assist exports – in other words to create capacity for exportable production. This can only be done in one way at a given level of GDP: if one thing is raised, something else has to fall. Consequently, the relative proportions of consumption have to be reduced. Within consumption, it is desirable for the cut to be in state consumption, budget-financed consumption, rather than in the extra-budgetary sphere. And another desirable change is for imports to fall. To be more precise, looking at all this in dynamic terms, the part that grows dynamically and relatively faster should be exports and investment, while the part growing far more slowly, or even stagnating for a while, should be imports. This will restore equilibrium to the balance of payments, primarily the trade and current-account balances. These are the desirable structural changes.

I would like to avoid the question as put in an 'either–or' form, because I disagree with this approach. 'Choose sides', people say. 'Are you a stabilization-ite or a growth-ite?' But neither would I like to fall into a kind of Orwellian double-speak, twisting things round so as to say that what is good for one is good for the other – we want both at once – and then acting as if this were self-evident. Stabilization and growth are complementary objectives, to some extent, but there is also a conflict between them. That is why it is so difficult to pursue economic policy and comment responsibly on it. But what are these things that preclude each other? We cannot say on the one hand that we will now set the balance of payments quickly to rights – or rather, just get it into a tolerable shape – and on the other hand say at the same moment that we will go full steam ahead with boosting production by fiscal means, and produce some immediate spectacular results. Anyone promising both of these at once is being frivolous and irresponsible. So I did not promise or recommend both at once. Nor would I recommend anyone to make such a promise now. I consider it important to use a kind of parallel thinking, which must first be understood and then applied consistently.

What do you mean by parallel thinking?

There are some measures to encourage growth which need to be taken now, which cannot be postponed, and which will not conflict with the stabilization tasks now urgently on the agenda. I begin with an example of something contained in the government package: development and support of special banking institutions to back up exports and imports. This is extremely important, and eventually, if not immediately, it will help to produce export-led growth. Provision of long-term credit for investment has been an unresolved problem for years. This requires building up a credit system – and a start has been made here, but it is not proceeding with sufficient force, I think – to promote the extension of long-term investment credit. Some measures to boost investment have now been built into the tax system, but these may well need augmenting with further measures. With the customs surcharge – and this too has already happened in part – it may be possible to give preference to imports for investment purposes, and so on. There are many measures whose postponement would retard the onset of growth; these have to be taken now and there is plenty of room for them in a short-term package of government measures. Here let me voice one of my misgivings. I have the impression that the medium and long term are not receiving enough attention. Perhaps they are emphasized in the actions taken – I cannot follow these sufficiently closely to judge. But they are certainly not underlined enough in discussions or in statements intended for publication. Somehow everyone has been gripped by the fever of doing and debating the immediate and short-term tasks. The champions of the present government package and its critics, both moderate and strong, are all arguing about the short-term problems, forgetting that the country has medium and long-term problems as well. Even if the short-term programme succeeds as well as it possibly could, there will still be several matters outstanding. I would make it compulsory – and I mean this partly in jest but partly seriously – for everyone, from the prime minister, through the finance minister, down to the trade-union leaders and members of parliament, to devote a specific percentage of their working day to dealing with the country's medium- and long-term problems, joining in discussions, helping to compile and debate information that looks beyond 1995 and 1996, and to contribute boldly – for no small courage is required here – to the medium- and long-term tasks.

This kind of long-term thinking is all the more necessary because the talk so far has generally been confined to how drastic the measures are. You used to be a believer in gradualism. What do you say now to the suddenness with which they have been introduced?

I want to correct slightly one of the statements in your question, about what I used to be a believer in. Very often in debates of this kind people use two pigeon holes: one for those known as believers in gradualism and the other for those thought to be believers in swift, rapid answers, shock therapies and big-bang solutions. I feel that I do not fit easily into either category. Let me begin with an example. I recommended in the book I wrote in 1989[6] that privatization and the transformation of society should go ahead gradually, but at the same time I took the decided view that forceful and quick surgical operation was necessary in the matter of macro stabilization. Later I recommended gradualism over several questions and over macro affairs as well. I can only repeat in this respect what I mentioned before – that I am neither an advocate of gradualism nor an advocate of sudden, drastic action in everything, once and for all. My approach depends on the prevailing situation and the task concerned. Gradualism has many advantages. One is that it causes less upheaval to those affected by the measures proposed. It also makes adjustment easier. If a small, gradual step turns out not to have been made in quite the right direction, it is comparatively easy to correct. It is more difficult to correct sudden and major steps. On the other hand there are circumstances in which a drastic step is inevitable. That is the case when a measure cannot be postponed any longer, because further loss of time will cause mounting problems. That is the case in Hungary now: we have to move quickly to avoid greater trouble. The other case, which also has to be considered in relation to this country, is when the very force and courage of a measure has a favourable effect in itself. I think this is most important for Hungary. The world is watching anxiously the various countries undergoing post-socialist transition – or other kinds of transitions from dictatorship to democracy – and it has occasional doubts about whether they will succeed. Hungary has a national interest in demonstrating its commitment to setting its house in order. So the commitment behind a move is in itself an economic factor.

But will this set of measures be capable of restoring the confidence of the international public and international investors?
Many of the Hungarian public feel that we pay too much heed to international public opinion, that Hungarian public opinion is far more important. They consider it a kind of servile humiliation to pay any attention to international opinion whatever. I think this is a rather childish attitude. The question of paying heed to foreign opinion is not one of national pride or national awareness at all. The world, as is said, has globalized. The economic activities of the world have become interwoven. Hungary needs the foreign business world as a creditor – for we have a constant need to raise loans, among other reasons because some of our debt servicing is done by borrowing. We also need investors. We need the kind of buyers in the privatization process who can bring in new technology. We also need foreign partners as exporters and importers. So we have a strong national interest in ensuring that we retain

---

[6] Kornai (1990) [1989].

the confidence of the world around us. And if the country's macroeconomic figures are in a very bad state, it will help greatly to restore or maintain confidence if people feel the Hungarian government has set about overcoming the problems energetically.

But I imagine a restoration of confidence is necessary here at home as well as abroad, on an international plane.
Quite so. And here let me emphasize a connection that is usually forgotten. When investors are mentioned, almost everyone thinks only of foreign investors, although domestic investors are just as important to us. It is time we gave up drawing this sharp dividing line between them. Money, whether for investment or lending, does not need to apply for a visa or show a passport. If a Hungarian investor's faith in the Hungarian economy should be shaken and he or she feels there is some great problem threatening, there are ways of withdrawing the money, legally or illegally. It is possible to slow down or confine this flight by administrative means, but not really to prevent it, and it is not worth doing that in any case. The way to keep domestic investors' money in the country is not to forbid them to export it – if administrative restrictions are necessary, they have to be applied, but that can never become the main means. The way to keep it is to ensure that investors feel their money is in a good place and will bring them a yield.

The government measures which have aroused the most protest are those that will whittle down the welfare provisions. Often quoted in this connection is an expression you used in 1992: a 'premature welfare state'.[7] What did you mean by it?
What I meant and still mean by a premature welfare state is a country ahead of itself by comparison with its realistic economic potential.

And this has happened in our case, at least in the social, the welfare sector?
Yes, and it has not happened all at once. Today's welfare system has been built up over a long period – a period of one, two or three decades. It began back in the 1970s and 1980s, and it continued in the 1990s. So it started while the country's production was tending upwards, but continued when production began to stagnate and then fall. This opened still wider the gap between the country's load-bearing capacity and the state's activity in providing welfare services. I am not a believer in winding up the welfare state and I am certainly no enemy of it. On the contrary, I consider the welfare state one of the great achievements of twentieth-century civilization, a something of value that must be preserved, and something for us, as members of Western

[7] See Kornai (1992b).

civilization, to be proud of. But it is one thing to say this is an achievement which must be preserved, and another to think it must be preserved in an unchanged form and on an unchanged scale. The welfare state has outgrown its desirable extent. It needs cutting back and reforming, and at the same time preserving to the extent that is desirable and needful.

Your 1994 article referred to applying the principle of need.[8] *This has now been incorporated almost word for word into the government programme. But what is the principle of need and how can it be applied?*
There are many different ways of influencing the distribution of income. The state has many ways in which it can intervene in this, and it has to decide whom to favour and at whose expense. Redistribution does not mean that the state just distributes money benevolently from an infinite fund. When it gives money to one person, it takes money away from someone else. Underlining the principle of need means that the state should refrain if possible from giving money to those who are not in need. Expressing the principle in negative terms like this makes its ethical content clear. There is no point in extending state bounty and benefits to those with no need of them, because if they are included, the needy are deprived – the money does not fall like manna from the sky. Nor can we continue indefinitely to fund these disbursements with foreign loans, as this amounts to depriving future generations. So that is what the principle of need means. Another principle is that most economists, myself included, look critically on all mechanisms based on a monopoly situation. The trouble with the welfare system developed in this country is that it has a monopoly. It used to be an exclusive state monopoly. Later it passed in some areas from the hands of the state into the hands of structures of a corporatist nature, the social security boards. But these also have the backing of the state, and they are absolutely centralized, with a full or almost full monopoly. I am convinced that monopolies are not a good thing, for several reasons. First they reduce efficiency. If an organization has an absolute monopoly, it has no inducement to perform its task as well as possible, and there is no real way of gauging this in any case, as it cannot be compared with the activity of any other, competing organization. The individuals supplied by monopolies are at their mercy, without any freedom of choice. A Hungarian pensioner is at the mercy of the pensions institution. And the pensions institution is always at the mercy of the parliament and government in a given year, which decides whether pensions are to be raised by 11 per cent, 9.5 per cent or 14.75 per cent. The pensioner rightly feels that his or her pension does not depend on how he/she worked throughout life and what happened to his/her money, but on what decision is reached by politi-

[8] See Chapter 2.

cians, the government, the opposition, or the political forces which happen to be engaged in day-to-day struggle. This defencelessness has to be lessened by the reform of the welfare system.

And how can this monopoly situation be changed?
The way to eliminate it is not just to have a single state-controlled or semi-state-controlled welfare, social-insurance system, but to have non-profit institutions and enterprises working on a commercial, profit-making basis alongside it. So in this sense a three-sector form is needed. There is a need for a state-controlled redistributive welfare system whose revenue side is covered by levies collected in the same way as public taxation. But there is also a need for non-profit institutions based on voluntary contributions by employers and employees, and for institutions operating on a commercial, regular market basis. These three sectors have to complement each other, but to some extent they have to compete with each other as well. In ten or twenty years' time, when the multi-sector system is quite developed and operating in a mature form, members of the Hungarian public should have a choice about how far they want to rely on the state service, and if they are able and prepared to devote their savings to it, in what ways they can improve on it.

But for most of the public, the whittling down of social expenditure comes as a curtailment, because the institutions you mentioned still only exist as initiatives.
These institutions cannot spring up from one day to the next. Establishment of them can only be gradual. Basically they have to rest on the self-interest of the actors in the economy – by which I mean the firms, the employers, and the employees – and the principle of voluntary action has to apply. This requires time. So I do not imagine them being able to fulfil from tomorrow the role they have to play. But perhaps this is a good example of what I said earlier, of how we cannot neglect the long-term tasks as we deal with the short-term ones. I think it is most regrettable that development of this non-state sector of the welfare sphere should only be coming on to the agenda now. We have wasted several fruitless years in this respect. If it had been placed on the agenda in 1990, how much further ahead we would be now! If only questions of reforming the welfare system had not been treated as taboo for four years; if only people had not tiptoed around them! Nobody dared discuss them. Every politician approved in a general way, saying there was certainly a need to reform the public-finance system, but no one dared stick his neck out and say what this meant. Unfortunately there is no way to avoid there being losers while this transition takes place – people who lose by it temporarily and those who lose by it permanently. The aim must be to ensure this occurs in a differentiated way. The reform must be done tactfully and

humanely, with understanding of people's problems and consultation. Though there are painful aspects of the transformation, let it take place in a way that mitigates the pain as far as possible, not in a brutal way.

You mentioned that politicians did not dare to or want to lay hands on the welfare state. Perhaps this was also because of an image in the public's mind, whereby anyone touching the welfare state is in effect sinning against the employees, the workers.
When I hear the word 'employee' or 'worker', coupled with questions about income or earnings, the first question that comes to my mind is how much real income working people are receiving for their work. How much are they paid for working? We have not overburdened this conversation of ours with statistics, but let me quote one figure here. In 1960, 80 per cent of total real income was derived from work. This proportion has been falling year by year ever since, and by 1992 it was down to 52 per cent. I think this is a staggering figure. It deserves a great deal of thought. It means that just one forint in two of the income of a Hungarian worker derives directly from work. Now I ask you, how can this be squared with respect for work? How can it be squared with a set of values whose prime object is to reward and encourage work and performance? It is high time – absolutely inescapable from the economic and incentive points of view, and from the ethical point of view – for work to receive greater respect and for earned income to achieve a greater proportion of total income.

This would require, on the other hand, the availability of work. Unemployment in Hungary has risen to a very high rate. Can this problem be solved?
A certain degree of unemployment is a concomitant of a market-economy system. But it is not immaterial whether this is 3, 5, 10 or 20 per cent. The present rate of unemployment in Hungary is high, although there are European countries where it is higher. The first goal we have to strive for now is defensive: we have to prevent the Hungarian economy from catastrophe, entering a production crisis in which production began to plunge. That would bring much higher unemployment than today's. The other goal is to reduce unemployment. We shall become permanently and reliably able to bring the customary level of unemployment down to much lower than the present level if Hungary embarks on a growth path and if the country manages to increase its GDP at a rate of at least 3–4 per cent over several years. This will lead to a lasting reduction in unemployment.

Finally, referring to the title of this interview, when can we actually begin to climb the steep road ahead of us?

That depends on how we measure its gradient. I am a prisoner of my own metaphor here, for I have played with the word 'road' in so many of my earlier writings. On the one hand, we are already on it; we can feel its gradient, if gradient is taken to mean that we experience the fatigue of climbing. Anyone climbing and doing something else at the same time begins to pant and gasp – this we can feel, and in that sense we are on the steep road already. And we also feel that it has become steeper; we were on a flatter road before. We often said about the road we were on that our feet were squelching in the mud and we were floundering about. It was also often said that we were just dawdling along this road. Now we suddenly feel it has become steeper.

Of course 'upwards' can mean something else as well. When will the Statistical Office announce, not just once, but several years in succession, that the country's production is growing, the country's consumption is growing, and the average per capita consumption is growing as well? All I can answer is that I do not know. I would not like to make any kind of forecast in this respect. And I would warn anyone else against announcing now that there is only a year or two to go, and then there will be lasting growth. Growth is a process determined by anonymous, unnamed forces, and it would take a prophet to predict it. GDP growth, production growth and consumption growth are the ultimate result of activities in which millions take part – in which a part is played by the government, by every member of parliament, by every union leader, by every member of the press, and by every Hungarian employer and employee. Growth depends on the combined performance of all these. Every one of them can singly or together commit small mistakes or fatal blunders. And in that case we shall still be where we are now in three years' time, or in an even worse position. But I do not exclude the possibility of all the participants doing what they have to do in this difficult situation, on this steep road. In this case the results will soon be apparent, not necessarily straight away, in every index, but in several indices, and not straight away for everyone, but as soon as possible for the benefit of as many as possible. The chances are there; the rest depends on us.

4.   The dilemmas of Hungarian economic policy: an analysis of the stabilization programme[1]

1.   INTRODUCTION

I would like in this chapter to place the current problems of the Hungarian economic policy in a wider economic perspective. The point of departure is the package of stabilization measures announced on 12 March 1995, which consists of three main elements:

1.   There was an immediate, radical devaluation of the Hungarian forint, and a further course of steady devaluation was announced in advance, right up to the end of the year. In addition, a significant import surcharge (supplementary customs duty) was introduced.
2.   A substantial fall in budgetary spending was prescribed. This extends to numerous estimates, including several items of welfare spending. The alterations will cut the budget deficit to a substantial extent in 1995 and still more in 1996.
3.   The government wishes to curb the rise in nominal wages and earnings. Strict limits were accordingly set for personal incomes paid by the budget-financed sector and for wage rises in enterprises in majority state ownership. The programme assumes that this conduct by the state sector will curb the rise in wages in the private sector as well.

As I write (June 1995), three months have passed since the announcement, and the government's intentions have become manifest, initially in a succession

[1] The study was prepared as part of a National Scientific Research Foundation (OTKA) research programme entitled 'The Interaction of Politics and the Economy in the Period of Post-Socialist Transformation' and with the support of Collegium Budapest. I delivered an earlier version as a lecture at the Budapest University of Economics and at a Friedrich Ebert Foundation event, where the contributions made were instructive to me. Among those with whom I consulted during the research were László Akar, Zsolt Ámon, Rudolf Andorka, Francis Bator, Michael Bruno, Richard Cooper, Zsuzsa Dániel, Tibor Erdős, Endre Gács, Stanley Fischer, Eszter Hamza, György Kopits, Álmos Kovács, Judit Neményi, Robert Solow, György Surányi, Márton Tardos, and László Urbán, all of whom I thank for their valuable comments.

of government measures and later in the Stabilization Act passed by the majority of the parliament. To this extent, the stabilization programme of 12 March has joined the facts of Hungarian economic life, exerting a strong influence on the future course of events. But this does not mean the programme will henceforth determine the path of the economy. One question to be considered concerns the extent to which the government's measures and the stabilization legislation will be implemented, and the consistency with which this will be done. Another question is what other factors beyond the stabilization decisions will exert an effect on the economy. What goes on in the Hungarian economy does not depend solely on the government and parliament. It also depends on the apparatus of state, the organizations representing various interest groups, the employers and employees, and not least the outside world, governments, international organizations, foreign banks and companies, all of which will react in some way to the 12 March measures. The future path of the economy is full of junctions, where the actors in the economy will have to choose between alternatives. Connected with each choice there are dilemmas, and I would like to examine a few of these more closely.

This chapter deals mainly with macroeconomic problems. Clearly there are many dilemmas that present themselves on a micro level, and there are numerous other problems to do with the transformation of institutions and property relations. These fall outside the range of this exposition.

Under the circumstances of the post-socialist transition in Hungary, three grave and burdensome tasks remain: (i) securing or at least improving the external equilibrium; (ii) securing or at least improving the domestic financial equilibrium; and (iii) deciding how to prevent the fall in real production and how to promote a recovery of production and lasting growth in the economy. One of the fundamental dilemmas is to establish the relative importance of these three tasks in relation to one another; in addition, each of them separately poses a succession of dilemmas. The chapter treats each problem in turn. Finally, it deals with dilemmas of another type – connections between political and economic stability, and interaction between politics and economic policy.

2. THE EXTERNAL EQUILIBRIUM

I take the view that for now and the immediate future the problems of the external balance – the trade balance, current-account balance and foreign debt – should receive the greatest attention in considerations of short-term economic policy.

I would like here to make a short diversion, asking whether the statement I have just advanced constitutes inconsistency and abandonment of the economic principles I have previously published.[2] In my view it does not. A distinction has to be drawn between the *ultimate* goals of economic effort – the underlying, permanent objectives, the general values serving as the basis for the position taken – and the *interim* goals and operative targets. As far as the former are concerned, my position is unaltered in this respect; I might say my 'economic philosophy' is unchanged. I am convinced that the prime objective of economic policy is to ensure lasting economic growth. Only this can produce a permanent, systemic rise in material welfare for all. Lasting growth is a requirement for modernizing the economy and living conditions, and enhancing the competitiveness of the country's production. It offers far more favourable conditions for the kind of structural changes that can prevent the reproduction of grave imbalances and make debt servicing easier to bear. It is another matter to decide what should be done at present to promote this unaltered general objective and what relative weights should be attached to the various interim targets. In my view this has to be tailored to circumstances. What could (and in my view should) have been done, let us say two and a half or three years ago, can no longer be accomplished now in quite the way I recommended at the time. This is partly because the last government was neglectful of some tasks for several years, and the new government elected in 1994 has been neglectful of some in the last nine months. A car driver can decide on a destination, but cannot decide once and for all to prefer the accelerator to the brake or left turns to right turns. The question of whether to accelerate or brake, or to turn left or right, must depend on the traffic conditions, traffic lights, and so on.

Let us return to the external equilibrium. Why did I think, even in August 1994, that this was a problem at most equal in rank with the others, and why do I think it is the primary problem at present? When there were only the figures for a single calendar year to suggest the unfavourable situation in this respect, it remained possible to consider weighting the tasks in a different way. But once similarly poor results had been reported for a second complete calendar year, it seemed impossible to avoid intervening primarily on this count, and doing so radically.

The main figures appear in Table 4.1, which shows exports growing strongly again in 1994 after a sharp setback in 1993. Unfortunately, the growth in imports hardly slackened, so that the balance of trade in both 1993 and 1994 was strongly negative. This was the main reason why the current-account deficit in two successive years attained and then exceeded 9 per cent of GDP

---

[2] I have dealt with current issues of Hungarian economic policy on the macro level in several recent publications (Kornai 1992c, 1993b and Chapter 2, this volume). Here I contrast my present position with these earlier writings.

Table 4.1   Hungary's foreign trade, 1990–94

Indices	1990	1991	1992	1993	1994
1. Exports					
a. US$ bn[a]	9.6	10.2	10.7	8.9	10.7
Change over previous year					
b. Volume index (%)	–4.1	–4.9	1.0	–13.1	16.6
c. Value index (%)	5.7	24.3	10.4	–2.8	37.7
2. Imports					
a. US$ bn	8.6	11.4	11.1	12.5	14.6
Change over previous year					
b. Volume index (%)	–5.2	5.5	–7.6	20.9	14.5
c. Value index (%)	4.1	53.9	1.6	32.3	32.2
3. Balance of foreign trade					
a. US$ bn	0.9	–1.2	–0.4	–3.6	–3.9
b. Percentage of GDP	2.7	–3.6	–1.1	–9.4	–9.5

Notes:
The table has been revised during compilation of this volume. The figures include trade on both the convertible and non-convertible accounts. The 1993 figures also include the arms imports from Russia delivered as repayment of earlier debt.
[a] bn = thousand million.

Sources: National Bank of Hungary (1995a), pp. 172, 180–81 and 221, and Central Statistical Office (1991), p. 60.

(Table 4.2). This figure is unfavourable to an almost unprecedented extent, and it means that the country has entered a danger zone. It was primarily this signal, along with the postponement of devaluation and other corrective measures, that was behind the deterioration in Hungary's credit rating in the eyes of international finance. Although Hungary so far has met all its financial commitments in full, potential lenders see this as proof of goodwill, not of real solvency. If a country overspends to such an extent over a lengthy period, potential creditors start to worry lest the debtor, in spite of good intentions, becomes simply unable to pay.

This brings us to the first dilemma. Every statement that can be made about Hungary's payments position is provisional and conditional. Luckily so far there has not been a catastrophe to prove conclusively that the external equilibrium is the primary problem today. Those less concerned by it may argue that export performance has improved and Hungary has sizeable foreign-exchange reserves. So they still question whether it would not be more expedient to allow the debt burden to remain at its present level or even

Table 4.2   Hungary's current-account balance in convertible currency

Year	Balance on current account	
	US$ m	Percentage of GDP
1991	267	0.8
1992	324	0.9
1993	−3455	−9.0
1994	−3911	−9.6

Note: The table has been revised during compilation of this volume.

Source: National Bank of Hungary (1995a), pp. 172 and 234.

accept some further deterioration, and help to stimulate production by drawing in outside resources to a greater extent.

This argument cannot be refuted directly with facts from Hungary's experience. No one can say precisely how far we could go with the earlier practice in handling the balance of payments. It will have to be taken into account, when resolving the dilemma, that the international financial world has always been subject to unexpected, unpredictable events. For instance, there may be a sudden, hysterical turn away from some country or other, a lightning loss of confidence, a panic capital flight, or a speculative attack on the country's currency. The destructive effects of such chains of events are apparent from the debt crises in Latin America.[3] Suddenly the channels of credit are blocked and foreign direct investment stops, so that the reserves swiftly run out and the country becomes unable to meet its payments. That gives it a worse name still and plunges it further into the payments crisis. There is a grave fall in imports, which drags production and exports down as well. The recession may even reach 10–15 per cent and last one or two years, which rapidly drives up unemployment.

The prime task for the stabilization package is to avert an upheaval of this kind. Although it will be some time before anything certain can be reported, the chances of avoiding a debt crisis can already be said to have substantially improved.[4] Let us sum up the measures that will tend to improve substantially Hungary's external balances.

[3] On the Latin American debt crises, see Larrain and Selowsky (1991), Sachs (1989), Sunkel (1993) and Williamson (1990).
[4] *New note*: Due to the stabilization programme, the dangerous previous trend did not continue: the deficit on the current account fell substantially. The rapid rise in exports was maintained, while the rise in imports slowed down. See Table 6.1.

1. The radical devaluation and prior announcement of the future course of nominal devaluation will stimulate Hungarian exporters and curb imports.
2. Domestic and foreign experts debate strongly the advantages and drawbacks of various exchange-rate regimes. The regime now chosen by Hungary's financial authorities – the pre-announced crawling peg – has certain advantages; above all, it makes the intentions of the policymakers plain and clear. It makes a prior commitment to keep the actual exchange rate within a designated band. This tends to take the edge off speculation and forestall the extra imports engendered by devaluation expectations. To this extent, if successfully applied, it will contribute to improving the trade and current-account balances. But such an exchange-rate regime entails dangers and risks as well. It ties the hands of the monetary authorities, reducing their room for manoeuvre. It depends on whether events largely independent of the monetary authorities, notably the rate of inflation, remain consistent with the exchange-rate trend announced in advance. (I shall return to this later.)
3. A fall in imports is being encouraged not only by the exchange-rate alteration, but by the customs surcharge on imports and a few other measures as well. This concurrently improves the competitive position of Hungarian production compared with imports. Let me note here that the question of what factors are causing a substantial growth in import intensity in every area of domestic absorption has not yet been analysed sufficiently. The exchange-rate adjustment and customs surcharge will presumably not suffice in themselves to halt and partially reverse this trend.
4. By restricting domestic demand, the stabilization package steadily induces producers to show export-oriented behaviour – it almost obliges them to do so.
5. The curb placed on rises in wages (and the levies proportionate to them) will improve the competitiveness of Hungarian products on the home market relative to imports, and on foreign markets relative to rival countries.
6. The opportunities of convertibility have grown in the corporate sphere. The change encourages enterprises more strongly than before to keep their money in Hungary, and not to feel induced all the time to part with their forints, since they can be easily converted into foreign currency at any time. So the holders of money are less tempted to turn their forints into foreign exchange and keep it abroad.
7. It is now easier for banks and firms to raise foreign loans independently and directly. This decentralization will improve the composition of Hungarian debt and ease the problems of the government and the central bank.

8. Exports are receiving stimuli and assistance in numerous forms. For instance, financial institutions specializing in foreign-trade credit have been formed.

International experience shows that devaluations and other measures affecting foreign trade normally exert their influence only after a lag of several months. It can be hoped that the 12 March 1995 package will be benefiting the external equilibrium by the second half of the year. If it should turn out that the change is not strong enough, there should be no hesitation, in my view, about taking further measures. It will be a year or two before the kind of profound structural change in Hungarian production, investment, consumption and foreign trade that can permanently improve the position of the trade and payments balances is complete. For my part, I would not set numerical macroeconomic threshold values beyond which the country's external equilibrium situation could be called reassuring. Qualitative criteria should be designated instead.

The debt crisis must be given a wide berth, not just narrowly avoided. Full confidence in the country's creditworthiness must be restored. The country's credit rating, along with the assessment of the business prospects for investments in Hungary and of the risk entailed in loans to this country, must be restored to a level no lower than it reached in its best years in the last decade.

3.   INTERNAL FINANCIAL EQUILIBRIUM

The price to be paid for improving the external equilibrium will be a deterioration in other extremely important macro variables. The devaluation and import surcharge will hitch up the price level. It is too early to measure the effect, but dearer imports must certainly be expected to raise costs and thus to spill over into prices. The first problem that arises here is to assess the relative importance of the tasks. Is a likely improvement in the external equilibrium worth the burden that a likely rise in the price level will place on the economy? The answer in my view must be affirmative, since the first serves to avert a catastrophe, while the inflation rate, even if it rises somewhat, will still fall far short of catastrophic hyperinflation. It is still affirmative even though it is clear that some acceleration of inflation will cause losses to very many citizens and bear heaviest on those least able to defend themselves. Of course, the assessment also depends on how great the inflationary thrust will be, and still more on whether the *acceleration*, that is the increase in the rate of inflation, continues or not. Its continuance would be a serious problem. A view of the course of inflation so far is given in Table 4.3. It would be desirable if the rate of inflation were to slow down after the initial push delivered by the devaluation.

Table 4.3   Consumer price indices in Hungary, 1980–95

Year	Average annual change (%)
1980	9.1
1981	4.6
1982	6.9
1983	7.3
1984	8.3
1985	7.0
1986	5.3
1987	8.6
1988	15.5
1989	17.0
1990	28.9
1991	35.0
1992	23.0
1993	22.5
1994	18.8
1995 January–March[a]	24.5
April[a]	29.2
May[a]	30.8
June[a]	31.0

Note: [a] Compared with the same period of the previous year.

Sources: 1980–87: Central Statistical Office (1991), p. 218; 1988–94: Central Statistical Office (1995a), p. 40; 1995: Central Statistical Office (1995b), pp. 31 and 37, and information from the Central Statistical Office.

Under prevailing conditions in Hungary, the permissible measure of inflation is limited by the commitments made by the government and the central bank concerning the exchange rate. The financial authorities announced in advance precisely what the forint exchange rate was going to be up to 31 December 1995. This exchange-rate policy will only achieve its purpose if the buyers and sellers on the Hungarian foreign-exchange market, which is fairly open and free, acquiesce to it not just verbally, but in the exchange-rate terms appearing in their transactions. Without going into the technical details, I would like to emphasize the implications for inflation. The planned trend in the exchange rate is based on a forecast of the widening of the gap between Hungarian inflation and inflation in the foreign currencies which play the main part in Hungarian foreign trade. According to the calculations of the Finance Ministry and the National Bank of Hungary, the pre-announced

exchange-rate course leaves room for the following normative limit on inflation measured in terms of the consumer price index: the consumer price level
at the end of the year may exceed the price level at a similar time last year by
a maximum of 28–29 per cent. This sum constitutes a normative requirement,
not a forecast. It is an upper limit that must not be exceeded if the pre-
announced exchange rate is to be maintained.

Should the Hungarian inflation rate turn out to be higher than this implicit
inflation, a real appreciation of the Hungarian forint would take place: the
National Bank of Hungary would have to give more dollars or marks for
forints than they were really worth. When the currency market sensed the real
appreciation, it would start expecting a devaluation sooner or later, a greater
devaluation than was previously announced. So devaluation expectations would
revive, which is just what prior announcement of the exchange-rate trend was
supposed to avoid. One of the key issues in Hungarian economic policy is not
to allow inflation to overstep the permissible limit.[5] (If inflation should be
less than the upper limit set by the exchange rate, that would have a favourable effect, of course.) Whether inflation can be retained within this band
depends mainly on two factors: wages and the budget deficit.

3.1 Wages

Hungary has experienced for many years an inertial inflation, in which expectations of price rises have fuelled wage increases, and the increase in
wages and other cost factors (or expectations of such an increase) have
induced price rises. The question is whether the increase in the price of
imports will filter through fully or to a large extent into wages. Devaluation
usually meets with success where such filtering is impeded, at least for a
while.[6,7] For this it is normally necessary to have a formal agreement between
the government on the one hand and the employers' and employees' organizations on the other. No such agreement has been reached in Hungary. Can
this requirement be met without a formal agreement? Can it be forced by
reduction of domestic demand, fear of higher unemployment, and recognition
of the difficulties of the economic situation? It seems the answer differs from
sector to sector. The wage pressure is far lower where the firm is close to the
market, that is, in the competitive sphere making tradable goods. It is stronger,

[5] *New note*: This condition was met. Although inflation increased substantially, it did not
exceed the prescribed limit. See Table 6.1.
[6] This was one of the reasons for the success of the Israeli stabilization in 1984. On this see
Bruno (1993), Fischer (1987) and Razin and Sadka (1993).
[7] *New note*: The Hungarian stabilization met the target from this macroeconomic point of view:
the rise in nominal wages was far below the rise in prices. This means that real wages fell
substantially (see Table 6.1). The severely distorted proportions could only be rectified at the
cost of grave sacrifices by employees.

however, in the branches where there are no rivals, and where the wage rise need not be endorsed by the market, but simply demanded from the government. Among cases that can be listed here are the monopoly or near-monopoly branches currently in state ownership, such as the railways and electricity generation.

If wages start to swing, the devaluation will become almost ineffectual, and this country, like others, may be caught up in a mindless, destructive vortex, a vicious circle of devaluation, inflationary surge, and further devaluation.

All employers and employees, and also employers' associations and union leaders, must respond conscientiously to the choices relating to wage policy. Responsible behaviour depends on the availability of clear information about macroeconomic policy, including the relationship between exchange-rate policy and wage policy. Those concerned can rightfully expect not only to receive enlightenment on the general macro relations between these, but for such relations to be conveyed to them in a transparent, numerical form.

3.2 The Budget

A budget deficit normally fuels inflation. There are exceptions to this – combinations of internal and external circumstances that allow a lasting budget deficit to coincide with a very low rate of inflation.[8] Hungary is not one of the exceptions: there is a strong connection between the budget deficit and inflation.

One such connection arises when the budget deficit is paid for directly by the central bank in the form of credits. This is customarily called financing the deficit by 'printing money'. Hungarian legislation sets an upper limit to this form of financing, although to some extent this can be treated flexibly, since the limit can be temporarily raised by passing occasional legislation. Whatever the case, the inflation-stoking effect can be exerted up to the set limit.

The deficit can also be financed if the state raises credit not from the central bank, but by issuing government securities and selling them to investors at home and abroad.[9] This has increasingly become the main source of financing the deficit in recent years. (Table 4.4 presents the size of the budget deficit and the sources for financing it.)[10] The method differs from printing

---

[8] This is the situation in the United States, for instance, above all because domestic and foreign holders of money have so far been willing to invest their savings in gilt-edged American securities. The state debt, having swollen to vast proportions, is a big problem even there, and the question of cutting the budget deficit has come to the political forefront.

[9] From the macroeconomic point of view, a precisely equivalent procedure is when a loan is taken up directly by the central bank from a foreign creditor and lent onwards as credit to the budget.

[10] Pioneering work with retrospective processing, classification and analysis of the data on Hungarian public debt was done by Borbély and Neményi (1994 and 1995).

Struggle and hope

Table 4.4   Indices of public debt

Indices	1991	1992	1993	1994
1. Increase in gross public debt[a] (current prices, HFt bn)	415.3	244.1	1040.0	641.3
a. to domestic creditors	63.4	217.7	467.3	202.2
b. to foreign creditors	351.9	26.4	572.7	439.1
2. Increase in monetary base (current prices, HFt bn)	179.9	188.3	172.1	178.6
3. Proportion of deficit financed by increasing public debt to financing of total deficit (%)	69.8	56.5	85.8	78.2
4. Proportion of deficit financed by broadening of monetary base to financing of total deficit (%)	30.2	43.5	14.2	21.8
5. Total domestic debt of consolidated public finance[b] as proportion of GDP (%)	71.1	74.9	84.5	83.2

Notes:
[a] State debt calculated by adding the gross debt of the budget and of the National Bank of Hungary.
[b] Including devaluation debt. For an explanation of this, see Borbély and Neményi (1995), pp. 142–3.

Source: Borbély and Neményi (1995), pp. 139 and 145, and further calculations by Neményi.

money in not directly increasing the money supply (or more precisely the monetary base, which is the main force behind expansion and contraction of the money supply), but it has several other effects which can contribute indirectly to maintaining and even accelerating inflation. Let us ignore here the foreign loans, which were mentioned earlier. The domestic public debt has also grown to a threatening extent in recent years, which in itself deserves special attention (Table 4.4). When the budget makes a very large demand on the domestic credit market, the price of credit – interest – is pushed up. The high nominal rate of interest will then be built into the inflationary expectations, keeping inflation high (or even increasing it in the case of a mounting deficit).

Another dangerous vicious circle has been created. The high rate of interest raises the interest burden on the public debt, which comes to form a growing proportion of the budget deficit. The growing deficit, on the other hand, encourages the raising of new loans, and promises of yet higher interest to satisfy the mounting demand. This again pushes the interest rate up, with a reciprocal effect on the deficit, and so on.

There is nothing alarming in itself about a country having a sizeable public debt. It is customary not only at lower or medium levels of development, but also in many mature market economies. What has to be avoided is a mounting rate of increase in the state debt – a vortex of debt. This will ensue if the public debt increases faster than GDP for a long period, so that the increase in the ratio of public debt to GDP is accelerating. In this case, it is obvious that tax revenues will sooner or later be unable to cover judicial, public-order and defence costs and welfare spending, since they will all go on financing debt repayments and interest, and beyond a certain point they will not even suffice for those. Hungary has not reached that stage, but several simulation calculations have shown that if the trend before 12 March 1995 had continued, the country would have entered such a debt vortex in the foreseeable future and careered on toward financial ruin.[11]

We cannot resign ourselves to a vicious circle of budget deficit, high interest rates, and mounting state debt. But slowing the process down and eventually halting it will require a whole range of measures. The credit demand from the budget is not the only factor affecting the interest rate, of course. Much depends on the interest policy of the central bank and the commercial banks, on the efficiency of the banking sector, on institutional reforms to encourage personal savings (such as developing a system of voluntary pension and health-care funds), and on several other circumstances. I shall not go into these now. What can be said in any case is that reduction of the large budget deficit is a necessary condition for easing the demand pressure on the credit market. This will entail a great many changes on both sides of the budget.

On the expenditure side, the 12 March 1995 package can be considered a forceful *initial step*. As such, it was brave of the government and the majority in parliament to take this first step in the face of so many kinds of opposition. There was a need for the radicalism and forcefulness of the initial moves, to show that the government and the majority in parliament had ceased their hesitation and postponement of hard tasks and committed themselves to action. They had the courage also to tackle such taboos as state welfare spending. This marked a turning-point in the history of Hungarian economic policy.[12]

Unfortunately, when choosing the measures of the first package, the following question was not addressed: how to achieve the necessary savings

---

[11] Long before the present stabilization programme, the theoretical connections and numerical simulation of these processes were dealt with by Oblath and Valentinyi (1993). More recent calculations can be found in World Bank (1995a).

[12] See Chapter 5.

with the minimum sacrifice and consequently the least public resistance. The stabilization programme was presented in a way that failed to explain sufficiently clearly and convincingly what its motives and likely results were. At the time the package was announced, the government had no reform programme of economic and social transformation that looked a long way ahead, and to this day only the very first steps have been taken to work one out and initiate broad debate. So the 12 March 1995 measures were merely concentrated on overcoming the immediate concerns. They were not integrated into any deeper, more comprehensive long-term plan of reform.

Let us hope the part of the stabilization package dealing with the budget is only the start of a reform of the whole system of public finance. Although at this stage in the discussion I have only raised the question of government expenditure in relation to inflation and the budget deficit, there is a deeper question: how great should the role of the state in the economy and society be? Before the 12 March 1995 package, Hungary was devoting the highest proportion of GDP to budgetary expenditure of any country in the post-socialist region (Table 4.5). Let people decide for themselves whether they approve of keeping this 'leading role'. Although I would not join those taking an extreme libertarian view, seeking to reduce the state's role to the minimum, I consider the role the state performs today (and still more yesterday) to be strongly out of proportion. A less centralized and more efficient administration is required.

Table 4.5 *General government expenditure as a percentage of GDP: an international comparison*

Country	General government expenditure as a proportion of GDP (%)		
	1991	1992	1993
Bulgaria[a]	50.7	43.9	41.7
Czech Republic	54.2	52.8	48.5
Hungary	58.3	63.4	60.5
Poland[a]	48.0	50.7	48.4
Romania	40.4	42.2	31.0

Notes:
The figures for general government expenditure include central and local-government expenditure, and expenditure of extra-budgetary funds. The figures reflect the consolidated budget; expenditure includes interest payments, but not debt repayments.
[a] Spending does not include interest payments due, but not yet paid.

Source: Tyrie (1995), pp. 138–42.

This need for a smaller, cheaper, but more efficient state that can be supported on less tax should be the guiding idea behind the reform of public finance, in my view. One constituent of the reform is an overhaul of the welfare system. I would not recommend a complete withdrawal by the state. As I have also underlined in earlier writings, I certainly do not subscribe to the idea of demolishing the welfare state. The development of the welfare state is one of modern civilization's great achievements, which has to be preserved; but it would be worth reducing its sphere and adding other mechanisms of provision.[13] I take the view that the role of centralized state participation in the welfare sphere, financed from compulsory taxation, should be reduced to more modest proportions, not ended. Welfare redistribution by the state needs augmenting to a far greater extent by non-profit insurance and welfare service institutions based on voluntary employer and employee contributions. For those prepared to pay for them, there should be wider and more closely monitored services and insurance schemes available on a commercial basis. There is no room here to treat the reform of the welfare system in detail. I just wanted to point to the macroeconomic aspect of it, for this great and difficult social-policy problem has a strong bearing on the question of overcoming the budget deficit.[14]

The parts of the stabilization package concerned with public finance, including welfare spending, seem especially open to the criticism made earlier about the package as a whole, that the regulations have not been incorporated into a comprehensive plan of reform. It would be worth preparing much more thoroughly for the subsequent measures, by paying close attention to the experts and representative organizations in specific fields and choosing much more carefully on which items to reduce spending. Each cut raises a whole succession of specific dilemmas; it will take many tough decisions to determine who will be the direct losers and winners. When the regulations are being drawn up and a timetable decided for introducing them, it is not enough just to aim to cut the budget deficit. The prime consideration has to be how best to dovetail the alterations into the overall reform of the welfare sector. The reduction in the state's obligations, the drop in taxes and the compulsory contributions to finance them, as well as the establishment of new organizations based on voluntary payments, should all take place concurrently, complementing one another in a coordinated way. The greatest care must be taken to minimize the sacrifice accompanying the process and ensure that it takes place as tactfully and humanely as possible. Citizens need to feel that, in the

---

[13] This is also emphasized by the Swedish economists critical of the excessive dimensions of the welfare system in the country that epitomizes the welfare state. They propose reforming the system by a considered reduction in the state's welfare spending, along with other measures to make up for it, not a merciless elimination of it. See Lindbeck *et al.* (1994).

[14] On reform of the welfare sector, see Chapters 7 and 8.

longer term, even though the range of entitlements guaranteed by the state will be narrowing, the tax burdens will also be less, so that the autonomy of the individual and the family grows and a higher proportion of income is at their disposal instead of the state's. It must be explained with great patience, compassion and understanding that the reform of the welfare system will be in the long-term interests of the whole of Hungarian society. Regrettably, these requirements were not met when the first group of measures to alter the welfare system was devised and announced. The omission contributed to the outcry and widespread opposition these measures encountered.

On the other side of the budget, tax revenues must rise. Development of the fiscal system has been one of the weakest points in Hungary's post-socialist transformation. In the struggle between tax evaders and tax officials, the former have proved much the sharper and more resourceful. For every change by the tax authorities, new loopholes have opened and new tricks have been found by citizens intent on avoiding tax. The sections of the stabilization programme dealing with taxation contained too much improvisation and sabre-rattling, and too many empty promises. Spreading tax burdens produces losers, just as withdrawing welfare services and benefits does. No one disputes in theory the principle of sharing tax burdens fairly. The arguments start when it comes to deciding specifically who pays more tax or pays tax on a hitherto untaxed item of income or wealth. I would recommend first and foremost broadening the tax base. The sphere of tax exemptions and concessions must be reduced and tax gathered from those intent on avoiding it.[15] This will make it possible on the one hand to cut the deficit and on the other to lower the tax rates. Here at last a 'beneficial' or 'virtuous' circle can emerge. If tax morality improves and the tax base widens, tax rates can be lowered. For it is above all these almost insupportably high rates that have prompted people to evade tax and lurk in the grey economy. So tax cuts will broaden the tax base.

The question is often put as to what division of labour there should be between fiscal policy and monetary policy in dealing with inflation. Some say the monetary policy should be far more restrictive, to make sure inflation is kept down, even with an unchanged deficit. In my view this procedure is too costly and too brutal. A Draconian cut in the aggregate money supply by one

---

[15] It is widely thought that the payment of tax and compulsory contributions is refused mainly by the black economy. I would prefer to keep the term 'black' for those who can be called real criminals in the legal and moral sense, and pay no tax anywhere in the world, of course. The big problem during the transition is with the grey and off-white areas of fundamentally honest citizens, who would like to live legally, but who withdraw some of their income from taxation, or at least connive with others in doing so. It would exceed the bounds of this chapter to look at how to turn this stratum (which I suspect covers the majority of society) into consistent, law-abiding taxpayers. I would like to note, however, that it cannot be done solely by policing methods.

of the main methods – a radical rise in the prime interest rates set by the central bank – would have a detrimental effect on production and investment. It would weigh not only on loss-making, inefficient, non-viable enterprises, but on profitable, efficient, viable ones as well. In my view the course of not simply controlling but dramatically restricting the credit supply should be treated as an emergency brake for a case in which inflation suddenly rises inordinately or a process of this kind threatens to get out of control.

This leads to the next subject, the prospects for real production.

4.   RECESSION OR RECOVERY AND LASTING GROWTH

There has been widespread debate in recent years, in Hungary and internationally, about the causes of the recession that has developed during the post-socialist transition and the conditions required for short-term recovery and for lasting growth.[16] In the winter of 1992–93 I hoped the time for recovery had come. It was too early. The government of the day confined itself to popular acts that would stimulate the economy, setting about expanding the credit supply and aggregate domestic demand in general, for instance, while failing to implement necessary but unpopular measures. For example, it did not carry out the currency devaluation many economists (including myself) were recommending, and actually continued a policy of real appreciation of the forint. This was among the factors behind the appearance of ambivalent phenomena in the economy in 1994. Though the factors tending toward recovery strengthened, and there was real growth for the first time in many years, as mentioned earlier the equilibrium tensions heightened as well.

The debate over the question of contracting or expanding real production continues. Two extreme views can be noted. One sees a need for drastic contraction of production as the only way of curbing the import hunger and setting the trade and current-account balances to rights. Its adherents consider the contraction of production not as a negative, possibly inescapable side-effect of a combined therapy, but as the therapy itself. The view at the opposite end of the spectrum is that the present (or even higher) level of budget deficit must be accepted, along with a further deterioration on the current account, for the sake of speeding up, rather than throttling, the recovery of production.

The 12 March 1995 stabilization programme, or at least the published quantitative projections, eschews both these extremes. It does not contain

---

[16] For the debate in Hungary see Balassa (1994), Békesi (1995), Csaba (1995), Erdős (1994), Kopits (1994) and Köves (1995a). Of the foreign contributions I would pick the following: Berg (1994), Calvo and Coricelli (1993), Holzmann, Gács and Winckler (1995), Kolodko (1993) and Saunders (1995).

immediate measures to promote directly an upswing of production. Instead, for the time being, the programme is content, due to the gravity of the foreign-trade and financial tensions, with far more modest production goals than could have been undertaken if the macroeconomic policy of the last two or three years had been more balanced. It aims at *no fall* in GDP; even, if possible, a continuation of last year's growth of 1–2 per cent. At this production level it envisages a *restructuring* in the utilization of production, with the share of exports and investment rising and that of consumption, especially collective, budget-financed consumption, falling. As far as the origin of total domestic absorption is concerned, there should be a growth in the share of domestically produced products and services and a fall in the share of imports[17] (Table 4.6). The speed and depth of restructuring depends on several

Table 4.6   Utilization of GDP

Indices	As a percentage of GDP				
	1991	1992	1993	1994	1995
1. Household consumption	68.6	72.8	74.0	72.4	68.3
2. Collective consumption[a]	9.4	12.0	14.4	11.7	11.4
3. Total final consumption[b] (1 + 2)	80.6	84.8	88.4	85.0	79.7
4. Total investment	20.4	15.5	19.9	21.5	22.4
5. Domestic absorption (3 + 4)	101.1	100.3	108.2	106.4	102.1
6. Balance of foreign trade	−1.1	−0.3	−8.2	−6.4	−2.1
Exports	–	31.5	26.5	–	34.9
Imports	–	31.8	34.7	–	37.0

Notes:
The table has been revised during compilation of this volume.
[a] The 1993 figures include arms imports from Russia in repayment of earlier debt.
[b] For lack of sources of data, the sum total of final consumption in 1991 includes the bank dividend of HFt 64.4 bn, or 2.6% of GDP, not distributed between households and the state budget.

Sources: 1991: Central Statistical Office (1994f), pp. 72–3; 1992–93: Central Statistical Office (1995a), pp. 107–8; 1994: Central Statistical Office (1995d), p. 76; 1995: Central Statistical Office (1996d), p. 3.

[17] The requirement of rapid *restructuring* within a growth target already set at a more modest level was one of the fundamental ideas running through the article I published in the summer of 1994 (see Chapter 2). So far as I can judge, the 12 March 1995 programme is very close in this respect to the proposal I made then. Another idea in the article also found a place in the programme's rationale: the need for *parallel concurrence* of moves to improve the equilibrium and measures to support growth. More will be said on this later.

factors, among them the measures presented in this chapter so far. Experience will show how fast the restructuring can take place. I do not wish to disguise the fact that I have many worries and uncertainties about this. Will the measures not overshoot the target, causing a sudden, excessive fall in aggregate demand? Will this not be accompanied by a bigger contraction in production than expected? If this happens, will it not lead to a fall in tax revenues that will undermine the original objective of reducing the budget deficit?

Another cause for serious concern connected with the contraction of production is the conflict of short-term and long-term thinking. Hungary has to navigate today under extremely difficult conditions. As has already emerged from this chapter, the country has to be steered between several Scyllas and Charybdises at once. The danger is that the leaders responsible for the economy will be almost entirely taken up with the short-term problems. This is a practice that cannot be accepted, if for no other reason than that it is constant postponement of the long-term tasks that has led to the present accumulation of troubles. There is a range of tasks that have to be done *now* so that they can contribute to lasting growth after a longish gestation period. It is most important to assess every urgent task today, not simply from the fire-fighting point of view of averting catastrophe, but in terms of deeper, systemic, transformation-oriented reforms and lasting growth, so that decisions are reached after weighing up 'short-term versus long-term' dilemmas. Here are a few examples:

1. Present-day budget revenue is a major factor in reaching decisions on privatization, but it cannot be the sole criterion. No less important are the commitments a potential new owner will make to increasing capital, accomplishing investment projects, and bringing in new technologies.
2. In developing the financial sector, it is worth bearing in mind how the banks can contribute to resolving today's problems of external and internal equilibrium. But it is not less important to establish the institutions for long-term lending and expand the credit available for production and housing investment. This ties up with establishing the conditions required for long-term deposits to become widespread, building up a network of voluntary pension and health funds, and developing more lively investment activity by these funds and private insurance companies.
3. While attention must go to reducing state spending, it would be worth increasing the proportion within such spending of the sums expended on investment.
4. However tough the measures required for reducing the budget deficit, the lesson of the most modern growth theories must not be forgotten. Among the most important factors behind growth are research designed to assist production, enhancement of the skills of the workforce and

modernization of professional knowledge. The development of these factors, however, requires constant financing, and this must not be restricted, even temporarily.

Moreover, stress on long-term considerations can help to win political acceptance for the stabilization programme. Though the radicalism of these measures and their speed of introduction arose mainly out of a need to avert the short-term troubles and a still greater trauma in the future, this argument remains incapable of persuading millions to accept great sacrifices which would cause woe and suffering over a long period. If they are willing to accept this at all, it will be in the hope of a better future. Yet any convincing presentation of such a future has been almost wholly absent from the arguments in favour of the stabilization programme.[18] This leads to the last problem area covered in the study, the relationship between the economy and politics.

5. ECONOMIC AND POLITICAL STABILITY

The sections of this chapter so far have dealt with conflicts among different economic requirements. They have covered trade-offs of a kind where the more one economic criterion is satisfied, the greater the concession that has to be made in respect of another. There is, however, a still graver conflict regarding the different requirements of economic and political stability.

Once the democratic political system in a country has consolidated and the economy has begun a course of lasting growth, it becomes possible to overcome this conflict, so that the economic and political stability mutually reinforce each other. Conflict between these two aims, however, is all too common in the world of post-socialist transformation. When the economy stagnates or even shrinks, and society suffers convulsions, the conflict can be dangerously heightened.

I have already mentioned that the components of the 12 March 1995 stabilization package were not sufficiently well selected from either the political or the economic point of view. The programme was presented clumsily, sometimes in an almost insensitive, insulting way, and neither the motives nor the likely effects of it were sufficiently explained to society. But even if

---

[18] The prime minister publicly announced in May 1995 that the first draft of the government's medium- and long-term programme of reform had been prepared. Yet this remains unknown even to the narrow profession of economics, let alone to the wider public. It was a grave omission to postpone this task for so long. It would have been far more fortunate if the country could have learned simultaneously about the short-, medium- and long-term programmes and it had emerged that they were integrated.

the programme had been compiled more thoughtfully and presented in a much more convincing fashion, that would not have changed the fact that it caused tangible losses to very many people indeed, by reducing their standard of living and undermining their sense of security. So the great opposition to it was unsurprising. Here I refer not only to the opposition protests in parliament, which are normal occurrences in a parliamentary democracy, but to the intense extra-parliamentary protests of various kinds. Almost every stratum and interest group in society protested against or at least sharply criticized the programme. The few weeks following the announcement of the package gave us a taste of almost every form of mass protest, from public condemnations on television and in the press to street demonstrations and deputations to parliament, and from strike threats to the first real strike. An article in the press of the radical right wing outside parliament urged the public to resort to civil disobedience and withholding of taxes. And this was just the start, for implementation of the programme had yet to have an appreciable effect. So the question arises whether the stabilization package is feasible at all – not economically, but politically.

Will the Socialist–Free Democrat coalition government of today's Hungary prove able to carry out a strict programme, of which we are still only at the beginning? And will it be able to do so while preserving the achievements of parliamentary democracy intact, as the parties in power have made an express commitment to do?

A curious reversal of roles has now taken place in Hungary. To simplify somewhat, the Socialist Party, having won the elections by emphasizing its social sensitivity, is now implementing a 'Thatcherite' programme. Meanwhile, politicians of the forces that describe themselves as right-of-centre conservative have brought out social democratic arguments in favour of the extended welfare state and the wage demands of employees. How long can both sides keep up this reversal of roles? I cannot make a forecast, and I do not want to. Instead, in line with the title of this study, I am stating the dilemma.

Hungarian society, in the first phase of implementation of the stabilization programme, provides an almost classic example of the case known to game theory as the 'prisoner's dilemma', to which there are two solutions in theory.

One is the non-cooperative solution. In the game-theoretical model, each prisoner wants to assert his own interests, and this has a self-destructive effect. If each stratum and interest group in society wants to escape paying its share and retain or even improve the financial position it has enjoyed so far at the expense of the other strata and interest groups, then everyone together fares worse. The equilibrium cannot be restored and production cannot grow. The country's reputation will fall further. Neither creditors nor investors (whether foreign or Hungarian) will believe that this country, racked by mass protests and strikes, is a good place for their money. The political instability leads to further destabilization of the economy. The more strenuously and effectively each group struggles for its own interests at the expense of the other groups, the more destructive the combined consequences of the struggle will be.

Game theory (and day-to-day common sense rising above group interests) clearly points to an alternative, cooperative solution. In the prisoners' dilemma, the prisoners have to agree with each other. Each has to make a concession. None achieves what is best from his own point of view, yet together they do better than they would by non-cooperative behaviour. All Hungarian citizens are prisoners of the current situation. Is every affected group, profession, branch and region capable of conceding something, making a sacrifice, resigning itself to the loss or reduction of certain privileges and benefits – and not just expecting others to do so? Are we mature enough to choose the cooperative solution? This is a dilemma to which all the parties, movements, organizations and individuals in society must respond for themselves, as their own consciences dictate.

5. Paying the bill for goulash communism: Hungarian development and macro stabilization in a political-economy perspective[1]

1. INTRODUCTION: FOUR CHARACTERISTICS

The Hungarian economy's road from a centralized, planned economy to a market economy displays a number of features that distinguish it from other post-socialist countries, despite the underlying similarities. Without aiming to provide a complete picture, I shall pick out four important features. One or other of these may occur singly in other countries in the region as well, or more precisely in a few countries in particular periods. The specific feature of Hungarian development is the lasting coexistence of these four characteristics.

First, Hungary, in its economic-policy priorities, placed great weight on raising present-day material welfare, and in the subsequent period of mounting economic problems and stagnating or declining production, on curbing the fall in living standards. Conditions in Hungary had earlier been christened 'goulash communism'. The policy for several years after the change of political system continued the previous one in this respect, and can aptly be called 'goulash post-communism'.

Second, a paternalist 'welfare state' covering the entire population was developed over several decades. Hungary can vie with the most developed Scandinavian countries in the range of codified entitlements to benefits and in the proportion of GDP devoted to social spending, whereas *per capita* production is only a small fraction of theirs. Although similar tendencies

[1] My research was supported by the Hungarian National Scientific Research Foundation (OTKA), by Collegium Budapest, Institute for Advanced Study and by the World Bank. Among those with whom I consulted during the research were László Akar, Zsolt Ámon, Rudolf Andorka, Francis Bator, Tamás Bauer, Lajos Bokros, Katalin Bossányi, Michael Bruno, Richard Cooper, Zsuzsa Dániel, Tibor Erdős, Endre Gács, Alan Gelb, Béla Greskovits, Stanley Fischer, Eszter Hamza, György Kopits, Álmos Kovács, Judit Neményi, András Simonovits, Robert Solow, György Surányi, Katalin Szabó, Márton Tardos and László Urbán, all of whom I thank for their valuable comments.

arose at the time in all Eastern European countries, Hungary went furthest by far, and in this respect stands alone in the region.

Third, the process of transformation in Hungary has extended over several decades; the initial steps were taken back in the 1960s. Though a few milestones can be mentioned, the process as a whole has been notable for its gradualism. Similar gradual development in this respect has only occurred in Slovenia.[2] In the eyes of those who distinguish 'shock therapy' or 'big-bang' strategy from 'gradualist' strategy, Hungary represents an extreme and special case of the latter: 'gradualism Hungarian style'.

Finally, Hungary has been marked for decades by a relative political calm. While the transformation in some countries has been accompanied by civil warfare, here not a shot has been fired. While the change of political system in some countries took place at lightning speed amidst spectacular circumstances (collapse of the Berlin Wall, mass demonstrations in the streets of Prague, execution of the Romanian dictator), Hungary continued restrained negotiations over an extended period, with the ruling politicians of the old order and the hitherto repressed opposition reaching agreement on free elections and a new constitution. For decades there were hardly any strikes or street demonstrations. Though the economic problems have worsened, successive governments have preferred to muddle through rather than resolve on measures that would arouse strong opposition and entail a risk of political destabilization.

These four characteristics together form the specific difference of the Hungarian transformation. This chapter sets out to contribute to an understanding of why these four characteristics came about, how they have affected each other, and what favourable and detrimental effects they have exerted.

I employ the approach of political economy to examine the economic phenomena. The thinking of politicians and mentality of the public are shaped by history, in which politics and the economy are embedded. This context and the interaction between politics and the economy are often ignored in economic-policy analysis and recommendations characterized by technocratic approaches. I would like to contribute to offsetting this biased approach.[3]

In some places I draw comparisons with other countries. These, however, are designed solely to shed light on some feature of Hungarian development.

---

[2] Yugoslavia set about dismantling the command economy before Hungary did, and in this sense the reform process has a longer history there. Slovenia is the only successor state of former Yugoslavia where the change of political system has been uninterrupted. Ruptures have occurred in all the others due to the conflicts and wars between successor states or ethnic groups.

[3] The chapter is not intended to cover all the essential themes of the Hungarian reform and transformation. Several very important questions are mentioned only in passing or not at all (like inflation, or joining the European Union).

I also refrain from judging which country is following the better road, and which country's politicians have been making wiser decisions.

2. A SURVEY OF POLITICAL HISTORY

From the point of view of my subject, the last four decades of Hungarian history can be divided into periods, as shown in Figure 5.1.

2.1 The Revolution of 1956 and the Years of Reprisals

Singled out in Figure 5.1 from the socialist period, as a date of great import, is 23 October 1956, the day the Hungarian revolution broke out. Hungary was the only country in the history of the socialist world which experienced an armed rebellion against the prevailing political order and Soviet occupation.[4] The revolutionary forces took power, if only for a brief period. Those few days of freedom sufficed for parties to organize. A multi-party government that revived the coalition before the communist assumption of power was formed under the leadership of a reform communist, Imre Nagy.

Though sporadic, there were cases of anti-communist lynching during the revolution. Harassment or replacement of the heads of many factories and public offices began. The fear engendered by all this left indelible memories in the minds of the party-state's leading stratum.

Hardly two weeks later, the revolution was crushed by the Soviet army. A one-party system with the communist party holding a monopoly of power was reimposed under the leadership of János Kádár. Armed resistance to the Soviet tanks lasted a short while and a general strike went on for some weeks before that was abandoned as well. Then came the reprisals. Imre Nagy and his associates and many other active participants in the revolution were executed; altogether 229 death sentences were carried out.[5] Thousands were imprisoned or detained in internment camps, and tens of thousands sacked from their jobs. The intimidation extended to a large part of the population. Hundreds of thousands had expressed their sincere opinions and begun to organize into non-communist and anti-communist movements and parties

---

[4] There were tumultuous events in East Berlin in 1953 and in Poland in 1956. The peaceful Prague Spring of 1968 was terminated by the tanks of the Warsaw Pact. Yet Hungary was the only country where an armed uprising had led to the collapse of the single-party political organization and the formation of a multi-party coalition, even if only for a few days.

[5] Based on the verdicts of the courts, 123 death sentences were carried out in reprisals after the 1848–49 Revolution and War of Independence, 65 after the defeat of the communist regime of 1919, and 189 for fascist acts during the Second World War. See Szakolczai (1994), p. 239.

Events	Periods in the political sphere	Periods in the economic sphere	
		Economic-policy priorities	Transformation of property relations and institutions
23 October 1956 Outbreak of revolution	Revolution		
4 November 1956 Beginning of Soviet intervention	Reprisals		
22 March 1963 Political amnesty	Softening of dictatorship	Priority given to current welfare, security and calm	Gradualist transformation — Reform-socialist phase
1 January 1968 Beginning of 'new economic mechanism'			
13 June 1989 Beginning of negotiations between communist party and opposition	Change to multi-party system		
23 May 1990 First sitting of democratically elected parliament	Parliamentary democracy	Measures to restore macro equilibrium	Post-socialist phase
12 March 1995 Announcement of stabilization programme			

Figure 5.1   The last four decades of Hungarian history, divided into periods

during the days of revolutionary freedom. Now they could all feel that reprisals might strike at any minute.

Memories of 1956 and the ensuing period have to be recalled, for as we shall see later, they explain much about the characteristics of Hungary's process of reform.

2.2 'Softening' of Dictatorship and the Political Turning-point

Let us jump forward a few years, to the period when the numb fear gradually relaxed and the brutality and mercilessness of the repression eased. In 1963, some years after the mass executions, a general amnesty was declared; those who had been imprisoned for the part they had played in the revolution were released. A 'softening' of the dictatorship began. The name of János Kádár, the man who had directed the reprisals, is also linked to this policy of gradually easing the political repression.

But as this curious, inconsistent, hesitant 'liberalization' continued, so did the erosion of the communist system, founded on repression. The process speeded up in 1989, when even those in power felt that the political monopoly of the communist party could no longer be sustained. Negotiations began with the opposition forces, which were now organizing themselves openly. In a few months, if not a few days, enormous strides were taken in the political sphere. The one-party system was replaced by a multi-party system; a new constitution came into force; in the spring of 1990 free elections with the participation of rival parties were held for the first time in 43 years; a government chosen by the new parliament was formed; the governing parties and the parliamentary opposition stated their intention of protecting and developing private ownership, freedom of contract and a market economy.

The beginning of parliamentary democracy is dated in Figure 5.1 from the day of the first sitting of the democratically elected parliament (23 May 1990). In the political sphere, this point in time (or, to be more accurate, the 1989–90 period of the talks on changing the political regime, the drafting of the constitution and the holding of the first free elections) marked a real turning-point. But the initial and terminal dates of the characteristic periods in the *economic* sphere fell at different points of calendar time from those in the *political* sphere.

3. PRIORITY FOR TODAY'S WELFARE, SECURITY AND CALM

One of the main propositions of this chapter is that a curious continuity prevailed in the priorities motivating Hungarian economic policy, extending beyond the political turning-point of 1989–90 (Figure 5.1). The same orientation persisted for 25–30 years. Only the announcement of the stabilization programme on 12 March 1995 broke this continuity. Sections 3.1–3.3 of this chapter analyse the period 1963–95; Section 3.4 deals with the stabilization programme.

3.1 Avoidance of Upheavals and Conflicts

From the outset, those directing and playing an active part in Hungary's economic transformation, both before and after the political turning-point of 1989–90, have been guided by a resolve to avoid upheavals and conflicts.

The roots of this stance go back, in my view, to 1956. The days of revolution and subsequent years of reprisals caused a grave trauma. The ruling elite of the time, the communist 'cadres', looked back in terror on the revolution, the mass demonstrations before 23 October, the street fighting and the popular fury vented against the secret police and party functionaries. They felt they had to be on much better terms with the masses in future, lest they rebel again. The multitude of average people, if not the heroes who had worked actively for the revolution and stood by its ideals, had also been scared by the upheaval – by both the revolution and its subsequent suppression. They were intimidated by the harassment and persecution of relatives, friends and colleagues. So there was an intense desire for peace and calm among the leading stratum and the millions of ordinary people alike. This climate of public opinion explains the psychological motivation behind Hungarian economic policy. Euphemistically this could be called moderation and ability to compromise, the pursuit of consensus. A pejorative description would be appeasement and cowardice. Both verdicts contain elements of truth.

Such was the motivation at the beginning of the process, when those who had been through 1956 were still present and active. But this climate of opinion, routine of behaviour and system of moral norms caused by the grave national trauma became ingrained, persisting even after 1956 had become a remote historical event in the minds of younger people.

So what is the prime factor here? Is it a mass concern to avoid upheaval, to which politicians react? Or is it the other way round: politicians fearful of possible mass protest and open confrontation with their opponents seeking to forestall them? Do cringing, bargaining politicians bring society up to behave the same way? Presumably there are effects in both directions.

Poland in 1956 did not go as far as an armed uprising and bloody street fighting, but, 20–25 years later, millions were prepared to strike and Solidarity was formed, with a militancy that not even military intervention could stifle for good. The struggle began with the customary trade-union demands in defence of real wages and jobs. Confrontation between those in power and

the masses heightened. Concurrently in Hungary, 20–25 years after a defeated revolution, the attention of the leading stratum and the millions of
ordinary people turned not towards strikes and political struggles, but calmly
towards the economy. Ordinary people chased around after extra earnings,
built houses and grew vegetables.

There was an almost logical continuation of this after 1990. Poland underwent another great flare-up under a Solidarity-led government prepared to
implement a radical package of stabilization and liberalization, demanding
great sacrifice. Hungary's governing coalition was not so prepared. Indeed
the victorious party in the first free elections, the Hungarian Democratic
Forum, had declared in its campaign that it would follow the policies of a
'calm force', which had been one of its electoral attractions.

In October 1990, early in the new government's term, a peculiar mass
demonstration broke out. Taxi-drivers protesting at a petrol-price rise planned
by the government blockaded Budapest's main intersections and brought
traffic to a halt. Bargaining between the representatives of the taxi-drivers
and the government took place before the television cameras. The opposition
of the day, instead of supporting the legitimate government intent on maintaining law and order and imposing an unpopular but necessary price increase, backed the organizers of the blockade instead. Eventually the
government retreated and a compromise was reached.[6] The episode acted as a
precedent. The Antall and Boross governments of 1990–94 never again ven-
tured an action that would elicit mass opposition, and the Horn government
that took power in 1994 behaved the same way for several months.

Looking back on a period of three decades since the mid-1960s, it can be
seen that whenever an economic conflict threatened, whether it was a strike
or a mass demonstration, the tension would practically always be defused by
bargaining and compromise. Confrontation was avoided, more successfully,
in fact, than in many established market economies.

The successive governments were imbued with very different ideologies.
In the final years before 1990, the reform wing of the communist party was in
power. In 1990–94 there was a coalition with a national and Christian democratic orientation. Since 1994 there has been a coalition of socialists and
liberals. Yet there was almost complete continuity until March 1995 in maintaining the tradition of compromise and conflict evasion, based on making
concessions to the dissatisfied.

---

[6] For the history of the taxi-drivers' blockade, see Bozóki and Kovács (1991), Kurtán, Sándor
and Vass (1991), and Rockenbauer (1991).

3.2   The Now-or-Later Problem

Hungarian economic policy from the early 1960s onwards was *pro-consumption*. This marked a sharp break from the Stalinist, classical socialist priorities of economic policy, in which investment, a forced pace of growth and the fastest possible acquisition of strong industrial and military might were the top priorities. In Hungary, for instance, this entailed a relegation of consumption.

It is not my province to analyse the psychology of individual politicians. What induced them to be consumption-oriented? Sincere concern for people's material welfare, or political Machiavellianism? It is clear from what has been said so far that the prominence given to material welfare could again be related to the trauma of 1956. If the communist powers wanted to be on good terms with the masses they ruled, they had to pay much more heed to their material standard of living; they had to content them. That would smooth over the conflicts; that was the best way to prevent protests, demonstrations and uprisings. Ultimately the degree to which the two posited mentalities applied to politicians is immaterial to the economic effect.

This new economic-policy orientation had a golden age between 1966 and 1975, with household consumption rising year after year without recession or stagnation, by an annual average of 5.3 per cent (Table 5.1). This was the

Table 5.1   *Absorption of GDP in Hungary, 1960–93 (annual average rates of growth, %)*

Period	GDP	Final consumption		Gross investment	
		Total	of which: total household consumption	Total	of which: accumulation of fixed assets
1961–65	4.4	3.7	3.4	5.2	5.1
1966–75	6.3	5.3	5.3	8.5	9.1
1976–87	2.7	2.3	2.2	0.1	0.8
1981–91	−4.0	−2.5	−2.9	−7.3	−5.1
1988–93[a]	−3.3	−0.7	−1.7	−4.1	−3.7

Notes:
The table has been updated for this book.
[a] The 1993 figure for total final consumption includes arms imports from Russia received as debt repayment.

Source: Central Statistical Office (1995d), p. 2.

time in many families' lives when they bought their first refrigerator, their first Trabant car, and later on took their first trip to the West. This was when most of the Hungarian public came to associate reform with growing welfare. This was when the West began to develop a partly true, partly distorted picture of the Kádár regime as 'the happiest barrack in the camp'. This was the *offensive* phase of consumption-oriented economic policy.

Production at that time was still growing fast – faster than consumption. However, under a Stalinist economic policy the gap between the growth rates of production and consumption would have been much higher. The leadership would have used the surge of growth to achieve a higher investment rate, and thus a much higher growth rate of GDP. Meanwhile it would have been contented with a far more modest improvement in consumption. One more point to make (and this will be discussed later in the chapter) is that the growth in production, and consumption, began in the 1970s to be gained partly at the price of accumulating foreign debt.

The proportions of the domestic utilization of GDP began to change in the late 1970s, with consumption's share rising and investment's falling. The growth in production steadily slowed down, remaining near to stagnation for a long time, and then starting to fall sharply in 1991. This is just the sort of situation that tests what weight consumption has in the priorities of economic policy. The consumption-oriented economic policy continued persistently against a stagnating and even shrinking economy. This it did before, during and after the change of political system, by then in a *defensive* manner. 'If a fall in consumption is inevitable, let it fall as slowly and as little as possible,' was the attitude (Table 5.2). This aim was plainly apparent in the period 1988–93, when GDP fell by an average of 3.3 per cent a year, while the fall in total household consumption averaged only 1.7 per cent a year (Table 5.1). Investment, not consumption, acted as the residual variable under the 'pro-consumption' policy of the late Kádár period and in the first five years of parliamentary democracy. This can be seen clearly in Table 5.1, where the accumulation of fixed assets first slows down and then declines faster than GDP.

This presents a special case of the well-known time-preference problem of 'now or later'. The main aim of Hungarian economic policy for at least two decades could be described as seeking at any time to maximize consumption in the present and immediate future, at the expense of debt that would devolve on later periods. Initially this ensured a rapid growth of consumption, but it was already beginning to backfire to some extent after a decade: the rise in production, and with it consumption, began to slow down. Later a decline in production and consumption set in, partly because of the policy in previous years resulting in debt accumulation. Yet the objective function, maximization of short-term consumption, was still unchanged. It continued,

Struggle and hope

Table 5.2   *Trends in GDP, consumption, real income and real wages in*
            Hungary (1987=100)

Year	GDP[a]	*Per capita* real consumption	*Per capita* real income	Real wages per earner[b]
1988	100	100	99	95
1989	101	106	102	96
1990	97	100	101	92
1991	85	91	99	86
1992	83	91	95	85
1993	82	93	91	81
1994	85	–	95	87

Notes:
The table has been updated during compilation of this book.
[a] The GDP figure does not show GDP *per capita*.
[b] Up to 1990, the figures cover only the category of workers and employees, excluding workers on agricultural cooperatives. The latter are included from 1991 onwards.

Source: Central Statistical Office (1995d), pp. 2 and 11.

of course, with its sign changed, as minimization of the fall in consumption, and the price of this aim was still accepted: further accumulation of debt.

Here I use the concept of debt in its broadest sense. This comprehensive interpretation has already been employed by several authors.[7] Let us look at its main components.

First, debt is what the country owes abroad. With this kind of debt, the connection is obvious: consumption today is being financed abroad, but this will have to be repaid tomorrow at the expense of tomorrow's consumption.[8] This kind of debt is oppressively large in Hungary's case (Table 5.3). The defensive policy of curbing the reduction of consumption has been implemented primarily at the expense of foreign debt.

Among other factors contributing to the build-up of foreign debt is the fact that the exchange-rate policy pursued has tended to overvalue the currency, which has weakened the incentive to export and allowed excessive import

[7] See Kornai (1972) and Krugman (1994). The latter uses the expression 'hidden deficit' on pp. 161–9.
[8] It is well known from the literature on the subject that the situation is different with state debt incurred to domestic creditors. At the time of repayment, the Hungarian creditors entitled to instalments and interest will receive money at the expense of Hungarian citizens paying tax at that time. Here there is a continual redistribution taking place within the Hungarian public, and it does not necessarily entail the dilemma of 'consume now, pay later' for society as a whole.

Table 5.3   *Indices of Hungary's convertible-currency foreign debt and debt servicing*

Year	Gross debt (US$ bn)	*Per capita* gross debt (US$)	Debt servicing/goods exports (%)
1975	3.9	369	25.3
1980	9.1	850	41.4
1985	14.0	1326	85.6
1990	21.3	2057	62.7
1993	24.6	2393	44.5
1994	28.5	2782	–

Sources: Gross debt, 1975–81: United Nations Economic Commission for Europe (1993), p. 130; 1982–93: National Bank of Hungary (1994), p. 137; *per capita* gross debt: Central Statistical Office (1994f), p. 1 and (1995a), p. 9; debt servicing/goods exports: National Bank of Hungary (1994), p. 269 and (1995a), p. 108.

demand to develop. It was apparent in several periods, most recently from 1993 up to 12 March 1995, that the financial authorities were postponing an increasingly inevitable devaluation.[9] This fitted in well with the economic policy of always postponing unpopular measures to the last minute. Devaluation, especially when coupled with a tighter wage policy, is known for cutting deep into living standards.

Second, let us start by assuming it is possible to determine what proportion of GDP must be invested to ensure the maintenance and a modest but acceptable expansion of national wealth, on the one hand, and a modest but acceptable expansion of production on the other.[10] If the proportion is lower, some tasks that should be done now will be omitted and left for later. The arrears formed by the postponed acts of investment are a form of debt, which a later generation will have to pay instead of the present one. So they can be considered as part of the debt in the broader sense.

Since no exact calculation has been made of the size and trend of the investment proportion required for lasting growth and technical development,

[9] In periods when a populist government ruled in certain Latin American countries, a tendency for the exchange rate to appreciate was apparent in every case.

[10] Determining the desirable proportion of investment is one of the central issues in growth theory. Its size depends, among other factors, on the period in which consumption is to be maximized and how steep the economy's growth path is to be.

A satisfactory conclusion has yet to be reached; there is still no theoretical consensus on the problem. Rather than becoming embroiled in a theoretical debate at this juncture, I have chosen a means of expression to which less exception may be taken. All I say is that 'modest' growth would be absolutely necessary. This would seem to suffice for the line of argument in this chapter, since it allows an idea of the problem of 'investment postponement' to be conveyed.

I can give no estimates of the size of the investment arrears. All I can do is convey the gravity of them indirectly.

Table 5.4 compares the trend of persistently high investment proportions in some moderately developed, fast-growing countries with the declining trend over time in Hungary's investment proportion. I am not saying Hungary should necessarily have maintained its earlier high proportion of invest-ment,[11] but the very great extent of the decrease demonstrates the line of thinking above: an accumulation of investment arrears.

Table 5.4   Trends in gross domestic investment in fast-growing developing countries and in Hungary, 1980–93 (as percentage of GDP)

Year	Hungary	Indonesia	South Korea	China	Malaysia	Thailand
1980	30.7	24.3	32.0	30.1	30.4	29.1
1985	25.0	28.0	29.6	38.6	27.6	28.2
1990	25.4	30.1	36.9	33.2	31.5	41.4
1991	20.4	29.4	38.9	32.7	37.0	42.2
1992	15.2	28.7	36.6	34.4	33.8	39.6
1993	19.7	28.3	34.3	41.2	33.2	40.0

Source: World Bank (1995c), pp. 58–61.

Expenditure in Hungary on maintenance and renovation of housing and infrastructural facilities (roads, railways, bridges and so on) has fallen sharply. Let me take housing construction as an example. This has been declining for two decades, and in recent years the volume of housing constructed has positively plunged. This is offset in part by the fact that far fewer dwellings than before are being removed from the housing stock: dwellings ready for demolition are being retained.[12]

Especially menacing is the drop in certain slow-return investment projects which have a long gestation period. Infrastructural investment and the devel-opment of scientific research fall into this group.[13]

[11] The fall in the proportion of investment would have been justified from an economic point of view if it had coincided with a rise in the efficiency of investment. Unfortunately this was not the case. On the contrary, a great many very costly investment projects of low efficiency were carried out.

[12] The average annual number of dwellings removed in the 1991–93 period fell to a quarter of the figure for the period 1976–80 (see Central Statistical Office, 1994b, p. 25).

[13] To give a single example, the sum spent on research and development in 1993, at constant prices, was less than a third of the maximum level of such spending in 1987. As a proportion of GDP, the sum fell from 2.32 per cent to 1.01 per cent (Central Statistical Office, 1989, p. 13 and 1994c, p. 13).

Third, another component of debt in the broader sense is formed by legis-lative commitments to future consumption. These include promises of legally guaranteed pensions, family allowances, maternity benefits, sick pay and all other welfare payments. These are promissory notes from the present genera-tion which the next generation will have to redeem. When they are eventually redeemed, they too will compete for resources with the investment required for economic development, and so it is justified to consider them a compo-nent of debt.[14] In what follows I shall call these three kinds of debt *social debt*.[15]

At the beginning of the section I mentioned pro-consumption economic policy. The points made subsequently have helped to show that a *short-sighted* pro-consumption stance and a very high social discount rate prevails. By pushing a snowball of social debt before us, we prevent a higher standard of consumption later.

All this sounds familiar to older generations of Hungarians. Once upon a time, Mátyás Rákosi, the leading figure in Hungarian Stalinism, argued in these terms for the very high proportion of investment in the economic plan: let us be sure not to kill the goose that will lay the golden eggs. The Kádár regime gained popularity by laying this 'Rákosi-ite' doctrine aside and set-ting about consuming the goose. Much of the public still greets any call for sacrifice with suspicion and rejection.

Table 5.5 cites an opinion poll that reflects very well the despondency, the mood of 'no thought for the morrow' and the mounting tendency towards hedonism. Even when the bitter outcome of the short-sighted, short-term preferences applied earlier have become clear, with slower growth and then a decline in consumption, attitudes do not change. They even undergo a self-destructive enhancement: people become yet more impatient and still less willing to make sacrifices.[16]

---

[14] I will exemplify the vast scale of such postponed commitments with a single piece of data, the calculation made by the World Bank of the size of Hungary's 'pension debt'. This is the name given to the discounted present value of all pensions to be paid in the future under the laws and regulations that currently apply. It emerged that the pension debt is equivalent to 263 per cent of 1994 GDP. Similar calculations were made recently for seven OECD countries, of which Italy had the highest 'pension debt'. The Hungarian figure is close to the Italian one. See World Bank (1995a), p. 36 and (1995b), p. 127. The idea that the state's 'pension debt' is part of the hidden debt was first suggested by Martin Feldstein.

[15] The three items just discussed do not cover the *whole* social debt, which has other compo-nents as well. Examples include postponed environmental-protection tasks or postponed repair of environmental damage.

[16] The well-known argument for a gradualist transformation over a long period is that if the steady development bears fruit soon enough, it will gain the reform supporters who will back subsequent, less pleasant measures of reform as well (Roland, 1994a). This really applied initially; the 'golden age' of 1966–75 provided the moral capital for later reform. But in this sense Hungary's early start with reform becomes a drawback. Depletion of the initial moral capital began early as well, and it had largely run out by the time the change of political system arrived.

Table 5.5   *Opinions on more distant goals in life and on ideals and values*
              (%)

Statement	Year	Respondents' attitude to statement			Total
		Disagree	Partly agree	Wholly agree	
'Everything is changing	1978	46	33	21	100
so fast that people do not	1990	17	35	48	100
know what to believe in.'	1994	13	38	49	100
'People live from one	1978	69	17	14	100
day to the next; there is	1990	17	35	48	100
no sense in making	1994	20	34	46	100
plans in advance.'					

Source: Andorka (1994), Table 5.4.

What is the relationship between the main characteristics of Hungarian development? How do the gradual nature of the transformation, the marked preference for 'now' and the desire for political calm fit together? The compromises and conflict avoidance required for gradualism require the pursuit of an *attractive* policy. Politicians are not prepared to put forward unpopular 'belt-tightening' programmes. The Ceauşescu regime used brutal repression. This allowed it to repay its previous debts, even at the cost of grave public deprivation. The soft dictatorship of the Kádár regime, on the other hand, eschewed brutal means of oppression for its last decade or two, which partly explains why it had to pursue an economic policy which courted popularity.

The same macroeconomic dilemma faced the new, democratically elected parliaments and governments. The politicians who came to power in Poland and Czechoslovakia judged this historic moment of euphoria to be a time when the public would be willing to make great sacrifices. The opportunity had to be seized to adjust the macroeconomic proportions.[17] The Hungarian government, on the other hand, was not prepared to do the same. Why not? Perhaps it was guided by political realism, finding that the Hungarian public was now accustomed to an easing of repression and thought extensions of its rights and freedoms only natural, so that it displayed no marked euphoria

[17] One of the fundamental arguments of the 'big-bang' supporters is that if the 'window of opportunity' opens, you have to reach in. See the account of the debate by Gérard Roland (1994a).

over the change of political system, simply noting it with calm satisfaction. Perhaps it was also because the new government's behaviour was obeying the old reflex – by no means alien to experienced politicians in parliamentary democracies either – in not undertaking anything that was going to be unpopular, or even elicit mass protest. Whatever the case, the Hungarian government rejected all versions of shock therapy, radical stabilization surgery or belt-tightening programmes of cuts, in favour of continued maximization of consumption (or more precisely, minimization of the fall in consumption). Table 5.6 shows the trend in real wages, signifying the degree to which Czechoslovakia, and later the Czech Republic and Slovakia, accompanied by Poland and Slovenia, differed in this from Hungary, where gradualism applied. To this day I cannot reconcile myself to the idea that the first democratic Hungarian government missed a historic, unrepeatable opportunity in 1990.[18]

Table 5.6   Real wages: an international comparison, 1990–93

Country	Real wages (% change over previous year)				1993 as a percentage of 1989
	1990	1991	1992	1993	
Czech Republic	–5.4	–23.7	10.1	4.1	82.7
Hungary[a]	–3.5	–6.8	–1.5	–4.0	85.0
Poland	–24.4	–0.3	–2.7	–1.8	72.0
Slovakia	–5.9	–25.6	8.9	–3.9	73.3
Slovenia	–26.5	–15.1	–2.8	16.0	70.4

Note: [a] The figure for 1990 covers only the category of workers and employees, excluding workers on agricultural cooperatives. The latter are included from 1991 onwards.

Sources: 1990–93: United Nations Economic Commission for Europe (1994a), p. 79 and (1994b), p. 41; Hungary, 1990–93: Central Statistical Office (1994f), p. 11; Czech Republic and Slovakia 1990–91: World Economy Research Institute (1994), p. 37.

[18] In a book I wrote in 1989, before the free elections (Kornai, 1990 [1989]), I recommended to the future Hungarian parliament and government a radical surgery for stabilization and liberalization, similar in many ways to Poland's. This was to cover, among other things, various unpopular measures, including a rise in tax revenues, an end to the budget deficit and strict control on wages. With this part of my proposals I was left more or less isolated; most tone-setting economists in the democratic parties, which were still in opposition, rejected them. The search for popularity and fear of upheaval characteristic of the previous period were deeply embedded in the economics profession.

The new government's first finance minister, Ferenc Rabár, was prepared to draw up a radical package of stabilization and liberalization measures. This radicalism of his, along with other conflicts, meant he soon had to resign.

Since then there has been another great historical occasion: the sweeping electoral victory of the Socialist Party in 1994; the Socialist Party, along with its liberal coalition partner, which was prepared to support radical measures, won a 72 per cent majority in parliament. The 'now-or-later' dilemma posed itself more sharply than ever when the new government came to power. There is a well-known rule of thumb in parliamentary democracies, that a government with unpopular measures to take should take them at the start of the parliamentary cycle. By the next elections the voters will have forgotten them, and it may even be possible by then to discern the benefits of the rigorous measures taken several years before. Of course this was not such a dramatically historic opportunity as 1990, when democracy arrived. This was just a normal chance offered by the beginning of a new parliamentary cycle. None the less, the new government let the opportunity slip again, hesitating for another nine months. All that the leading party of the coalition, the socialist party that had grown out of the reform wing of the old communist party, did in this case was to obey the established reflexes of its predecessor. For months there was a tug-of-war between the trade-union and party opponents of further sacrifices on one side and the more radical economist reformers, prepared for a tougher economic policy, on the other. In the end it was always the latter who made the concessions, and the economic policy of muddling through continued as before.

Analogies with populism inevitably spring to mind.[19] The economic policy described – subordination of the long-term interests of economic development to the requirements of political popularity and the unilateral concern for living standards – bears a clear resemblance to it. Still, I do not think it would be right to see this simply as an Eastern European version of populism. Latin American populism (and earlier populist trends in Europe) employed aggressive demagogy and pursued economic policies of unbridled irresponsibility. The economic policy I have described as typical of Hungarian development for decades was less reckless. It was cautious rather than tub-thumping, attempting repeatedly to strike a compromise between the public's living-standard expectations and the legitimate long-term macroeconomic requirements. Yet it can be said that the economic policy steadily incorporated features resembling populism,[20] and a leaning towards populism has always haunted and strongly influenced political decision-makers.

---

[19] See Bozóki (1994), Bozóki and Sükösd (1992), Dornbusch and Edwards (1990), Greskovits (1994), Hausner (1992) and Kaufman and Stallings (1991).
[20] This also distinguishes the situation from that in Latin America, where some countries undergo a cycle of events. Populism rules for a time and then falls, but may well return to power later.

3.3 Redistribution and Paternalism

The previous section examined economic-policy priorities as aggregate categories, focusing on the question of 'consumption versus social debt'. Now let us examine what redistribution processes govern consumption.

Table 5.7 shows that if household income in Hungary is taken as a whole, the proportion of income earned from work is steadily falling. Meanwhile the proportion of income received through state and social-security redistribution is tending to rise.

Table 5.8 presents another cross-section. Attention was drawn in a study by Assar Lindbeck (1990) to a dangerous trend in the Swedish economy: the proportion of employed whose income derives from the market is falling fast, while the proportion of those whose income derives from the state budget is rising. Hungarian figures for 1993 were compiled for a comparison, with astonishing results: the Hungarian ratio of 1:1.65 far exceeds the Swedish ratio of 1:1.32 that Lindbeck found alarming. Not even the country to go

Table 5.7   Household income by main sources of income in Hungary, 1960–92 (% of total income)

Year	Income from work	Social benefits in cash	in kind	Together	Income from other sources
1960	80.4	7.0	11.4	18.4	1.2
1970	76.1	11.3	11.3	22.6	1.3
1975	71.5	15.5	11.7	27.2	1.3
1980	68.0	18.9	13.1	32.0	0.1
1985	65.6	19.9	14.1	34.0	0.4
1990	58.1	22.6	16.6	39.2	2.7
1992	52.8	25.0	16.4	41.4	5.8

Note: 'Income from work' means the sum, within the net income of households, of the income in money and in kind directly connected with the performance of work. It covers income from employment, cooperative membership, and household, auxiliary and private farming, including personal income from entrepreneurial activity, and the value of work done by households in their own homes. 'Social benefits in cash' denotes the part of the net money income of households received under social insurance and other social-policy measures, and financed out of social insurance, central and local-government budgets, and to a lesser extent by business organizations. 'Social benefits in kind' are the part of consumption by households for which they do not pay, these benefits being financed out of the budget, social insurance, or business organizations. See Central Statistical Office (1994a), p. 232.

Sources: 1960: Central Statistical Office (1971), p. 387; 1970 and 1975: Central Statistical Office (1981), p. 356; 1980 and 1985: Central Statistical Office (1986), p. 240; 1990 and 1992: Central Statistical Office (1994a), p. 30.

*Table 5.8   Number of participants in the market and non-market sectors in
             Sweden and in Hungary*

Activity	Number of participants (thousands)		
	Sweden		Hungary
	1970	1989	1993
1. Public administration and services	806	1427	875
2. Pensioners	1135	1899	2647
3. Unemployed	59	62	694
4. Employed in labour-market programmes	69	144	54
5. On sick leave	264	317	150
6. On parenthood leave	28	126	262
7. Total of 1–6	2361	3975	4682
8. Employed in market sector	3106	3020	2842
9. *Ratio of 7 to 8*	*0.76*	*1.32*	*1.65*

Notes:
Row 1: For Hungary, the figure refers to employment in budget-financed institutions.
Row 2: Figures include old-age pensioners and early retirees; for Hungary the figure omits
employed pensioners (223 000 in 1993), who are not included in any of the other market or
non-market categories either.
Row 3: For Hungary, registered unemployed only.
Row 4: For Hungary, the figure is the sum of those undergoing retraining and in public-works
employment.
Row 5: For Hungary, the proportion of employees and industrial-cooperative members on sick
leave (5.1 per cent) was projected on to active earners in the market sphere. Workers in the
budget-financed sector on sick leave do not feature in the figure for those on sick leave, to
prevent double counting. The figure for active earners in the market sphere does not include
those on sick leave.
Row 8: This includes state-owned firms and public utilities.

Sources: Sweden: Lindbeck (1990), p. 23; Hungary, Rows 1 and 2: Central Statistical Office
(1994f), pp. 14 and 54; Rows 3 and 4, Labour Research Institute (1994), p. 45; Row 5: Central
Statistical Office (1994f), p. 54, and (1994d), p. 22; Rows 6 and 8: Central Statistical Office
(1994f), p. 54.

furthest of any mature market economy in state and social-security redistribution attains Hungary's ratio of those 'living off the state budget' to those
'living off the market'.

Section 3.2 contained a mention of the defensive period of economic
policy, when the aim was to slow down the fall in living standards. This
attempt was not directed at real wages, which fell to roughly the same extent

as production (see Table 5.2). On the other hand, while the country's economic situation steadily deteriorated, the system of transfers tended to expand. Family allowances grew more ubiquitous; maternity allowances became generous, at least in the length of entitlement. The system of unemployment benefits in Hungary provided a wider range of entitlement than in many developed market economies. Hungary's proportion of welfare spending to GDP far exceeds the OECD average.[21]

To use an expression I coined in an earlier piece of writing, Hungary became a premature welfare state.[22] The countries with very high proportions of welfare spending surpass Hungary in economic development many times over.[23] So why did Hungary undertake to finance state welfare transfers beyond its capabilities? It is most important to the government at any time to reassure people. The paternalist redistribution certainly has a soothing effect, compensating to a large extent for the reduction in, and uncertainty about, real wages earned legally in the market sector.

I would like to emphasize in particular the problem of uncertainty. The characteristic feature of Hungary in the last two or three decades has not simply been that more weight was given to the economic-policy priority of *consumption*. Similar weight was attached to the requirement of socioeconomic *security*. The market economy, which increases uncertainty, and the paternalist redistribution system, which decreases it, developed in parallel.[24] Increasing redistribution fitted in better with the prevailing socialist ideology and the power aspirations of the leading group than putting higher income at the disposal of households would have done. It was left to the central authorities to decide who should share in the redistribution transfers, when and to what extent.

The shift in proportions just described did not derive from a forward-looking, long-term government programme. It arose out of improvisation, through rivalry between distributive claims. First one group, stratum or trade, then another, would demand more, or at least struggle against curtailment of

[21] For a comparison and statistical analysis of welfare spending in Hungary and in the OECD countries, see Tóth's article (1994). See also Figure 2.2, this volume.

[22] I call the Hungarian welfare state 'premature' because, in my view, given the country's medium level of development, serious fiscal problems and extremely high level of taxation, it cannot allow itself to take on such a burden of state redistribution. Some economists and sociologists specializing in welfare issues take just the opposite view, for instance Kowalik (1992) and Ferge (1994), arguing that because the problems caused by the transition are so grave, these post-socialist countries cannot afford not to make great social transfers.

[23] The statement does not apply in reverse. Not all developed countries have high proportions of welfare spending. It is notably low, for instance, in the United States and Japan. See Tóth (1994).

[24] These trends do not apply to the development of the housing sector. There the steady rise in the proportion of private building entailed a relative reduction in the role of bureaucratic–paternalist distribution.

its existing rights. This was done by every ministry and every office in the bureaucracy, every trade union and other special-interest group, and, on behalf of their district, by members of parliament and party officials. A great many dissatisfied groups could be silenced if the state undertook a new legal obligation that would always apply in the future, not just in the following year. In many cases the discontented could be pacified by a recurrent softening of the budget constraint: a firm, bank or local government would be saved from bankruptcy by a fiscal grant or a soft bank loan.

This *distributive appeasement* of dissatisfaction is one of the main factors explaining the financial disequilibria and tensions in the economy.[25] The budget deficit is augmented by pushing welfare spending up to levels that tax revenues cannot cover, and by using state subsidies to bail out firms, banks and local authorities in distress, so as to save jobs. Weakening of wage controls and softening of the budget constraint with soft loans fuel inflation, and so, of course, does monetization of the budget deficit, that is, financing it by the central bank. The growing cost of servicing the external debt contributes to the deficit on the current account. The connection between this and the one-sided consumption orientation of economic policy was discussed in the previous section.

There is a connection in the opposite direction as well. Once the financial disequilibria have emerged, it becomes impossible for a government whose policy is hallmarked by 'consumption-protection', paternalist state care and distributive appeasement to bring itself to take the drastic restrictive measures required.[26] Here again there was continuity after the 1990 change of system,[27] right up to 12 March 1995.

The steady spread of redistribution, with a steady stream of successive little concessions, also led to 'gradualism Hungarian style'. The changes were made in tiny fragmented, concurrent and consecutive stages, step by step. All this also saved the political sphere from traumatic upheavals and contributed to the relatively calm political atmosphere.

---

[25] This connection is well known from the literature on the financial crises and stabilization attempts of the developing countries: the distributive demands push up the budget deficit, thereby contributing to inflation and other financial tensions. See Haggard and Kaufman (1992a), pp. 273–5.

[26] This is not specific to the period of post-socialist transition. Governments everywhere use compensation designed to ease restrictive measures of stabilization as a means of dispelling protest (see Nelson, 1988).

[27] To quote Iván Szabó, the last finance minister of the 1990–94 coalition government, which described itself as moderately right-wing conservative: 'It is strange, but it was a social democratic, rather than a conservative programme that we carried out at the time' (Szabó, 1995, p. 15). On another occasion Szabó remarked that 'over-consumption occurred in the country by comparison with the level of income, of GDP attained. This was the sacrifice the government made for the sake of political stability in the country' (Szabó, 1994, p. 16).

3.4 A Departure: The Stabilization Programme of Spring 1995

The Hungarian government announced a stabilization programme on 12 March 1995. I do not attempt in this chapter to analyse this programme from the economic point of view. I examine the question using exclusively an approach based on political economy, analysing, in other words, the mutual effects of politics and economic policy. As a reminder, let me sum up the main components of the programme:[28]

1.   There was an immediate, substantial devaluation of 9 per cent, followed by introduction of the system of a pre-announced crawling peg. A substantial surcharge of 8 per cent was placed on imports.
2.   Restrictions on budgetary spending were introduced, including cuts in certain items of welfare spending.
3.   The government sought to achieve a sharp reduction in real wages. It therefore placed strict limits on the incomes paid in the public sector and on wages in state-owned firms. It was assumed that this would curb wage rises in the private sector as well.

The implementation of the stabilization programme has been going on for more than a year at this time of writing. However, it is too early to make a full assessment of the programme from the point of view of political economy.[29] Since the rest of the chapter analyses the general features spanning 20–30 years, it would be out of proportion and hasty to examine the experiences of a short period in the same depth. The mere announcement of the programme was a significant development and the government has been following its declared policy quite consistently. The programme marks a clean break with the four main features that have typified the Hungarian road of reform and systemic change hitherto.

---

[28] Of the analyses of the Hungarian macroeconomic situation, I would emphasize Antal (1994), Békesi (1993, 1994 and 1995), Csaba (1995), Erdős (1994), Köves (1995a and b), Lányi (1994–95), Oblath (1995), and World Bank (1995b).
　　For the view of those directing the stabilization programme, see Bokros (1995a, b and 1996), and Surányi (1995a, b and 1996).

[29] The programme's macroeconomic results are undoubtedly remarkable. The main macroeconomic indicators are presented in Table 6.1. In 1995, as compared with 1994, the deficit on the current account and the General Financial Statistics (GFS) budget deficit – as a percentage of GDP – decreased by 4 and 3.4 percentage points respectively. What happened in Hungary was clearly an export-led adjustment: the decrease in final consumption was accompanied by a considerable expansion of exports, allowing for some growth in aggregate demand. Thus the external financial and debt crisis was avoided without a recession, and GDP grew by 1.5 per cent in 1995. However, the country had to pay a high price. Inflation increased by about 10 percentage points, and real wages decreased by 12.2 per cent (see also Chapter 6).

First, consumption is replaced as the top priority by the aim of restoring the seriously upset macroeconomic balance, so as to establish the conditions for lasting growth and, at a later stage, for growing consumption. The defensive action to ward off the decline in consumption has been suspended. A sudden change has been made in the time preference of economic policy. Up to now the future has been sacrificed to the present. Now sacrifices are being demanded of the present for the sake of the future. Up to now the accumulation of social debt has been accepted for the sake of present consumption (slowing of the fall in consumption, or possibly stagnation or a slight rise in consumption). Now a reduction in present consumption has been undertaken to prevent a further build-up of social debt.[30]

Second, the paternalist welfare transfers by the state and the welfare entitlements of the public were taboo until 12 March 1995. There was no political force ready to recommend a well-specified reduction in them. Now a change has occurred. It has been shown to be possible not only to grant entitlements, but to revoke them as well. Since the announcement of the stabilization programme the issue of reforming the welfare state has come to the fore in political debate and intellectual discussions. Furthermore, the first steps to reduce welfare entitlements have been taken. For instance, tuition fees were introduced for higher education; the principle of need became a guiding principle in distributing certain welfare benefits, and so on.

Third, in sharp contrast to the gradualism, hesitancy and piecemeal policies characteristic of recent decades, a package of measures with traumatic effects has been introduced with dramatic suddenness. True, this is a far less comprehensive programme than the earlier shock therapy in Poland, the Czech Republic or Russia, but that is partly justified by the difference in Hungary's situation in 1995. Yet a degree of similarity remains: the break with continuity, the sudden reversal, and the trauma.

Finally, the stabilization package has brought the political calm to an immediate end. No one could imagine that the 12 March 1995 measures had a consensus in support of them. On the contrary, they have been greeted by the widest variety of interest groups and political forces at best with doubt and criticism, and at worst with vehement protest.

Why did the government that took office in July 1994 hesitate for nine months?[31] To answer this means going back to the results of Hungary's last general election in May 1994, and asking the following question: Who voted

[30] What made the 12 March stabilization programme so urgent were the threats to Hungary on the international financial market. In so far as the programme averted a credit crisis and its concomitant catastrophic effects, the present generation is already reaping the benefits, of course. The consumption sacrifice averts the threat of a much deeper fall in consumption.
[31] See Gombár (1995), Kéri (1994) and Lengyel (1995).

for the winning Socialist Party and why?[32] Why did the coalition that had won a large parliamentary majority four years before suffer a grave electoral defeat? Let me suggest a couple of answers. One of the motives of the electorate was undoubtedly negative in character: many simply wanted to vote *against* the ruling coalition, because of the bad economic situation. Contributing to this was the arrogant tone adopted by many government members and leading politicians. The socialists were expected to display more modest, rather plebeian behaviour. Many politicians in power were amateurs at governing. The socialists with experience in administering the state and the economy were expected to show more expertise.

The Socialist Party's constituency was very varied. The party gained backing from many employees, mainly (though not exclusively) blue-collar workers. Large numbers of pensioners voted for them. So did many members of the intelligentsia, either from a social democratic conviction or because they were repelled by the nationalist, anti-Semitic, pro-Horthy manifestations under the previous government.[33] Also among the socialist supporters were many entrepreneurs and managers, whose transfer from the party *nomenklatura* into the business world of the market economy had taken place not long before, so that they had retained their connections with their old associates. This list, which is far from complete, shows that the party's constituency included groups not only in agreement with each other, but also with strong conflicts of interest between them.

The Socialist Party's campaign was ambivalent. Its professional technocrats tried to point out frankly to voters that the country was in a difficult position and miracles could not be expected. But certain statements by party speakers left room for the assumption that the Socialist Party could promise a swift improvement in living conditions. What is more important, whether such an improvement was promised to the voters or not, is that many people voted for the Socialist Party hoping that it stood for socialist ideas. The party would be 'left-wing'. It would take sides with the poor, not the rich. It would soon set about improving the living conditions of the workers, the needy and the pensioners. Voters hoped the party would defend the state system of paternalist care, and perhaps even restore full employment and job security. Similar expectations in several other post-socialist countries have also given electoral success to socialist and social democratic parties derived from communist parties. It is all the more understandable that this should have been expected in Hungary, since Hungarian reform socialism went furthest in serving the interests of material welfare and social security.

[32] On the political and sociological background of the 1994 elections see Ágh (1995), Gazsó and Stumpf (1995), and Sükösd (1995).
[33] Miklós Horthy was the head of state during the right-wing, ultra-conservative regime in the period 1919–44.

After the elections, the Socialist Party entered a coalition with the Alliance of Free Democrats, whose history goes back to the dissident movement before the change of system. It is a quirk of history that the opposition and their successors, and those who harassed them and their successors, should now be in the same cabinet, voting together. The Free Democrats had been calling for a radical restoration of macroeconomic equilibrium in the previous two years, and they said the same during the elections. They did not disguise the fact that the country has grave economic difficulties and that restrictive measures demanding sacrifices will be required. Their ideas mainly cover European liberal thinking, but some of the party's supporters are not averse to social democratic principles either.[34]

The coalition of the two parties has 72 per cent of the seats in parliament. This is enough to vote through the government's proposals even on legislation requiring a qualified, two-thirds majority. Looking just at the proportions of seats, it might be thought that the coalition parties could immediately push through anything they set their minds on. But it was just this – the need for governmental resolve, agreement between the two parties, and above all unity within the Socialist Party – that caused problems in the nine months after the election. This returns us to the question of stabilization.

It is clear from what has been said that the Socialist Party did not have a mandate from its voters to introduce a stabilization programme of severe restrictions and austerity. Most of the socialist politicians tried to avoid the task through the kind of routine behaviour imprinted on them in the past. They dared not face their voters. Not only was division apparent at discussions within the Socialist Party and negotiations with the trade unions, but the opponents of a radical programme of stabilization appeared to be stronger than the supporters. For months the government was dogged by hesitation, equivocation and almost total uncertainty on fundamental questions of economic policy.

The government finally decided it could hesitate no longer. It had to begin paying the bill for the overconsumption of previous generations. One might ask why this had to wait until March 1995 to happen; and why precisely in March 1995? Why did the present leadership not try to continue with the policy of muddling through? I do not know what went on behind the scenes of the political process, and so I can only outline some hypotheses. Perhaps the disquieting economic statistics had a sobering effect. To mention just one of them, Hungary's deficit on the current account in 1993 was equal to 9 per cent of GDP; despite hopes of improvement, it increased to 9.5 per cent in 1994. Perhaps the events in Mexico caused the alarm. The Hungarian situation is certainly more favourable in many respects; for example, the debt

---

[34] On the coalition formed in 1994, see Kis (1994) and Körösényi (1995).

consists mainly of long-term credits. Yet the sight of a financial crash in a country that was seemingly developing well may have spread fears among Hungary's leaders. Finally, there was another factor: the foreign assessment of Hungary was becoming increasingly negative. As long as the leaders of the Hungarian economy were only in dispute with the IMF, it was possible to think of this as just the usual kind of dispute between the IMF, insisting on rigour, and a small country in difficulties. But condemnations began to multiply in the international financial press, in analyses by prestigious credit-rating institutions and large foreign private banks, and in conversations with leading politicians of other countries. Hungary, the model pupil of Eastern Europe, more and more frequently received a bad report. All these, and perhaps some other factors as well, led the Hungarian political leadership to take a sudden decision to announce a strict and very unpopular programme. After decades of conflict avoidance, it undertook to face the inevitable mass indignation.

Having chosen its course of action, the government went about it almost like a *coup*. It did not submit the 12 March announcement beforehand to wider forums in the Socialist Party. It did not request prior agreement from the socialist faction in parliament or the unions sympathetic to the party. It did not consult with social-policy experts in the state bureaucracy. Deterred by the example of earlier barren negotiations, the government tried to present its supporters with a *fait accompli*.

So what kind of rearguard political defence can the programme expect? To an extent it can rely on groups of technocratic experts and some sections of the liberal intelligentsia with influence over public opinion. The entrepreneurs more or less agree with the programme, with many reservations and criticisms, and can be expected to support it so long as it opens up the road to growth, from which they expect greater and safer earnings. It can hope for tolerance, if not support, from employees in expanding branches and firms, and at work places where surplus labour has already been shed, in other words from employees who do not feel their direct interests are infringed. Will this level of support or passive endurance suffice?

A dispassionate observer cannot give any other answer to this vital question than to say it is uncertain. The first year brought encouraging initial results in the most important *macroeconomic* indices: the monthly budget deficit fell, inflation slowed down again after the initial spurt of price rises, and the monthly deficit on the current account decreased considerably (see Table 6.1). These, however, are all the kinds of sign that only economists respect. The public do not feel them in their daily lives, whereas the fall in real wages is already hurting, and they are bitter about the reduction in some redistributive benefits. The *political and social* reaction to the programme by broad sections of society is rejection. The various professional groups and representative bodies are protesting one after the other. The programme is being attacked strongly by the opposition, inside and outside parliament, while there is much dissension and criticism from within the ranks of the main governing party. The Constitutional Court has annulled several essential components of the Stabilization Act.

The criticism and protest came in a great variety of forms. There were those people who only objected to the details of the programme's implementation and above all the way it had been announced. They were not convinced that the package had been compiled with sufficient care. Many people thought that the decisions on the trade-offs were mistaken: the amount of the reduction in the fiscal deficit did not compensate for the mass protest it had provoked. Many were angry because the government failed to explain patiently and convincingly why the measures were necessary. The restrictive measures were announced in an unfeeling style, devoid of compassion for those who would lose by them. There was indignation in the leading ranks of the Socialist Party and among the trade-union bureaucracy, which is tied to them by many strands, because these weighty measures were taken almost in the form of a *coup*, without the prior consultation to which they claimed an entitlement. The question remains: Would the rejection have been so intense if the mistakes of detail and of communication with the public had been avoided, but the essence, the restriction and the start made on whittling down paternalist welfare expenditure had remained? The answer to this is all the more important because the country is still only at the beginning of the programme. Releasing macroeconomic tensions that have built up over 20 or 30 years is not achieved by a single, energetic action over a few months. Correcting the deeper disproportions behind the constant reproduction of current-account and budget deficits, reducing the debt, permanently and substantially curbing inflation, and undertaking a comprehensive reform of the welfare sector – these are tasks that will take years, and will often demand sacrifices from many people.

The atmosphere is calming down now and people are becoming used to the new situation. Could a large part of society come to see the economic need for the measures, or at least put up with them without strong protest? Or will the mass protest grow stronger again, leading to comprehensive, long-lasting strikes and large street demonstrations that undermine the economic results of the stabilization? These questions conclude my initial comments on the political background to the stabilization programme. I return to these questions in the final section of the chapter.

4. GRADUAL TRANSFORMATION OF PROPERTY RELATIONS AND INSTITUTIONS

Reform of the Hungarian economy's property relations and institutions began in the second half of the 1960s, after the relaxation in the political and ideological spheres. Let us look again at Figure 5.1. Preparations for the first measures of reform took several years. On 1 January 1968 a milestone was reached when the classical command economy suddenly ended, and a curious hybrid form took over.[35]

This was the only sudden leap in the history of Hungarian economic reform. Ever since, the transformation of property relations and institutions has taken place gradually, in a series of small steps. The slow economic reform had been progressing for 22 years when the tempestuous political change of 1989–90 occurred. This, however, did not end the gradualism of the transformation taking place in the field of property relations and institutions, although the changes speeded up considerably.

Bearing in mind this political turning-point, the course of institutional change in the economy can be divided into two phases: a slow and less radical, 'reform-socialist' phase (1968–89), and a faster, more radical 'post-socialist' phase that still persists.[36] The border between the political periods, however, did not bring a sudden, dramatic change to the institutional structure of the Hungarian economy.

4.1   The Historical Conditions and Political Background

At the beginning of the post-socialist transition, a debate began over the desirable speed of transformation.[37] Two extreme positions emerged. One was represented earliest and most consistently by Jeffrey Sachs,[38] who believed that most of the transformation should be implemented over a very

---

[35] This took place much later in all other socialist countries except Yugoslavia.

[36] Like many other authors, I made a terminological distinction between the two phases in my earlier writings, notably in my 1992 book *The Socialist System*. The first I called a 'reform' (as it was directed at modifying the socialist system) and the second a 'post-socialist transition'. I have to concede, however, that in daily political language and professional parlance, the changes since 1990 are called a 'reform' as well.

[37] The debate was initially confined almost exclusively to the normative plane: recommendation against recommendation. Later came the first theoretical models. A survey of the debate appears in Funke (1993). Among the participants in the debate at the beginning of the 1990s whose views he sums up are Rüdiger Dornbusch, Stanley Fischer, Alan Gelb, Cheryl W. Gray, Michael Hinds, David Lipton, Ronald J. McKinnon, Domenico Nuti, Gérard Roland, Jeffrey Sachs and Horst Sieberst. For a survey of political-economy arguments in the debate see Roland (1994a). A few examples of theoretical models are Aghion and Blanchard (1993), Dewatripont and Roland (1992) and Murrell and Wang (1993).

[38] See Sachs (1990 and 1993), and Lipton and Sachs (1990).

short period. He himself borrowed the expression 'shock therapy' from psy-
chiatry for the programme he recommended, but the term 'big bang', known
from cosmology, became widespread as well.[39] In the early stage of the
debate, the most prominent representative of the opposing position was Peter
Murrell, who argued that the transformation would take place gradually, by
an evolutionary path, and this was as it should be.[40] This programme is
usually called 'gradualism' in the literature on the subject.

The debate at the time covered both the speed at which to overcome the
inherited macroeconomic disequilibria and the speed at which to transform
property relations and institutions. Since the first of these has been covered in
Section 3, discussion here will be confined to the second.

Some participants in the debate of the time declared allegiance to one of
the two 'pure' programmes. Others took up intermediate positions. Different
speeds were recommended for the various dimensions of the transformation,[41] or the choice of the time schedule was made dependent on various
specific conditions.[42]

Five or six years have gone by since the post-socialist transition began.
Experience already shows that the transformation of property relations and
institutions has been taking place at different speeds in the region's various
countries.[43] Hungary's road to transforming property relations and building
up the institutions of a market economy can be described in various ways:
organic development, cautious, moderate or considered progress, or hobbling
towards a market economy hampered by frequent hesitation and protest. It is
debatable which description fits best (all of them do to some extent), but no
one could ever say Hungary had taken a *leap* towards a market economy.

It is tempting to put the differences between countries down to different
philosophies among leading figures or perhaps leading groups of a few people, or even to the schools to which the advisers whose recommendations
were adopted belonged. These certainly had a part to play. I think, however,
that the decisive influences were the dissimilar historical antecedents and the
political power relations, structure of society and public mentality – in other
words factors that limited and affected the choice of political leaders between

[39] The study by Brabant (1993) convincingly explains how far from apposite these established
expressions are.
[40] See Murrell (1990). One of the intellectual sources of the argument was conservative philosophy, for instance Burke (1982) [1790], and other evolutionary theories in economics, for
instance Nelson and Winter (1982).
[41] I would place in this category my first work on the subject of post-socialist transition
(Kornai, 1990 [1989]), where I recommended a rapid transformation for macro stabilization
and liberalization and gradual transformation for privatization and other aspects of social
transformation.
[42] See Roland (1994b), for instance.
[43] See, for example, Brabant (1993), Portes (1994) and Rosati (1994).

alternative courses of action. Before entering into more detail about Hungary's transformation, let me say something about these historical and political factors. Once again, the intention is not to offer a complete analysis, but simply to pick out a few examples.

The 'reform of the economic mechanism', the gradual process of transforming Hungary's property relations and economic institutions that began in the 1960s, was part of a reaction to the trauma of 1956 by the leading political stratum and the whole of society. Perhaps only the blindest of party cadres could believe that people had been brought to rebellion in 1956 solely by the incitement of counter-revolutionaries. Very many members of the governing élite at the time were shaken in their faith as they set about restoring the socialist system. This was the intellectual soil that the idea of market-socialist reform managed to fertilize. Right up until the system collapsed in 1990, this kind of thinking led to a search for some acceptable hybrid. The élite wanted to take market coordination (or some of it) over from capitalism, and perhaps something of property relations (as long as it was on a small scale), but without giving up their power. This meant maintaining the political and military alliance with the Soviet Union, sole rule by the communist party, dominance by the state in controlling the economy, and state ownership of enterprises. There remained in the leading political and economic stratum an extremist type of diehard Stalinist, but this became rare after 1956. The vast majority of the élite showed ambivalence, or one might say political schizophrenia. On the one hand they wanted to save the communist system, to which they were bound by conviction and self-interest. On the other they realized the system had to be changed. So erosion of the system's political base took place first of all inside the minds of these people, as more and more of them abandoned the original, classical communist view on more and more issues, in favour of reform.

A contribution to formulating this idea of reform was made by a semi-deliberate, semi-unwitting change of world political orientation. Though the party cadres knew they had been restored to power by the armed might of the Soviet Union, anti-Soviet feelings arose in many of them. They looked down on the primitive nature of the Soviet system and felt embarrassed by its barbarity. Concurrently with the domestic reform, the country opened up progressively to Western influence. The public and the *nomenklatura* alike began to travel. They would have liked somehow to marry the efficiency and wealth they saw in the West with the Eastern system on which their power rested.

This curious erosion of old faith is the main reason why the change began early and took place gradually, in many small steps. The most enlightened reformers would put forward specific proposals. Initially these had to be made less radical. Later the opposition weakened, and they could apply more radical proposals as well. Many changes took place spontaneously, rather than by government order.

There is one further dimension in which the reform ties in with the response to 1956. The revolution had broken out as a political, not an economic protest. The post-1956 political leadership welcomed developments that distracted the attention of the public from politics, particularly the intelligentsia. One good substitute for pursuing politics was for economists, lawyers, engineers, state officials and managers to rack their brains about reforms and push fervently for their introduction. It was better still if the intelligentsia and the other strata in society concerned themselves with how to earn more money by extra work in the first economy and by various kinds of semi-legal, but tolerated activity in the second economy. This was probably the main mechanism for defusing the tensions, as it harnessed the energies of society's most active members.

Amidst all these changes, many people also changed their personal course. Within the old socialist society another, capitalist society began to take shape. Many individuals began to shift, partly or wholly, to a position consistent with the new society. The impetus may have come from a change in personal thinking, or from the attractions of an entrepreneurial lifestyle. There was a wide distribution in terms of who began to change careers and when, and in when the change was complete, which meant that for the whole set of the élite there was a continual, gradual transfer.

By the time the political liberation came in 1990, many things were already half-prepared for the development of a market economy. Table 5.9 shows changes had taken place in Hungary before 1990, of a kind that most countries in the region had to make after 1990. Perhaps more important still, far more people in Hungary had gained experience of how a market operates – in the 'market-socialist' state-owned enterprises, in the private sector or grey economy, or possibly by studying or working abroad.

The transformation speeded up considerably after the political renewal. The ideological barriers came down, and there was no more need for euphemism in discussing private property or capitalism, or concealment of private ownership of production assets. People were positively encouraged to become entrepreneurs and owners, and the passage of legislation to conform with a market economy speeded up greatly in the new democratic parliament. Yet this acceleration still did not produce a leap, most of all because leaps cannot be made in this field. Constraints on the mass production of legislation are imposed in a constitutional state by the capacity of the drafting and legislative organizations. It takes time to abolish old organizations and institute new ones. Even the far more violent communist change of system had taken years to accomplish. Moreover, the abolition of each organization and position of power provokes opposition of those with a vested interest in it, which again slows the process down.

Table 5.9   Chronology of reform measures

Reform measures introduced in Hungary before 1990	Hungary	Poland	Czechoslovakia[a]
Abolition of compulsory delivery system in agriculture	1956	1971	1960
Abolition of mandatory plans	1968	1982	1990
Abolition of central quotas	1968	1991	1990
First steps in price liberalization	1968[b]	1957, 1975[c]	1991
Uniform exchange rates	1981	1990	1991
Entry into IMF and World Bank	1982	1986	1990
Considerable freedom for entrepreneurship founding private companies	1982	No restrictions	1991
Bankruptcy legislation	1986[d]	1983[e]	1991, 1992
Two-tier banking system	1987	1988	1990
Personal income-tax system	1988	1992	1993
Value-added tax system	1988	1993	1991
Legislation on incorporated companies	1989	1990	1991
Liberalization of trade	1989	1990	1991
System of unemployment allowances	1989	1990	1991

Notes:
[a] The reform measures taken during the 'Prague Spring' of 1968, but withdrawn during the Husák restoration, are not indicated in this table.
[b] For example, 58 per cent of industrial producer prices became market prices, and market prices applied to 2 per cent of consumer goods in 1968.
[c] Gradual liberalization after 1957, with a surge in 1975, when 40–50 per cent of prices were liberalized.
[d] The first Bankruptcy Act was not enforced. A new Act was passed in October 1991.
[e] This Act was not enforced. Although it was tightened up in 1988, very few firms went bankrupt.

In this respect the Hungarian transformation backs up the gradualist principle that a coherent system of institutions and customs cannot be transformed all at once. If the 'half-ready' market economy of Hungary has taken years to mature and is still not fully developed, the same must be even more true of other countries which had not gone so far as the Hungarian reform initially. There is no country whose experience can refute this hypothesis.

'Gradualism Hungarian style' in transforming property relations and institutions was not a result of a grand master-plan. But neither would it be correct to accept the pace of Hungary's transformation uncritically as inevitable and determined just by blind fate. Very many aspects of it should have been started and completed earlier. The blame for every case of hesitation and protraction rests with those running the process and, ultimately, with the government of the day. But the retarding factors, like vacillation among the leadership, professional incompetence, inexperience, pliancy in the face of opposition, and of course the opposition itself, born of vested interests of various kinds, are all parts of historical reality.

4.2   Privatization of State-owned Enterprises[44]

By the abolition in 1968 of compulsory plan directives, part of one of the fundamental property rights, that of control, passed to the management of the state-owned enterprise. Yet the central authorities continued to intervene in enterprises in many indirect ways. Most importantly, selection, appointment, promotion and dismissal of managers remained in the party-state's hands.[45] But the managers became a much more influential force, and they became capable of asserting their own ownership interests, in the later, post-socialist period as well.

When privatization came on to the agenda after 1990 and new private firms arose on a mass scale, more and more strands tended to combine and merge the sociological groups of managers of state-owned and private firms and owners of independent firms and joint-stock or limited companies. A passage opened up between the roles of managers and owners. Ultimately these people together form the 'business class'. The former army of submissive party stalwarts carrying out plan directives gradually yields candidates for the business and manager stratum of today, which new people also join, of course. This transformation of the leading stratum takes place without bigger interruptions over a period of decades, and speeds up in the 1990s. The process is demonstrated in Table 5.10. Sociologist Iván Szelényi and his fellow researchers have shown the extent of the continuity in Hungary's economic élite,[46] despite the strongly anti-communist rhetoric of the coalition that took office in 1990 and its attempts to implant its party supporters in many business positions. Most of its own business people also came from the old economic élite.

Hungary in 1988 was the first socialist country to pass a so-called Company Act, whereby state-owned enterprises could commercialize and convert themselves into a modern company form. The first privatizations took place before 1990, but only after 1990 did privatization become one of the prominent features of government policy. Both the governing and the opposition parties agreed that the privatization should fundamentally take place by sale

---

[44] Limitations of space prevent me from analysing developments in property relations in the agricultural cooperatives, although they played an important part in the socialist system. They closely resembled the state-owned enterprises. For the same reason I do not cover the privatization of state farms or of state-(or local-government-)owned housing either.
[45] See Kornai (1986).
[46] See Szelényi (1994). See also Kende (1994) and Szalai (1994). Nagy (1994a) analyses how the old party élite has developed into the new élite.

Table 5.10   The origins of Hungary's new élites and new economic élite (%, 1993)

Position held in 1988	All new élites	New economic élite
Nomenklatura	32.7	34.8
Other high officials	47.5	54.7
Non-élite	19.8	10.5

Note: Based on life-history interviews with members of the economic, political and cultural élites in 1993. Samples: 783 (all) and 489 (economic).

Source: Szelényi (1994), p. 39.

on the market, not free distribution,[47] and this is what happened.[48] So the Hungarian road to privatization differs sharply, in its prior announcements and programmes and in the actual course of events, from that in other countries, above all the Czech Republic and Russia, where much state property was handed free of charge to citizens or to managers and employees of firms.[49]

Let me pick out some characteristics of the Hungarian privatization process.[50] Many commentators on events in Eastern Europe – politicians, journalists and sometimes even representatives of international financial

[47] I spoke out against the idea of free distribution in my book (Kornai, 1990 [1989]). Most Hungarian economists agreed, at least tacitly, and proposals for free distribution were only sporadic; see, for instance, Siklaky (1989). Though espoused briefly, at first by one opposition party and later in the government as well, the idea never gained conviction. Many Western economists, on the other hand, including notable figures like Milton Friedman and Harold Demsetz, recommended rapid, free distribution. The idea was taken up by many economists in several post-socialist countries, notably Poland, Czechoslovakia and Russia.
[48] The main exceptions need mentioning. (i) Those deprived of property under the previous regimes or persecuted for their political convictions, religious or ethnic affiliations or class status have received compensation in the form of a special voucher entitling them to modest amounts of state property free of charge. Redemption of these 'compensation vouchers' has been protracted and is far from over. (ii) The law stipulates that specified state property shall be transferred free of charge to the social-insurance system. Partial implementation of this recently began. Ultimately, these exceptions have had little effect on how property relations develop.
[49] On Czech privatization see Dlouhý and Mládek (1994) and Federal Ministry of Finance (1992), and on Russian, Boycko, Shleifer and Vishny (1995), these authors being advocates of free distribution. From more critical authors who were not active in initiating or implementing the privatization campaign, see Brom and Orenstein (1994), Hillion and Young (1995) and Stark and Bruszt (1995) in the case of Czech experience, and for analysis of the Russian situation, see Ash and Hare (1994), Bornstein (1994), Nelson and Kuzes (1994), Rutland (1994) and Slider (1994).
[50] Of the literature on privatization in Hungary, I would single out Bossányi (1995), Major and Mihályi (1994), Mihályi (1993 and 1994), Mizsei (1992) and Voszka (1992, 1993 and 1994).

organizations – have dwelt on a single index: the percentage of the original state sector that has been 'privatized', that is, no longer counts as state-owned enterprise. Taking this figure alone, roughly half the state-enterprise sector in Hungary had been privatized by July 1994 (Table 5.11). For about a year under the new government no further substantial progress had been made that would change this aggregate index.[51] At the end of 1995, however, the process accelerated spectacularly when large parts of the electricity, gas and oil sector and telecommunication had been privatized, mostly to foreign investors, and the privatization of the banking sector gained

Table 5.11   Degree of privatization in Hungary on 30 June 1994

Method of privatization or reducing state assets	Percentage of the total book value of state assets in 1990[a]
1. Total assets of companies 100% sold	11.5
2. Total assets of companies in majority private ownership	10.1
3. Privately held shares in companies in majority state ownership	4.5
4. Assets sold by enterprises or companies managed by the State Property Agency (ÁVÜ) or State Asset-Management PLC (ÁV Rt.), and assets these invested in new companies	4.4
5. Small-scale 'pre-privatization' sales[b]	0.9
6. Assets of firms in liquidation[c]	15.8
1–6. Degree of privatization; assets of the ÁVÜ and ÁV Rt. affected by privatization	*47.2*

Notes:
[a] The book value of the state's assets was established in 1990 by methods agreed with the World Bank. The total was put at HFt 2000 bn at the time.
[b] State assets sold under the Pre-privatization Act of 1990 (some 10 000 establishments, mainly commercial and catering premises).
[c] Assets of firms that underwent liquidation proceedings. There has been practically no privatization revenue from these.

Source: Hungarian Government (1994), p. 20.

[51] See Mihályi (1995).

momentum as well. The present government has promised to complete privatization by 1998.[52]

This single index in itself says little, however, for it may distort the true property relations, and poses many problems of measurement. A private owner with a mere 20–25 per cent of the shares may play a dominant role in a joint-stock company, if he or she sets the tone on the board and the representative of the state's stake remains passive. On the other hand there may be cross-ownership: the state as such is no longer the owner of the company, but there is a big stake and influence held by a state-owned bank.[53]

The main issue is not the proportion of assets privatized, but the results (permanent, not temporary) that some privatization strategy generates. Sections 4.2.1–4.2.6 attempt to clarify this by describing the experiences in Hungary.

4.2.1 Diverse property constellations

Privatization in Hungary is often linked with reorganization and restructuring. Many enterprises break down into smaller firms. Some of these pass into private ownership and some into mixed ownership. The remainder continue to be owned by the state, perhaps indirectly, with the reorganized firm becoming the property of other state-owned firms or banks (cross-ownership). There is a real proliferation of the most diverse property constellations, to use Stark's apt expression[54] – a recombination of property.

Privatization takes place in various legal and organizational forms, through a variety of techniques. The largest and most valuable enterprises are sold by the central agencies by competitive bidding or auction. For smaller and medium-sized firms there are several simplified procedures for transferring the property rights. Where possible, shares are sold for cash, but there are various credit schemes as well, some of which charge market interest rates. There are also credit schemes with preferential interest and repayment terms designed to promote purchases by domestic entrepreneurs. With some firms,

[52] According to Crane, based on information provided by the Hungarian privatization agency, 'Over 85 per cent of Hungary's productive capital stock should be in private hands by the end of 1997.' See Crane (1996), p. 14.

[53] Official Czech reports suggest the proportion of the former state-owned enterprise sector 'privatized' has risen to about two-thirds through coupon privatization. However, a majority of the shares have passed from the original coupon-holders into the hands of a few investment funds, where the large state-owned banks wield great influence among the owners (see Portes, 1994, pp. 1186–7 and the study by Stark and Bruszt, 1995). Most privatized firms are heavily in debt to the state-owned banks. So if real bankruptcy proceedings were applied, most of their property would revert to the state. The question is whether genuine private ownership prevails where the primary distribution of property transfers a nominal title of ownership to private citizens, but the state's partial property rights remain in an indirect form. This example shows how superficial it is to describe the state of privatization by a single aggregate percentage.

[54] See Stark (1994).

all or the majority of shares are sold at once, while with others they are offered gradually, in stages. There are special procedures to facilitate management or employees' buy-outs. Although it has rarely happened so far, there are plans for investment companies to take over the shares of several state-owned firms, so that buyers will be able to purchase mixed portfolios. All these forms have arisen by trial and error, not out of any preconceived, uniform plan or central directive. Sometimes consideration for the government's political popularity has caused some form or other to be promoted or relegated.

Hungarian privatization can certainly not be accused of proceeding in a 'constructivist' manner (to borrow Hayek's phrase). On the contrary, it is full of improvisation. Previously determined concepts may be withdrawn, and a campaign launched to speed events up, only for the delays to begin again, and so on. The experimentation on the one hand creates legal uncertainties and delay, protracting the process, which dampens the enthusiasm of buyers and investors. On the other hand it allows lessons to be learnt from mistakes and new methods to be tried, which many people consider one of the main advantages of evolutionary development.[55]

Unfortunately, several months passed after the formation of the new government in mid-1994 before it had assembled its privatization ideas and submitted a new privatization bill, which parliament then enacted.

The privatization process is a curious mixture of centralized and decentralized, bureaucratic and market actions. Gigantic central bureaucracies have been created, and they are seeking to seize the control for themselves in repeated campaigns, or at least obtain strict supervision over them. Yet time and again, events slip from their grasp.

4.2.2 'Crumbling away'

Some former state-owned enterprises in their original form have a negative market value, because they can only be run at a loss. This state property, worth a minus sum, has been crumbling away along the Hungarian road to privatization. The enterprise is wound up by judicial proceedings, and only its material assets are sold. Alternatively, part of the true commercial value, particularly the intangible parts of it (commercial goodwill, expertise or the routine of production, buying and selling), is siphoned off into private firms in legal or illegal ways. Both these processes form important components of the formal and informal privatization of the state's wealth. In evaluating the crumbling-away process, two closely connected aspects of it must be distinguished. One is the *decline in real wealth*. Some physical productive capital is lost irrevocably in the process of liquidation and change of ownership,

---

[55] See Murrell (1992).

while some intellectual capital becomes unusable as well. There are no reliable estimates for this, but expert observers are unanimous in stating that the loss of real wealth is very significant. It is far more common and on a greater scale than the structural change in the economy renders inevitable. The other, completely separable aspect, is the *loss of wealth by the state, as owner*. The wealth may remain, but the new, private owner has not given adequate compensation to the old owner, the state. To put it plainly, the state has had its pocket picked, even though the new owners may make good use of the appropriated wealth for their own benefit. I shall return to this phenomenon, confining myself here to emphasizing that the process of crumbling away provides clear opportunities for squandering the state's property on the seller's side, and for legalized theft of it on the buyer's.[56]

4.2.3   Revenue from privatization

Privatization has yielded substantial fiscal revenue, which has amounted to US$ 7427 million by the end of 1995[57] (Table 5.12). This is a major advantage of the sales strategy over free distribution, although the proceeds have been less than hoped for, with much being deducted by the high costs of privatization and the central agencies. None the less, the revenue makes no small contribution to a state with serious fiscal problems. Some of the most important Acts, including the privatization of electricity and gas production and distribution and the sale of oil and oil products, generated significant revenue.

The most important advantage, though, is not the 'tangible' fiscal revenue, but the favourable changes described under the next heading. ˙

Table 5.12   Privatization revenue, 1990–95 (US$ million)

Sources and forms of revenue	Direct privatization revenue from sales of existing assets			
	1990–93	1994	1995	Total, 1990–95
From foreign clients	1528	123	3122	4773
From domestic clients (cash)	609	228	195	1031
From domestic clients (credit)	354	279	30	663
Compensation vouchers	209	611	140	960
Total	*2700*	*1241*	*3486*	*7427*

Sources: State Property Agency (ÁVÜ), State Asset Management PLC (ÁV Rt.), and State Privatization and Property Management PLC (ÁPV Rt.); communication by Péter Mihályi.

[56] See Bossányi (1995).
[57] To give an indication of its size, it exceeds Hungary's total investment in 1994.

4.2.4 Real owners and injection of capital

Because money has to be paid for the assets of the state, a high proportion of cases involve the immediate appearance of real owners (individual or corporate, domestic or foreign), who exercise real control over the managers. (In the comparatively rare cases of management buy-out, the management and the owners become the same.) Even when a majority is not obtained, a strategic investor's influence will be much stronger than the share held, in many cases even in relation to a majority shareholding by the state. The presence of the new owner is felt particularly strongly where full or partial ownership has passed to a foreign firm or individual.

Privatization by sale produces favourable conditions and strong incentives for reorganization and a new, effective style of corporate governance. This contributes to the fact that privatized Hungarian firms soon surpass state-owned firms in their performance (Table 5.13).

Many state-owned enterprises are in a run-down condition and in great need of capital injection: they need investment for restructuring. A commitment by the buyer to invest new capital within a short time often appears in the terms of

Table 5.13   The profitability of privatized companies in 1992

Branch	Gross profitability[a]	
	Privatized companies	Branch average
Mining	1	−8
Metallurgy	−2	−12
Engineering	2	−11
Non–metallic ores	5	−1
Chemicals	15	5
Textiles and garments	9	−2
Timber, paper and printing	6	12
Food, beverages and tobacco	7	−1
Other manufacturing	−2	2
Construction	8	3
Agriculture	0	−4
Commerce	8	1
Accommodation, services	6	6
Transportation, warehousing	5	2

Note: [a] Index of gross profitability employed: cash flow (profit plus depreciation) over total assets.

Source: Vanicsek (1995).

the sales contract. Where there are several potential buyers, the amount of new investment promised often acts as a selection criterion, alongside the price offered. Even if this is not spelled out in the contract, the owners will normally be aware when they buy that the firm needs development, and set about it quickly. Countless examples of this have occurred in Hungarian practice. This is one of the most important advantages over free distribution, which transfers ownership to penniless people unwilling and unable to invest.

4.2.5 Shortages in the privatization supply

One argument often brought against the idea of privatization by sale was that the savings accumulated by the public were too small for them to buy the state's wealth. Disconcerting calculations appeared at the time showing how many decades it would take to sell all the assets, given the low initial stock of savings.

Experience has shown this is not the real bottleneck in the privatization process. There are potential foreign buyers with sufficient purchasing power, and savings have meanwhile been accumulating in the hands of Hungarian entrepreneurs and, more widely, the Hungarian public.

The real problem throughout has been to make the privatization supply attractive enough, and it worsens as the privatization process in Hungary continues. Many of the most coveted items in the supply have gone, apart from a few remaining large public utilities, purposely held back. Many of the foreign investors so far have preferred to make a 'green-field' investment in a new plant. Domestic investors tend to prefer to buy safe, high-yielding Hungarian government bonds with their money, put it in a foreign-currency account at a Hungarian bank, send it abroad illegally, or invest it in a newly established private Hungarian firm, rather than buy shares in firms under privatization. Even if the most favourable credit conditions and the biggest concessions are offered, bordering on free distribution, the demand for the less attractive enterprises is low. This suggests that the viability of many state-owned enterprises is questionable.

4.2.6 The purity of privatization

Events are constantly being affected by politics. Every political force that gains governmental power also constitutes a community of interests, intent on helping its clients to gain good positions. Augmenting this are similar endeavours by other political strands and various groups in the bureaucracy. In Hungarian society, as in every living social organism, various kinds of network operate, whose members are intent on helping on each other's careers in the hope of reciprocal assistance.[58] The owners of every newly

---

[58] See Stark (1990).

privatized firm, and new private firms, are glad to bring on to their boards both members of the old *nomenklatura* and members of the new, leading political groupings, for they know such people have valuable connections.

There is widely thought to have been a great deal of corruption during the privatization process. This is presumably true, although no specific case of corruption has been exposed. Certainly the suspicion of corruption and opaqueness in the process have helped cause a further fall in the popularity of privatization, from an already fairly low initial level.[59]

I shall not venture, even with hindsight, a simple 'yes' or 'no' to the question of whether Hungary's has been better or worse on the whole than other privatization strategies. To sum up, I can say only that the gradualism applied to privatization in Hungary, as a spontaneous, wildly proliferating, evolutionary process, presents clearly favourable and unfavourable, attractive and unattractive features. The expression 'gradualism of privatization, Hungarian style' contains a modicum of national pride, and at least as much self-mockery. But it certainly seems that the strategy *works* and will result, in the foreseeable future, in the privatization of the enterprises that are viable and that it is not expedient to retain in state ownership. Certainly the process might have been faster, even supposing the same general strategy had been employed, and if the administration at any time had been more forceful and skilful, and shown greater confidence in the decentralized mechanisms. However, even if these weaknesses of Hungarian privatization and the resistance to it mean it is not completed for another few years, it will still have taken place at lightning speed when compared with other changes of ownership relations in world history.

4.3 New Private Businesses

Like many other economists, I was convinced from the outset that the key factor in changing property relations, at least in Eastern Europe's smaller countries, was the appearance of new private undertakings.[60] This was different from the ideas of those who wanted to concentrate attention on privatizing the hitherto state-owned enterprises. I argued that even if the new private businesses only accounted initially for a smaller proportion of production, their vigour would make them the real engine of post-socialist transformation.

[59] According to a survey in 1994, 50 per cent of the adult population thought privatization should be speeded up or continue at the same pace, but 50 per cent thought it should be slowed or halted altogether. See Lengyel (1994), p. 98.
[60] See Kornai (1986, 1990 [1989] and 1992a).

An appreciable development of Hungary's private sector had begun before the change of political system (Tables 5.14 and 5.15). It was not alone in this, for East Germany, Poland and Yugoslavia also had sizeable private sectors, but the development in Hungary had gone further by 1990 than it had elsewhere. The process was moving along two parallel paths.

One path is development of the legal private sector.[61] The rigid anticapitalist prohibitions of classical, Stalinist socialism began slowly and almost

Table 5.14   *Number of active earners in Hungary engaged in individual businesses or non-incorporated business associations in 1981– 94 (thousands)*

Year (1 January)	Self-employed	Family members assisting	Employees	Altogether	As a percentage of all active earners
1981	118.2	61.8	0.3	180.3	3.6
1989	218.4	81.0	48.0	347.4	7.2
1992	466.0	97.4	144.0	707.4	16.7
1994	–	–	–	805.1	21.7

Source: Laky (1995), p. 686.

Table 5.15   *Trends in the number of incorporated business associations in Hungary, by main types, 1989–95*

Type of association	1989	1992	1994	1995
Enterprises[a]	2400	1733	821	761
Private limited companies	4484	57262	87957	102697
Joint-stock companies (PLCs)	307	1712	2896	3186
Cooperatives[b]	7076	7694	8252	8321

Notes:
The data refer to December of each year.
[a] The term 'enterprise' covers the former socialist-type state-owned enterprises. These were gradually converted into companies during the transition.
[b] Cooperatives include agricultural cooperatives, housing, savings and credit cooperatives, consumer cooperatives, and miscellaneous cooperatives. In April 1995, about a quarter of the cooperatives were engaged in agriculture, a quarter in the real-estate or housing markets, and over a third in manufacturing or construction.

Sources: Central Statistical Office (1994e), p. 115; (1996c), p. 120.

[61] See Gábor (1979 and 1985), Laky (1984) and Seleny (1993).

imperceptibly to ease in the reform-socialist period. The process began to speed up in 1982, when it became possible to found various forms of private companies, and conditions for self-employment also became more favourable.

There was a huge increase in the rate at which private businesses appeared after 1990 (see Tables 5.14 and 5.15).[62] This brought with it a structural transformation of production. The excessive concentration of production lessened; masses of small and medium-sized firms came into being. The relative proportions of the branches changed, with a rise in the weight of the services, after decades of neglect.

The other path by which the private sector develops is through the expansion of semi-legal and illegal activity. This was viewed kindly by advocates of the market economy before the political turning-point as the only way, in many fields, of circumventing the restrictions imposed by ideological bias. The 'shadow economy' was a kind of civil-disobedience movement against the bureaucratic constraints. The moral and political standing of the grey and black economy changed increasingly after 1990. It could be interpreted not as acceptable civil disobedience any longer, but as evasion of civic responsibilities, taxes, customs duties and social-insurance contributions.

According to the latest estimate, compiled with particular pains, 30 per cent of 'real' (registered and unregistered) GDP derives from the grey and black economies.[63] Unfortunately, continuity also applies to willingness to pay taxes. Moral norms and behavioural rules instilled over decades alter at a snail's pace. Indeed, if taxpaying morality is altering at all, it seems to be changing in many cases for the worse. Those who infringe regulations had more to fear from the dictatorial state. Moreover, the sums at stake have become much greater: tax fraud and utilization of legal loopholes can earn their perpetrators much greater sums. There is not just a handful of tax evaders at work, whom a strict fiscal authority can easily detect. There are not just organized criminals at work, whom the police have to catch. Almost the whole Hungarian population takes part, actively or tacitly. The 'savings' from evading tax and other levies are shared between seller and buyer, employer and employee, and the customs-evading professional smuggler or shopping tourist and the consumer of the smuggled goods. The question of extending taxation to the grey economy is political, not just economic. It would be popular if the police or tax office could catch a few very rich people in the act of tax fraud. But if they start applying more methodical controls – seeing whether traders and service providers give receipts, all employees are registered, or small and medium-scale entrepreneurs' declared incomes square

[62] The extremely rapid growth of self-employment is due partly to the fact that the tax burden is lighter on these earnings than on the wages paid to employees.
[63] See Árvay and Vértes (1994) and Lackó (1995).

with their lifestyles – they will arouse opposition. No government has attempted to do this, except for one or two hesitant experiments.

Privatization and the genesis of new private enterprise led between them to half of total (recorded and unrecorded) GDP being derived from the private sector by 1992 (Table 5.16), and the proportion has risen further since then. By 1994, the share of the private sector in the recorded GDP amounted to 60 per cent.[64] The private sector's share of employment is even greater.

Special mention needs to be made of how foreign capital is involved in the Hungarian private sector. Its share of recorded Hungarian GDP was 10.4 per cent in 1994,[65] but the effect of its appearance is disproportionally greater, making a big contribution to modernization of the economy. The volume of foreign direct investment in the 1990s has been far greater in Hungary than in the other post-socialist countries of Eastern Europe[66] (Table 5.17).[67] Statements by foreign investors suggest the attraction was mainly the consolidated state of Hungary's market economy.[68]

Table 5.16   Contributions of ownership sectors to total GDP, 1980–92

Ownership sector	Contribution to total GDP (%)					
	1980	1985	1989	1990	1991	1992
Public ownership	83	79	74	70	63	50
Private ownership	17	21	26	30	37	50
of which: Domestic	17	21	26	20	34	42
Foreign	0	0	0	1	3	8
Total	*100*	*100*	*100*	*100*	*100*	*100*

Note: Total GDP is the sum of the contributions of the recorded and unrecorded economy.

Source: Árvay and Vértes (1994), p. 18.

[64] Central Statistical Office (1996g), p. 141.
[65] Ibid.
[66] Reform socialist China deserves a special note. The absolute quantity of foreign direct investment entering China is several times as great as Hungary's. However, using relative indices (for example, investment/GDP or investment/per capita GDP), investment in Hungary is still much greater than in China.
[67] According to the data supplied by the Hungarian Privatization Agency, the cumulative total through 1994 was US$ 7956 million, which is significantly higher than the figure in Table 5.17, compiled by an international agency. In 1995 the total increased by the huge amount of US$ 4570 million (communication by the National Bank of Hungary), giving a cumulative total of US$ 12 526 million for 1990–95.
[68] Another important factor is that Hungary has always been an utterly reliable, punctual debtor, never requesting a moratorium on or rescheduling of its debts. This is reassuring to foreign investors.

Table 5.17   Foreign direct investment in the post-socialist countries, 1990–
94

Country	Cumulative totals (US$ mn)			FDI per capita in 1994
	1990	1992	1994	(US$)
Albania	–	20	116	36
Bulgaria	4	102	205	23
Croatia	–	16	104	22
Czech Republic	436	1951	3319	319
Hungary	526	3456	6941	670
Poland	94	495	1602	42
Romania	–	120	501	22
Slovakia	28	210	434	102
Slovenia	7	183	374	185
FYR of Macedonia	–	–	5	3
Eastern Europe	1095	6552	13608	126
Commonwealth of				
Independent States	–	1761	4622	22
Baltic States	–	111	811	102
Total	*1095*	*8424*	*19041*	*58*

Notes:
ᵃ Cumulations of inward foreign investment from 1988.
ᵇ European countries only.

Source: United Nations Economic Commission for Europe (1995), p. 151.

4.4   Liberalization and Reform of the Legal Infrastructure

By liberalization I mean all changes that rescind earlier legal restrictions, administrative constraints and bureaucratic regulations on economic activity. Without wholly coinciding with the categories of decentralization and de-regulation, the concept largely overlaps with them.

Liberalization of many provinces of economic decision-making has taken place gradually, in many small stages, in Hungary since 1968. The process of price and export liberalization speeded up markedly after 1990 and was concluded in a relatively short time.[69] The government cannot be said to have applied a sudden, shock-like liberalization, if for no other reason than be-

[69] For a numerical presentation of the process of price and import liberalization, see Tables 1.4, 1.5 and 1.6.

cause partial freeing of prices and imports had already occurred, and the bulk of import liberalization was accomplished in the four-year period of 1989–92.[70]

Central wage controls were abolished in 1992, quite soon after the change of political system. Nor was the special tax to curb the running away of wages retained. On the other hand, there was steady development of a central 'interest-arbitration' procedure between the government and the employers' and employees' organizations to influence wage trends. I shall return to this later.

Investment projects before the reform of 1968 were carried out by central state decision and financed out of the central budget. Decentralization of this sphere of decision-making also began decades ago (Table 5.18). After the change of system, the transformation of property relations went on to institutionalize the distribution of decision-making rights customary in a market economy, whereby the central state authorities only decide projects they finance themselves and have a say in decisions on projects they help to finance.

Table 5.18   The proportion of state-controlled investment, 1968–90

Year	Proportion of total investment spending decided by the state (%)
1968	51
1975	44
1980	46
1985	42
1989	33
1990	29

Note: With state-controlled investment, the decision was made at central state level and the funds came from the state budget. Remaining investment was decided at enterprise or cooperative level. It was funded partly from the enterprise or cooperative's own resources, and partly from credit.

Sources: 1968: Central Statistical Office (1974), p. 95; 1975: Central Statistical Office (1976), p. 80; 1980: Central Statistical Office (1981), p. 117; 1985, 1989 and 1990: Central Statistical Office (1991), p. 69.

[70] Several Hungarian economists criticized the import liberalization as being too fast, particularly in view of the failure to implement a drastic devaluation or impose stronger tariff protection at the same time. International experience with import liberalization does not contain an example of application of such an 'own-goal' policy, in which unilateral, radical liberalization was applied without replacing the effect of the administrative restrictions with tariffs, and/or a strong devaluation. See Gács (1994), Köves *et al.* (1993), Nagy (1994b) and Oblath (1991).

A measure of liberalization has also occurred in foreign-exchange management, most of it since 1990. The Hungarian forint became partially convertible in 1992 (for the current payment transactions of banks and enterprises), but international capital transactions remained subject to official permit. Under the new Exchange Act, the convertibility of the forint was extended in 1996, although certain restrictions on conversion transactions by individuals and on capital transactions remain. The official exchange rate has hitherto been determined centrally, although free-market (black) foreign-exchange trading has been tolerated. Periodic devaluations of the forint have been necessitated for years by inflation, but there was no rule of any kind to govern the timing or scale of devaluations before the stabilization programme was announced in March 1995. Since then, as mentioned before, there has been continual devaluation according to a detailed schedule announced in advance.

Not for a moment has the principle of *laissez-faire* applied in a pure and extreme form in Hungary. Agencies of the bureaucratic command economy gradually turned into agencies of state supervision and partial regulation. In many instances an earlier bureaucratic authority was abolished, and another, more market-compatible one eventually emerged, resembling more closely the supervisory and regulatory bodies of other market economies. For instance, the following agencies arose: the Economic Competition Office (an anti-trust agency), the Bank Inspectorate, Insurance Inspectorate, Securities Inspectorate, Ministry of Environmental Protection and Regional Development and National Labour Centre. A Tax and Financial Office was created for the collection of personal income tax and value-added tax, taxes that were patterned after the tax system in developed market economies.

The process of drafting legislation to conform with a market economy and repealing laws contrary to it began a good few years before the turning-point of 1990. Although transformation of the legal infrastructure has also taken place gradually, in several steps, the earlier start and intensive work done have allowed Hungary in this respect to retain several advantages over the other countries in the region. The most important legislation for the operation of a market economy was in place by 1992–93. The courts and other law-enforcement and judicial organizations, along with the lawyers representing firms and individuals, began to obtain experience in ensuring the implementation of these Acts.

I would not like to give the impression that an ideal combination of market and bureaucratic coordination has arisen in Hungary. It is doubtful, of course, whether such a combination exists anywhere. Certainly both the market and the bureaucracy in Hungary today operate with a great deal of friction. Adequate supervision and legal regulation are lacking in areas where they are clearly needed.[71] On the other hand there is still too much bureaucratic intervention in areas where it is superfluous and, in areas where bureaucracy is inevitable, it often works in a sluggish, unprofessional way.

4.5 Corporatist Formations

Trade unions under the socialist system had no great influence on the country's economic policy. They were confined to protecting employees' interests in job-related and enterprise matters. Trade-union leaders were appointed and supervised in their work by the communist party.

Political pluralism provided a chance for trade-union autonomy to develop. The legal successors of the official union movement of the old regime, eager to survive, sought to gain popularity by representing employees' interests as effectively as possible. New unions were created alongside the old, and competition for members among the various alternative unions began. Relatively little attention was paid to unionism by the new parties in parliament except for the socialists, although its influence is substantial, especially in times of heavy economic burdens on employees, with declining real wages and rising unemployment. The successor to the old official union (MSZOSZ) became the strongest of the rival union movements.

National employers' federations were also founded. They, however, have so far had less say than the employees' unions, perhaps because there is still not much interplay between politics and business. The legal and semi-legal methods for business people to influence elections and political power relations by contributing money have not yet developed. The government at any time is more afraid of the employees' than of the employers' organizations.

A central framework for coordinating the views of the government and the employees' and employers' organizations on economic policy came into being in 1988.[72] It is known as the Interest Conciliation Council. Here the union movement has been demanding more and more vehemently that close attention be paid to its views, not only on wage policy, but in the preparation of every other major economic-policy decision. The scope of central coordination of interests is not fully institutionalized, but it is heading in that direction. This adds a major corporatist component to the Hungarian political and economic system. Interplay between the state and unions was increased by the electoral alliance formed before the 1994 general elections by the Socialist Party and the MSZOSZ, several of whose senior officials were elected to parliament, where they have joined the governing Socialist Party's faction.

[71] Foreign tourists are surprised, for instance, by the 'wild capitalism' practised by taxi-drivers. Unlike most Western cities, Budapest has no clearly regulated system of taxi fares.
[72] On the emergence and problems of interest conciliation in Hungary see Greskovits's (1995) instructive analysis.

Closely related to this trend are the changes in the way Hungary's social-insurance system is organized. The pension system and the health-insurance system were both branches of the central bureaucracy of the state, and the so-called social-insurance contribution clearly a state tax. The expenditure of the pension and health-insurance systems was met in practice out of the state budget.

Some separation of the finances of these two great distribution systems from the central government budget had begun before the political change. The profound change, essential from the political and sociological point of view, came with legislation embodying the principle of self-governance for the two social-insurance systems (to cover pensions and health insurance). The law laid down that these two organizations were to be run jointly by representatives of the employers and the employees. For the employers, the employers' federations delegate the representatives, while the representatives of the employees are elected by those entitled to the provision. Under the special election procedures prescribed, the candidates are put up by the trade unions, not political parties. The first such elections brought a sweeping victory for the candidates of the MSZOSZ. Through this 'personal union' the dominant trade-union movement exercises a controlling influence over the two vast apparatuses. This, of course, has further legitimized the movement's demand for a greater say in the country's affairs, and strengthened the corporatist strands in the fabric of social and economic relations.

So far as I know, the course of development in Hungary is unique in this respect. There are extremely strong formal and informal strands binding together the government, the Socialist Party with its majority in parliament, the social-insurance system, and the strongest union federation. Perhaps only the social and economic structure of Israel has shown some similar features.[73]

The acquisition of corporatist traits is leaving its mark on Hungary's economic development. While the country continued on the well-trodden 'Hungarian road', the mutual willingness to compromise shown by the government, unions and employers fitted in well, not least because they concluded no agreement likely to arouse widespread public protest.

It was not surprising that, when the government announced its restrictive stabilization programme, it broke the established corporatist conventions. There was no prior agreement with the unions and employers before the programme was put forward. Negotiations had been going on in the previous months. The Interest Conciliation Council had met several times and the

---

[73] Some years ago an Israeli economist echoed the debate between Stalin and Trotsky in the ironical title of an article: 'Can Socialism Be Built in Half a Country?' The reference is to the trade-union control over half the economy. Though not in a fully developed form, a similar problem has arisen in Hungary.

On the negative effects of the Israeli economy's corporatist features, see Murphy (1993).

prospect of concluding a 'social and economic compact' was raised repeatedly. But they could not agree. In the end the government decided to present employees and employers alike with a *fait accompli*. Since then there have been some efforts on the side of the government to negotiate with the trade unions and other associations representing various interest groups, leading to partial agreements on some points. Still, there is no general 'social compact'. The question is how long this state of 'neither agreement nor confrontation' can be sustained.

5.   CONCLUDING REMARKS IN TERMS OF POLITICAL ECONOMY AND POLITICAL PHILOSOPHY

5.1   Positive Political Economy[74]

This chapter approaches the history of the Hungarian economy's development and transformation from the angle of positive political economy.[75] The question I have tried to answer is not whether the Hungarian road of post-socialist political and economic transition is good, better or worse than the ones down which governments with other programmes have taken their countries. I wanted to know *why* Hungary's transformation was on a different road. My answer is certainly not comprehensive and may contain mistakes, but I am sure it was justified and important to raise the question.

I have sometimes heard economists, who agreed to act as advisers and then found their advice was not followed, make statements like this: 'My proposals were correct, but these selfish and stupid politicians have subordinated economic rationalism to their own criteria,' or: 'The proposal was correct from an economic point of view, but it was not politically feasible.'

Though psychologically understandable, this reaction has nothing to do with a scientific approach.[76] The sphere of politics is not an external circumstance for the economy, but one of the main endogenous actors in it. For positive political economy, this is the axiomatic point of departure for analysis. The

---

[74] A survey of the new Western trends in positive political economy is given in Alt and Shepsle (1990).

[75] The trend known in Western literature for the last couple of decades as political economy, which examines the interaction of politics and economic policy, has few exponents in Hungary or the post-socialist region as a whole. (The old expression 'pol-econ' denoted a different trend subscribing to Marxist–Leninist doctrine.)

Pioneering work in applying political economy in the modern, Western, sense to Hungary was done by Greskovits (1993a, 1993b and 1994). I would also like to mention the writings of Bruszt (1992 and 1994a).

[76] 'Economic blueprints that treat politics as nothing but an extraneous nuisance are just bad economics', writes Przeworski (1993), p. 134.

quest is to find out what makes a proposal politically feasible. What kinds of behaviour are typical of the political sphere of the country concerned, and what are the typical solutions to its dilemmas? Or, to go a stage deeper, why have the particular typical political constraints and kinds of behaviour evolved? Why are the dilemmas solved in this way, and not in some other?

Economists brought up on welfare economics are inclined to take the welfare function for granted; they expect every government to strive to maximize this function, and criticize a government that departs from the optimum.

This chapter suggests another approach, to some extent by analogy with the theory of revealed preferences. A specific historical process occurred, in which governments took active part. Can a degree of consistency in time be observed in the actions of the governments? If so, let us construct subsequently the objective function that the political leaders actually maximized, or the preferences revealed in their actions.

By following this line of thought, the chapter has arrived at two conclusions: (i) there was a consistency in time in the economic policy of the successive, in many respects dissimilar, governments, from the 1960s right up to the spring of 1995; and (ii) they showed clearly discernible preferences. They wanted to avoid conflict. They wanted as far as possible to ensure the uninterrupted survival of the economic élite and continual additions to it of people from the new political forces. They were not prepared to take radical, unpopular action. They aimed at short-term maximization of consumption, accepting as a trade-off the accumulation of social debt.

These revealed preferences go a long way to explaining the macroeconomic proportions that emerged, the constant redistributive concessions, and the gradualism typifying Hungarian development.

The preference system of Hungary's economic politicians was consistent inasmuch as it accepted, at least implicitly, the time preference, that is, the point in the 'now-or-later' trade-off attractive to them.

On the other hand, I consider fairly inconsistent the position often taken by foreign observers, for instance several staff members of the International Monetary Fund and the World Bank. These economists were enthusiastic over a long period in praising the Hungarian reform, its gradualism, and the concomitant political consensus and calm, including the continuation of this policy after 1990. Hungary was the gradualist success story. Nowadays I have often heard the same economists say something like this: 'We are disillusioned with Hungary. It used to be the model country, but now its results are far worse than those of other, more successful post-socialist countries.'

The disillusioned fail to identify the essential causal connection. Hungary now displays an unfavourable macroeconomic performance *precisely because* it previously stuck to the road of Hungarian reform and 'gradualism Hungarian style'.

The revealed preferences of Hungarian policy can be deduced not from the programmes announced in advance by politicians, but by what occurred. Rhetoric can say one thing and deeds another. Neither is it certain that the politicians, individuals and groups succeeding each other in positions of power really wanted to see what actually ensued. It may be, for instance, that they never fully thought through the 'now-or-later' dilemma. They may have convinced themselves that they were only putting aside certain tasks temporarily, until they had solved some urgent problem. The approach in this chapter is not intended to interpret the politicians' psychology or the measure of their candour, deliberation and foresight, but the actual routines, conditioned reflexes and decision-making regularities revealed in their deeds.

5.2   Further Remarks on Intergenerational Time Preferences

Although it is not the main purpose of this chapter to assess past developments, I cannot avoid in these final remarks addressing the question of whether the preferences of successive Hungarian governments deserve approval. The first aspect to clarify is *whose* approval is concerned. Can historians or research economists analysing the period *ex post* seek to apply their own scale of values? They can do so, but let this be stated, and let the value system concerned be declared. I have not aimed in this chapter to judge the past by my scale of values. What has concerned me more is to try to find the *internal* value judgement in the society examined.

Let us again take as an example the problem of 'now or later', and compare in the light of it the life stories of two Hungarian citizens, *A* and *B*. *A* was born in 1920 and died in 1993.[77] He was starting out on his career when the first change of political regime began. By the time he was 70 he had lived under seven regimes.[78] The rule and collapse of most were accompanied by war, revolution, repression, bloodshed, imprisonment and executions. As far as I know, Hungary set a world record by squeezing seven regimes – six changes of system – into 47 years of modern history.[79] Well, it was a benefit

[77] According to demographic data, Hungarian men who were 50 in 1970 had a further life expectancy of 23 years (Central Statistical Office, 1994f, p. 37).

[78] 1. To 1944: nationalist–conservative, semi-authoritarian Horthy system. 2. 1944: Occupation by Hitler's army; reign of terror under Hungarian Nazis. 3. 1945 onwards: expulsion of Hitler's army and Hungarian Nazis by Soviet army; beginning of Soviet occupation; formation of multiparty, democratic coalition. 4. 1948 onwards: other parties ousted by communists; Stalinist dictatorship established. 5. 23 October 1956: revolution; formation of multi-party revolutionary government. 6. 4 November 1956 onwards: revolution crushed by Soviet army; Kádár regime takes power, brutally repressive initially, but steadily 'softening' and commencing reforms. 7. 1989–90: collapse of communist system; formation of parties, free elections, formation of new parliament and government.

[79] Americans, Britons and Australians contemporary with *A* underwent no change of regime. These were not changes of the kind occurring in the United States when the Democrats replace

to have relative calm in the last 30 years, during the majority of A's adult life. If his material welfare matched the Hungarian average, it improved greatly to start with and deteriorated relatively little later. He did not live to see the time when a start had to be made in paying the bill for the earlier policy preference.

B's life differs strongly from A's. He was born in 1970 and started work in 1993. Two years later, in the spring of 1995, he began to pay the bill for the short-sighted policies of the previous regime, and was likely to carry on doing so for a long time. As a working adult, however, he never felt that policy's relative benefits.

So what did Hungarian development in the last three decades, with its curious time preference, mean in terms of material welfare, security and calm? Let me repeat the question, now using the example: what did it mean to whom?[80] For the older A it was favourable, more favourable than if he had lived in a communist country which had set little store by the population's standard of living, and for that reason applied stronger repression. For the younger B, however, it was not favourable, because he inherited a bigger social debt than his contemporaries in countries where the political power had applied greater restriction.

Several general conclusions can be drawn from the line of thought so far. Consistent assessment of any past period must be based on normative postulates. Alternative postulates will yield different intergenerational distributive principles. In other words, divergent principles emerge for distributing the advantages and drawbacks, benefits and losses fairly between generations. At this point we touch upon the theoretically extremely difficult issues of interpersonal comparisons of individual utilities and the possibilities and limits of creating a social welfare function.[81] There is a rich, well-expanded literature on the ethics and economic applications of ethical theory for distribution within the same generation, but to my knowledge, dynamic generalization, in other words a normative theory of intergeneration distribution, is still comparatively immature. There are no well-elaborated principles of economic ethics to say what advance the present generation can be allowed to withdraw at the expense of the next, which will have to pay it back. In other words, there are no rules to say what positive or negative legacy the present generation is obliged (or permitted) to bequeath to the future.

the Republicans, or Labour the Tories in Britain. Hungary underwent traumatic changes of regime six times, causing deep upheavals in society.

[80] I put this question from the single angle of intergenerational choice, assuming that both individuals' living standard represented the national average. I left open the question of welfare distribution in the period concerned. There will clearly be relative winners and losers within the same age group as well.

[81] For a splendid survey of the debate on welfare judgements, social preferences, social choice and public choice, see Sen (1995).

When considering long-term economic development, economists, including myself, tend to take as axiomatic the social discount rate that should express the time preference of society. Yet we know what a decisive role this discount rate plays in every theoretical and quantitative model to determine the optimum savings and investment rate and the optimum path of growth.[82]

The problem is that the social discount rate is not given at all. The theory that it finds expression in the prevailing real market rate of interest is strongly disputed.[83] The earlier example of the time preferences of the two Hungarian citizens shows that behind the dilemma lies a deep ethical problem. It is not at all self-evident how one should 'average' the time preferences of people with different destinies.

Given these difficulties, who authorizes us, as economists taking positions on matters of economic policy, to adjudicate on this dilemma? What right have we to decide what weight to give, in the intergenerational welfare function – even if it is for the retrospective assessment of economic history – to the benefits enjoyed and losses incurred by the different generations? It is especially offensive that most of us, failing even to discern the ethical problem behind our historical judgements, brashly declare that Country X's policy was right and Country Y's was wrong.

Mention of 'authorization' leads to the question of the legitimacy of choice. When examining legitimacy, the analysis should again begin with a *positive* scientific approach. It is understandable psychologically for generations that have suffered much to disregard the legacy they leave to later generations. It is understandable that A and his contemporaries, having gone through so much suffering, wanted to secure themselves a slightly better, more peaceful life.

Of course most of those in Hungarian society have lived through a stretch of both periods and start to pay off the bill in their lifetime. Relative weighting of present and future value takes place in the thinking of these people themselves, and the spread is certainly wide. If the time preference differs from person to person, people under a democratic political structure have the right to express their preferences as a political choice. Many people try to do that in elections and by other political acts.

This leads to a fundamental question: to what extent can a government be expected to act always in the way the citizens expect it to? I would like now to present this problem not just in relation to the 'now-or-later' dilemma, but in more general terms, with special reference to the post-socialist transformation.

---

[82] For example, in earlier or present, more up-to-date versions of the various 'golden-rule' models. See, for instance, Blanchard and Fischer (1989).

[83] See Barro (1974).

5.3 With or Against the Stream?

Communist ideology has a messianic nature. Sincere believers in it are sure the system they want to apply is the only redeeming social system. The system must operate even though people have not realized what their true interests dictate. Stalinist socialism put the vast majority of Eastern Europeans off messianic doctrines for life. They want nothing more to do with systems that try to bestow happiness on them by force.

The Kádár regime marked a change in that it tried to confine such forced bestowal of happiness to narrower bounds. In Bolshevik terminology this was 'opportunism', a policy of 'following in the wake of the masses'. The Kádár regime was far from a political democracy, for which the underlying institutions were lacking. But Kádárite politicians resembled those of a parliamentary democracy in trying to form groups of supporters among certain sections of the population and represent their interests. This political endeavour reached fulfilment later, after 1990, when the success of every party and political movement, the seat of every member of parliament, and the acquisition of governmental positions came to depend on the voters.

A messianic politician feels authorized to impose his or her programme by force. The more democratic politics becomes, the more a politician needs mass support to implement a programme of any kind.

The Hungarian road of transition to a market economy, displaying the four characteristics described in this chapter, proved to be a policy that tended to receive mass support to a greater extent (or at least to be less likely to meet resistance) than ideas directed at a radical correction of macro tensions. This policy exacted a great price, however, with succeeding generations pushing before them an ever greater and more perilous quantity of social debt. But must happiness be bestowed on them against their wishes and will?

Here I would like to return to the stabilization programme announced in March 1995, in which the government departed from the road taken up to that point, turning away from it in terms of all four characteristics. The programme ended Hungary's relative political calm. It aroused passions. The government parties met with sharp resistance, even from their supporters. Their political popularity dived.

Justification for the radical programme of restriction can be made on several levels. The most obvious argument starts from the current position of the Hungarian economy. The grave macroeconomic tensions and the need to avert economic crisis speak in favour of drastic restriction, rightly, in my view.

Another level of argument reaches its conclusions from the angle of the medium- and long-term transformation of the Hungarian economy and society. The present package is only the first in a succession of measures to remove the barriers to long-term growth caused by the financial disruptions, improve the structures of production and foreign trade, and help to revise the role of the state, including a reform in the welfare sphere. I am convinced that these, too, are correct arguments.

All these arguments, however, fail to resolve a deep political and ethical dilemma: is it permissible to push through a reform despite opposition from most of the public? The initial answer comes easily. The government and the political parties and movements behind it should do much better at convincing the public, so that communication between the government and population improves. Preparation for the measures should be more circumspect. Greater consideration must be given to the economic benefit and political cost of each measure, the destabilizing effect of the discontent it engenders. These are justified demands, but it can be questioned whether even the best professional preparation and persuasion can ever make popular a restrictive programme that withdraws entitlements.[84] The dilemma cannot be side-stepped.

In my view it is one thing to *understand*, in a sense affected by positive political-economic analysis but also a sympathetic heart, why there is resistance, and another to *endorse* the resistance. More specifically, it is another matter for a responsible politician to bow to mass pressure, and drift along the stream, when this plainly runs great risks even in the short term, and in the long term aggravates the already large accumulated debt and causes yet greater harm.

We have arrived at a fundamental dilemma in political thinking, which arises not only in Hungary, but in every country where a government and the parties behind it and the legislature face unpopular decisions. I will therefore put the questions in a general way, not confined to a Hungarian context, and then try to answer them in line with my conscience.

If politicians defy resistance from the majority of the public, swimming against the tide, is this not a return to the messianic approach of ideological dictators? Is this permissible in a democracy? Can a reform be applied without consensus, or, to use a narrower criterion, without approval from the majority of the public at the time?[85] I believe it is permissible, but only if several conditions are strictly met:

1. The government in all conscience must be convinced there is no alternative. There is an inescapable need for the regulations, although they are opposed by the majority of the public.

[84] Greskovits (1993b and 1994), aptly describes the type of leader engaged in this as suffering from the 'reformer's loneliness'.
[85] 'Reform without consensus' is what the study by Sachs (1994) calls the situation just described. I agree with the view expressed there, that the situation is acceptable temporarily, under certain conditions, for want of a better course.

2.   The government is obliged to remain within the bounds of the constitutional, democratic system of law. This is not self-evident, because the situation, the knowledge that there is a 'state of emergency', may tempt a committed group of reformers to resort to unconstitutional, dictatorial methods.[86]

3.   The governing group must make a sincere commitment to subordinate itself unconditionally to the judgement of the public at the next elections. Furthermore, there must be political power relations and institutional guarantees that leave no room for doubt about the freedom and cleanliness of the next elections. In that case, through the elections the public can express *retrospectively* whether it approves or rejects what the government and parliamentary majority have done without widespread support.

Political direction that is ready to go against the stream and commit itself to unpopular measures, but subordinates itself to these conditions, is acknowledged as 'leadership' in American political jargon. Although I know this kind of reform without consensus departs from the usual 'popularity-maximizing' behaviour of many politicians in mature parliamentary democracies, I do not think it can be called anti-democratic in a normative sense, so long as the conditions mentioned are strictly met. Indeed there are difficult situations that require this kind of determined political behaviour, and the present Hungarian situation happens to be just such a one.

5.4   Three Scenarios

At the time of writing there is no way of predicting which way Hungary is bound. Several eventualities can be envisaged. I will confine myself here to outlining three clearly defined scenarios.

First scenario: return to the policy of muddling through. After a time, the present government or a reshuffled version of it returns to the well-trodden road. Substantial concessions are made to mass pressure, the stabilization programme is toned down and the pace of implementation slowed. Actions urgent from the economic point of view are further delayed. The reduction of state paternalism stalls at its present level. The government resigns itself to a slow rate of growth or even stagnation. With luck the policy does not end in catastrophe. (The bounds of this scenario are exceeded if it does.) It is not

[86] I urge the government to be forceful, decisive and consistent, but nothing is further from my intentions than to recommend disregard for the democratic rule of law and constitutionalism. Anyone who reads this into this chapter or any of my earlier writings misunderstands my position. Unfortunately such a misunderstanding has already occurred. See, for instance, the article by Elliott and Dowlah (1993).

impossible to imagine that the policy of muddling through could be continued for a good while after 1995, although it will lose the country its chance of
achieving rapid and lasting growth.

There are many forces working to persuade those in power to abandon the
course taken in the spring of 1995 and return to the old road. Apart from the
ingrained Hungarian habits of decades, parliamentary democracy entices politicians to behave in this way.

It is worth recalling here the example of the United States. American
democracy has proved incapable of coping with certain fundamental economic problems, such as the federal budget deficit or health-care reform,
because politicians have been unwilling to perform unpopular tasks, especially swift and radical solutions to them. If this is the case in the most
mature democracy of all, it is hardly surprising to find the same behaviour in
several half-mature Eastern European democracies. The experience of several
countries shows that the more the political scene fragments and the less the
long-term rule of some political grouping becomes institutionalized, the less
inclined is the prevailing government to take unpopular actions with a slow
political return. Anticipation of political defeat in the foreseeable future is no
incentive to embark on altruistic reforms with long-term prospects that entail
thinking ahead over decades. Politicians are even more inclined than the
general public to think in terms of the well-known Keynesian formula: 'In the
long run we are all dead.'

Second scenario: perseverance and political downfall. The present government perseveres with the strict principles of the stabilization programme
and is ready to carry it out consistently, but fails to obtain the political
support to do so. The resistance steadily grows, manifesting itself, perhaps, in
a wave of strikes that paralyses the economy or mass protest of other kinds.
This further damages the economic situation, making even stricter measures
necessary, so that society enters a self-destructive spiral of restriction and
resistance. On reaching a critical point, the process leads to the political
downfall of the present government policy.

It is not worthwhile in this chapter to speculate on when and how this might
happen. Would it come in 1998, at the next general elections? Or could it occur
earlier, when the government parties' members desert them on a critical vote? I
do not even include the possibility that the upheaval might bring down parliamentary democracy as well as the government, because I do not think there is a
realistic danger of this happening in present-day Hungary.[87]

If the government, adhering to the stabilization programme, succumbs
politically, its successor is quite likely (though not sure) to adopt a different

[87] However, I cannot exclude this eventuality under similar circumstances in some other post-
socialist countries, where parliamentary democracy is less firmly founded than in Hungary.

policy. It may return to the old Hungarian road of muddling through, for instance, or embark on a yet more perilous populist, adventurist policy, but this again points beyond the second scenario.

All who take an active part in the stabilization programme, and all who support it in Hungary or abroad, must realize that the programme's political downfall cannot be excluded.[88]

Third scenario: success after delay. Within this scenario there is a variety of alternatives. One is that savage, unpopular stabilization reforms have succeeded in a number of autocratic countries.[89] Protest was met with repression. Sooner or later, the economic results of the reforms arrived, and because there was no more protest, there was no more need for repression. The governments of such countries did not take on the inconveniences of democracy and freedom of speech and association until the reassuring economic results had been obtained. Often-cited examples are South Korea, Taiwan and Chile.

There is much debate among analysts of post-socialist transition about what was and what may be the best order in which to take political reform that leads to democracy and economic reform that leads to a market economy.[90] It certainly seems that if political reform is completed sooner or goes faster than economic reform, great political problems posed by the unpopular elements of economic transformation have to be faced.[91] The conclusion many draw from this is that it was unfortunate to rush the democracy. It would have been better to follow the Chinese strategy of entering a path of fast growth and rising living standards first.

I cannot agree. To my mind, democracy has intrinsic value, a greater and more fundamental value than anything else. Despite the economic troubles and the inconveniences of democracy, I rate Hungary's firm parliamentary democracy as a great achievement. Luckily it rules out the course of suppressing protest by force. So let us confine ourselves to a third scenario in which the events occur in a democratic framework.

---

[88] Many foreign observers take too little account in their calculations of this political risk. I consider this especially dangerous and maybe damaging in the case of those whose positions may give them influence over events in Hungary; for instance, those who participate in decisions relating to Hungary in foreign governments or international organizations. It depends on them as well whether the threat to Hungary described in the second scenario is averted. A breakdown of political stability would pull the rug from under economic stabilization, not to mention the direct economic damage caused by radical forms of mass protest.

[89] See Collier (1979), Evans (1979), Haggard (1990), Haggard and Kaufman (1989) and Waterbury (1989).

[90] See, for instance, Haggard and Kaufman (1992b), pp. 332–42.

[91] A few works from the rich body of writing that covers the chances and consequences of autocracy and democracy during the post-socialist transition are: Bruszt (1994a and b), Bunce and Csanádi (1992), Greskovits (1994), Offe (1991) and Przeworski (1991).

It is not unrealistic, in the knowledge of Hungarian conditions, to hope for a relatively favourable succession of events. The government may manage to explain better why and how the stabilization programme serves the public's interests. The resistance may not be so vehement. The storm of initial protest may blow itself out and patience come to prevail. The not too distant future may bring favourable trends in the living standards of broad groups in the population, so that the atmosphere improves.

The word 'may' makes the uncertainty plain. Much depends on how the stabilization programme's active participants behave – from government, parliament, political parties and interest groups, to employers and employees.

I do not see it as my task to weigh the chances for the three scenarios and the various intermediate and mixed cases, or put subjective odds on the alternatives. I would like to hope that the third scenario prevails, but I am ready to support the stabilization programme even if the second scenario threatens. I am convinced that the good of present and future Hungarian generations requires us to find a new road that ensures lasting development.

6. Adjustment without recession: a case study of Hungarian stabilization[1]

1. INTRODUCTION

On 12 March 1995, Hungary's government and central bank announced a tough programme of adjustment and stabilization. (I shall refer to this by the abbreviation ASP 95.)[2] At the time of writing (June 1996) the process of implementing the programme has been taking place for 15 months. This study is an attempt to assess and take stock of its results so far.

The terms 'adjustment and stabilization' are applied to economic-policy programmes of many different kinds. Along with other components, they usually include measures to reduce inflation. This, however, was not the case with the Hungarian programme, which belongs to a class designed mainly to overcome serious current-account and budget disequilibria and avert an external and internal debt crisis.

Fifteen months is a short time. So caution and moderation are called for in applauding the programme's early successes, because they could easily slip from our grasp. Indeed, it would be more accurate to entitle the chapter

[1] My research was supported by the Hungarian National Scientific Research Foundation (OTKA). The first version of this chapter was presented at the OECD–CCET Colloquium 'Economic Transformation and Development of Central and Eastern Europe: What Lessons from the 1990s?', 29–30 May 1996, Paris. I benefited from the consultations with László Csaba, Zsuzsa Dániel, Rüdiger Dornbusch, John McHale, Csaba László, Judit Neményi, Gábor Oblath, Jeffrey Sachs, György Surányi, Georg Winckler and Charles Wyplosz; some of these colleagues also read the first draft of this paper. I thank them for their valuable comments.
[2] Work on some parts of ASP 95 had begun under the previous finance minister, László Békesi. The programme was then drawn up under the direction of the new finance minister, Lajos Bokros, and the new president of the National Bank of Hungary, György Surányi. ASP 95 was announced to the country on television by Prime Minister Gyula Horn, accompanied by the finance minister and the president of the central bank.

For a year, Bokros played a prominent part in devising, explaining and implementing the programme, and it came to be known colloquially as the Bokros Package. I have preferred to use a 'non-personal' name here because responsibility for the programme was accepted throughout by the prime minister, and because the government, the majority in parliament and the central bank remain collectively responsible for what occurs under it – achievements and mistakes alike. Lajos Bokros resigned in February 1996; however, the new finance minister and the government committed themselves to continuing to implement the programme.

'Adjustment without recession *so far*'.[3] With this warning in mind, it is worthwhile to start to assess the developments up to June 1996.[4] I shall concentrate mainly on experiences that point beyond the specific case of Hungary and may be instructive elsewhere.

The chapter has the following structure. Section 2 considers the programme's results so far and the costs and sacrifices entailed in applying it. Section 3 examines the instruments the programme employs and the extent to which they can still be used in the future. Finally, Section 4 assesses the tasks ahead, the threats to what has been achieved so far, and the prospects for Hungary's development.

2.   ACHIEVEMENTS AND COSTS

The main macroeconomic indices appear in Table 6.1. I shall return to these subsequently.

2.1   Avoiding Imminent Catastrophe

Many favourable developments have occurred in the post-socialist Hungarian economy of the 1990s. To mention some of the most important ones, liberalization of prices and foreign trade is essentially complete, huge numbers of private firms have been founded, strides have been made in privatizing state-owned enterprises, massive structural transformation has occurred in the composition of production, and foreign trade has been adjusted to conditions after the collapse of Comecon. In 1994, GDP started to grow again, after the deep transformational recession resulting from the change of course in 1990.

However, the developments in Hungary had some disquieting features as well. The socialist system had bequeathed the country a dire macroeconomic heritage, above all a very high foreign debt. In this respect the starting-point for the Hungarian economy was worse than for most other post-socialist economies. There were many difficult tasks that the government in office in 1990–94 failed to perform, and the succeeding government, which took office in 1994, vacillated for several months before acting. By 1993, the

---

[3] Indeed it takes two or, more probably, three years before the effects of such a programme can be fully assessed. A study by Alesina and Perotti (1995), for instance, terms a fiscal adjustment successful if the public debt/GDP ratio shows a material improvement (of at least 5 per cent) in the third year after the firm measures were taken.

[4] Attempts at an overall assessment have been largely confined so far to articles in the Hungarian daily and weekly papers and internal reports by the government and the central bank. These I have tried to use in this chapter. See, for instance, National Bank of Hungary (1996a) and Ministry of Finance (1996a). Among the more detailed studies see Köves (1995b) and Oblath (1996).

Table 6.1   Macroeconomic indicators in Hungary, 1993–5

Indicator	1993	1994	1995
1. GDP (annual growth rate, %)	−0.6	2.9	1.5
2. GDP per capita (US$)[a]	3745.0	4046.0	4273.0
3. Household consumption (annual growth rate, %)[b]	1.9	−0.2	−6.6
4. Gross fixed investments (annual growth rate, %)	2.0	12.5	−4.3
5. Exports (annual volume indices)[c]	−13.1	16.6	8.4
6. Imports (annual volume indices)[c]	20.9	14.5	−3.9
7. Trade balance (US$ mn)[d]	−3267.0	−3635.0	−2442.0
8. Balance on current account (US$ mn)	−3455.0	−3911.0	−2480.0
9. Net convertible currency debt (US$ mn)[e]	14927.0	18936.0	16817.0
10. Convertible-currency reserves (% of annual imports on current account)[e]	59.4	60.2	78.8
11. Unemployment rate[f] (%)	12.1	10.4	10.4
12. Employment[g] (employees as percentage of population)	42.2	40.2	39.5
13. Balance of general government (GFS balance,[h] % of GDP)	−5.2	−7.6	−3.6
14. Inflation (annual consumer price index)	22.5	18.8	28.2
15. Gross average earnings[i] (annual growth rate, %)	21.9	24.9	16.8
16. Net average earnings[i] (annual growth rate, %)	17.7	27.3	12.6
17. Real wage per wage-earner (annual growth rate, %)	−3.9	7.2	−12.2

Notes: The table has been updated for the compilation of this book.
[a] Converted from Hungarian forints by the annual average of the official commercial exchange rate.
[b] Actual final consumption of GDP by households.
[c] Export and import data are based on customs statistics. The import data include 1993 arms imports from Russia in repayment of earlier debt.
[d] Trade-related payments on the current account.
[e] On 31 December.
[f] End-year registered unemployed as a percentage of the active (employed and unemployed) population in the previous year.
[g] On 1 January.
[h] For more detailed fiscal data and explanations, see Table 6.4.
[i] Gross average earnings of full-time employees; 1993–94 indices are calculated from data on organizations with over 20 employees, 1995 indices from data on those with over 10 employees.

Sources: Rows 1–10: Central Statistical Office (1996f); pages according to rows: 224, 223, 224, 276, 276, 324, 324, 325, 324-5; Row 11: National Bank of Hungary (1996b), p. 57; Row 12: Central Statistical Office (1995c), pp. 4–5; Row 13: National Bank of Hungary (1996c); Rows 14-17: as for Rows 1-10, pages, respectively: 313, 75, 77, 86.

current-account deficit had already reached 9.0 per cent of GDP. When this recurred in the following year, at 9.5 per cent, there was a real danger that the external finances of the country would get into serious trouble. Partly tied up with this was a mounting budget deficit, which reached 8.2 per cent of GDP in 1994, according to the national accounts.[5,6]

The equilibrium problems caused the rise in external and internal debt to accelerate. The growing costs of servicing this debt raised the current-account and budget deficits even more, so that further loans had to be raised to cover them. In the winter of 1994–95 the international financial world, on seeing the unfavourable financial macro indicators, began to lose confidence in Hungary, which had hitherto been a favourite in Eastern Europe for always paying its debts on time. The process I have outlined is well known to be self-propelling. The decline in Hungary's image became manifest in worse credit conditions, which pushed the country even closer to a debt spiral.

In Chapter 5 I analysed the historical, political and social reasons why successive governments wavered, why they protracted and postponed the increasingly inevitable radical measures. I shall not repeat these here. Furthermore, only future historians, looking behind the political scenes, will be able to discover what combination of effects eventually brought to an end the habitual conduct of decades, the policy of muddling through. A big part in steeling the Hungarian government to take radical action was certainly played by the deterrent lesson of the Mexican crisis in January 1996. It made oppressive reading to see the guesswork in the international financial press – which country was going to follow Mexico? – and find Hungary named as prime candidate.

What began in Hungary in March 1995 was *preventive* therapy. Its most important result was to avert a catastrophe that *would* have ensued if the programme of adjustment and stabilization had not been initiated. This point I try to convey in Table 6.2, which compares the courses of events in Mexico and Hungary, and Table 6.3, which features the course of crises in some other countries and shows episodes inherently resembling the situation in Hungary before ASP 95.[7]

---

5 The sources of the data are: National Bank of Hungary (1995a), pp. 172 and 234, and see also Tables 6.1, 6.2 and 6.4.
6 Of the analyses of the Hungarian macroeconomic situation that built up in 1993–95, I would emphasize Antal (1994), Békesi (1993, 1994 and 1995), Csaba (1995), Erdős (1994), Köves (1995a and b), Lányi (1994–95), Oblath (1995), and World Bank (1995b).
   For the view of those directing ASP 95, see Bokros (1995a, b and 1996), and Surányi (1995a, b and 1996).
   For my own views see Chapter 2, this volume, written before the announcement of ASP 95; see also Chapters 4 and 5, written during the implementation of the programme.
7 Of the literature on the Latin American crises and protracted financial disequilibria, I relied mainly on Cooper (1992), Dornbusch and Fischer (1993), Dornbusch, Goldfajn and Valdés (1995), Dornbusch and Werner (1994), Krugman (1991), Little *et al.* (1993), Sachs (1996), and Sachs, Tornell and Velasco (1995).

Table 6.2   Macroeconomic indicators: Hungary compared with Mexico

Indicators	Mexico		Hungary	
	1994	1995	1994	1995
1. GDP (annual growth rate, %)	4.5	−6.2	2.9	1.5
2. Real private consumption (annual growth rate, %)[b]	3.7	−12.9	−0.2	−6.6
3. Industrial production (annual growth rate, %)	4.8	−7.5	9.6	4.8
4. Employment in manufacturing (annual change in number of employees, %)[c]	1.0	−2.9	−9.1	−5.3
5. Real earnings (annual growth rate, %)[d]	4.1	−12.4	7.2	−12.2
6. Inflation[e]	7.1	51.9	18.8	28.2
7. Balance on current account/GDP (%)	−7.8	−0.3	−9.5	−5.4[a]
8. Net external debt/GDP (%)[f]	32.2	36.1	45.9	38.4

Notes:
The table has been updated for the compilation of this book.
[a] Preliminary data.
[b] For Hungary actual final consumption of GDP by households.
[c] December–December for Mexico. For Hungary average number of employees; the Hungarian 1995 figure refers to firms with more than 10 employees. Total national unemployment and employment data for Mexico, statistically comparable to the Hungarian data, are not available. For the Hungarian figures see Table 6.1, Rows 11 and 12, which show that the increase of manufacturing unemployment was associated with decreases in other sectors since total employment and the national unemployment rate remained almost unchanged. There is no available information about changes across sectors in Mexico.
[d] For Mexico, real monthly earnings in manufacturing. For Hungary, real wage per wage earner (see note j in Table 6.1).
[e] December–December for Mexico.
[f] Net external debt for Mexico includes public debt only; for Hungary it includes both public and private foreign debt.

Sources: Mexico: The data were collected or calculated by Miguel Messmacher from the following sources: Rows 1, 3 and 4: 1994: Banco de Mexico (1996), p. f, Tables II-16, II-3 and II-9; Row 2: OECD (1996), Table 3; Row 5: OECD (1997), p. 58; Row 6: Banco de Mexico (1996), Table III-1; Row 7: International Monetary Fund (1997), pp. 426–9 and Banco de Mexico (1996), Table IV-1b; Row 8: International Monetary Fund (1997), pp. 426-9, 1994: Mexican Ministry of Finance (1995), 1995: Mexican Ministry of Finance (1996). Hungary: Rows 1-2: as for Rows 1 and 3 of Table 6.1; Row 3: Central Statistical Office (1996e), p. 8; Row 4: 1994: Central Statistical Office (1995d), p. 143; 1995: National Bank of Hungary (1996b), p. 56; Row 5: as for Row 17 of Table 6.1; Row 6: as for Row 14 of Table 6.1; Rows 7 and 8: National Bank of Hungary (1996c).

Table 6.3, a–e   Episodes of crisis and adjustment in selected Latin American countries

General explanation of the tables. Year 0 is chosen to be the one with the largest current-account deficit during the period. This year is indicated for each country in the third column. The countries are listed in descending order according to the size of the largest GDP decline. (Chile is first with 14.1 per cent in 1982.) This order is retained in all the tables. The tables were compiled by Miguel Messmacher.

Table 6.3a   Annual growth rates of GDP (%) (growth positive, decline negative)

Country	Worst current-account deficit	Year of adjustment	−4	−3	−2	−1	0	1	2	3	4
Chile	1981	1982	9.9	8.2	8.3	7.8	5.5	−14.1	−0.7	6.4	2.5
Costa Rica	1981	1981	8.9	6.3	4.9	0.8	−2.3	−7.3	2.9	8.0	0.7
Argentina	1981	1981[a]	6.2	−3.3	7.3	1.5	−5.7	−3.1	3.7	1.8	−6.6
Brazil	1982	1983[a]	5.0	6.8	9.1	−4.4	0.6	−2.9	5.4	7.9	7.5
Mexico	1981	1982	3.4	8.3	9.2	8.3	7.9	−0.6	−4.2	3.6	2.6

Note: [a] Indicates the year of devaluation.

Source: International Monetary Fund (1995), respective country tables.

185

Table 6.3b Current-account balance/GDP (%) (deficit negative, surplus positive)

Country	Worst current-account deficit	Year of adjustment	−4	−3	−2	−1	0	1	2	3	4
Chile	1981	1982	−5.3	−7.1	−5.7	−7.1	−14.5	−9.5	−5.7	−11.0	−8.6
Costa Rica	1981	1981	−7.5	−10.3	−13.8	−13.7	−15.6	−10.4	−9.9	−6.9	−7.4
Argentina	1981	1981[a]	3.2	2.8	−0.5	−2.3	−2.8	−2.8	−2.3	−2.1	−1.1
Brazil	1982	1983[a]	−3.5	−4.8	−5.5	−4.5	−5.9	−3.5	0.0	−0.1	−2.0
Mexico	1981	1982	−2.2	−3.0	−4.0	−5.4	−6.5	−3.4	3.9	2.4	0.4

Note: [a] Indicates the year of devaluation.

Sources: International Monetary Fund (1995), pp. 154–5 and respective country pages. For Mexico, 1977–78: World Bank (1995c), pp. 464–6.

Table 6.3c   Growth rates of real exchange rates (%) (appreciation negative, depreciation positive)

Country	Worst current-account deficit	Year of adjustment	-4	-3	-2	-1	0	1	2	3	4
Chile	1981	1982	-10.6	-6.7	-4.2	-16.0	-7.9	81.9	-3.4	27.4	13.6
Costa Rica	1981	1981	2.2	0.9	2.3	-4.1	239.3	-37.5	-16.3	2.6	1.2
Argentina	1981	1981[a]	-16.0	-34.4	-30.8	-30.4	96.2	168.6	11.4	10.3	-39.9
Brazil	1982	1983[a]	1.1	48.2	-4.4	4.7	6.2	66.0	13.8	4.1	-40.9
Mexico	1981	1982	-5.9	-7.4	-6.9	-10.8	-3.3	96.5	-14.8	-12.3	22.2

Notes:
Growth rate of real exchange rates = (1 + rate of change at nominal exchange rate) x (1 + US inflation)/(1 + domestic inflation).
[a] Indicates the year of devaluation.

Source: International Monetary Fund (1995), respective country tables.

Table 6.3d   Inflation rate (%) (average annual change of the consumer price index, increase positive)

Country	Worst current-account deficit	Year of adjustment	-4	-3	-2	-1	0	1	2	3	4
Chile	1981	1982	91.1	40.1	33.4	35.1	19.7	9.9	27.3	19.9	30.7
Costa Rica	1981	1981	4.2	6.7	8.7	18.4	36.9	89.4	33.0	11.8	15.1
Argentina	1981	1981[a]	176.0	175.5	159.5	100.8	104.5	164.8	343.8	626.7	672.1
Brazil	1982	1983[a]	38.7	52.7	82.8	105.6	97.8	142.1	197.0	226.9	145.2
Mexico	1981	1982	29.0	16.2	20.0	29.8	28.7	98.8	80.8	59.2	63.7

Note: [a] Indicates the year of devaluation.

Source: International Monetary Fund (1995), pp. 122–3.

Table 6.3e Annual change in private consumption (%) (growth positive, decline negative)

Country	Worst current-account deficit	Year of adjustment	-4	-3	-2	-1	0	1	2	3	4
Chile	1981	1982	16.6	9.8	14.2	14.4	15.5	-35.6	-8.1	25.2	-5.6
Costa Rica	1981	1981	11.9	9.1	2.0	-2.5	-3.1	-7.9	3.7	7.5	3.1
Argentina[b]	1981	1981[a]	2.5	-1.4	14.0	8.0	-3.8	-6.2	4.1	3.8	-6.8
Brazil	1982	1983[a]	2.3	9.6	6.6	-4.2	3.9	0.7	5.2	2.7	6.8
Mexico	1981	1982	0.3	9.3	9.9	9.4	8.3	-6.5	-7.0	4.4	4.1

Notes:
[a] Indicates the year of devaluation.
[b] In Argentina's case, total consumption.

Source: World Bank (1995c), pp. 12–13 and 104–5.

I would not like to take the analogy too far. Each country has a history that is individual and, strictly speaking, unique. Still, there are some major similarities between the developments in Hungary and the episodes in the other countries featured in Tables 6.2 and 6.3:[8]

1. Each country suffered adverse phenomena in its trade, with imports running away by comparison with exports. In addition, the trade imbalance led to problems on the current account.
2. In some countries listed, the situation was worsened by the budget deficit.
3. Several analysts believe that one cause of the problems, perhaps the chief one, was the rise in the real exchange rate, and as a result the overvaluation of the domestic currency.
4. The countries had attracted large amounts of credit and investment in various forms; each had long been attractive to lenders and investors, on whose confidence the country's financial situation came greatly to depend.

These are the *antecedents* I would like to underline. They are the respects in which events in Hungary and the other countries in the tables resemble each other. There the similarity ends, however. For the catastrophe that overtook the others *did not occur in Hungary*.

Though the course of each was different, almost every episode of crisis was typically a cumulative process. These are events similar to fire breaking out in a crowded hall: panic spreads, and everyone rushes for the narrow doorway, meanwhile trampling on each other and blocking the exit.[9] In financial crises, people rush in alarm to withdraw their money and try to get rid of their investments, causing tumultuous capital flight. It is the panic that accelerates and reinforces the crisis, which is why the collapse is so sudden. This panic is what Hungary managed to avoid.[10]

When catastrophe ensues, the most dramatic consequence is the serious fall in production that occurs in a short time, and the concomitant abrupt rise in unemployment (see Tables 6.2 and 6.3). This is the brutal process that reduces domestic absorption through a rapid contraction in aggregate demand and rectifies the disproportion between absorption and production. The preventive ASP 95 allowed (or more cautiously, has so far allowed) Hungary to

[8] For the sake of brevity I did not include all indicators demonstrating similarities in Tables 6.2 and 6.3.

[9] See Kindleberger (1978).

[10] Economists watching the events in Mexico with concern, including myself, avoided alarming the public and hesitant politicians with threats of catastrophe. There was a danger that such warnings would become self-fulfilling prophecies by arousing panic. It was hard to reassure the Hungarian public and the international business world, in other words to avoid arousing panic, while mobilizing efforts to avert the crisis.

avoid this calamity of recession. It would have been particularly painful in Hungary's case, because the country has still not recovered from the problems caused by the transformational recession after 1990. If Table 6.1 is compared with Tables 6.2 and 6.3, it can be seen that Hungary's production in 1995, far from sinking, even rose to a modest extent, while unemployment remained basically unchanged instead of making a jump. Hungarian and foreign economists conversant with the history of crises and stabilization efforts have expressed respect for this achievement, but not the Hungarian public, even though it is the greatest success scored by ASP 95. For the man in the street, there is no sense of accomplishment in having averted a catastrophe outside his experience. Indeed, some have been irresponsible enough to suggest it would have been better if Hungary had shared Mexico's fate. In the end, runs the argument, the country would have been forgiven its debts and been pulled out of the mire, just as the United States, other developed countries and the international financial institutions rescued Mexico.[11] Apart from the grave doubts about how much help a far more distant Hungary could have expected from the United States, Mexico still paid a dreadful price for the catastrophe, in spite of the help it received.

2.2 Starting to Adjust the Macroeconomic Proportions

Apart from having short-term preventive effects, ASP 95 has already begun, in several essential ways, to rectify the macroeconomic disproportions that were the deep underlying cause of potential catastrophe. It is hoped that ASP 95 will have beneficial effects in the medium and long term as well. Let me draw attention to the following changes, which were presented numerically in Table 6.1:

1. The most important change is in the current-account deficit, which had remained obstinately at a very high level for two years. It was substantially lower in 1995 than in 1994, its proportion of GDP falling by four percentage points. The net debt/GDP ratio shows significant improvement (see Table 6.2, Rows 7 and 8).[12]
2. The volume of exports, which had already grown substantially in the previous year, rose by a further 8.4 per cent in 1995. Thus ASP 95 can

[11] These views are reported in the article by Kocsis (1995).

[12] The balance on current account does not contain the balance of medium- and long-term capital flows. Therefore a very important item, namely foreign direct investment, does not appear in the current account. However, while the large inflow of foreign direct investment does not improve the current account, it does show up in the improvement of the country's net external debt. When calculating *net* foreign debt, reserves are part of the asset side, and capital inflow contributes to the reserves. Therefore it is feasible to have a negative current account and at the same time a reduction of net external debt.

really count as an export-led adjustment. Meanwhile the volume of imports, having risen appreciably in the previous year, fell by 3.9 per cent (see Table 6.1).

3. A contraction occurred in domestic absorption, but, as I mentioned, without a fall in production, which rose somewhat. This was made possible by the change in proportions itself. On the demand side, there was a rise in the proportion of exports and, if only to a small extent, investment, while that of consumption fell. On the supply side, the proportion of domestic production rose and that of imports fell. This is shown in Figures 6.1 and 6.2.

4. The budget deficit (GFS balance,[13] in percentage of GDP) has been reduced by 4.0 percentage points.

5. The profitability of the business sector rose, on average from 3.8 per cent to 8.2 per cent.[14] The profits of profitable firms increased and the losses of loss-makers decreased. The state budget's share of total credit placement fell and the share of business rose. These circumstances all helped to raise the business sector's prospects of growth.

ASP 95 increased the financial world's confidence in Hungary. The credit ratings began to rise again, and the barriers to Hungarian borrowing were removed. The papers of consequence in the world and the big banks involved in Eastern European investment and lending gave the programme a positive assessment. A credit agreement was finally reached with the IMF and Hungary admitted into the OECD. These two events put an official seal of approval on Hungary's improved scores.

2.3 The Price of Adjustment

A heavy price had to be paid for adjusting the macroeconomic processes. Figure 6.3 shows how inflation accelerated after the devaluation and other measures decided before the programme (for instance, the increase of energy prices). However, it remained within the range of moderate and controlled inflation, and is now easing again after its post-ASP 95 peak.

---

[13] For an explanation of the General Financial Statistics (GFS) methodology, see the note to Table 6.4.

[14] The index number mentioned in the text is a quotient with the business sector's 'own resources for investment purposes' as numerator and GDP as denominator. The definition of own resources for investment purposes is depreciation plus pre-tax profit minus company taxation. The source of the data is Ministry of Finance (1996a), p. 20.

Szentgyörgyvári and Baár (1996), p. 18 take another definition: profitability before tax equals difference between total income and total costs, divided by total income. Taking the average for the whole business sector, this was –3.2 per cent in 1992, rising to 3.3 per cent in 1994, and to 7.2 per cent in 1995.

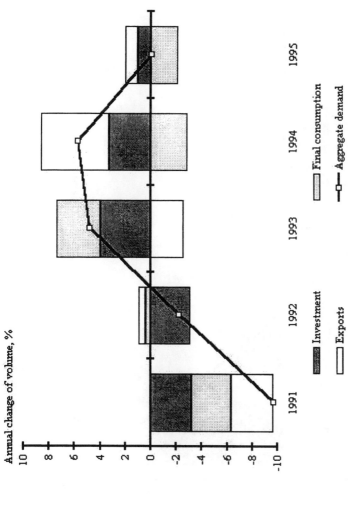

Annual change of volume, %

Investment ▨ Final consumption ▨

Exports ☐ Aggregate demand ⟶□⟶

Note: The figure has been updated for the compilation of this book. The underlying figures for 1995 are not consistent with the figures in Tables 6.1 and 6.2, because they are based on a different preliminary estimate, although the changes point in the same direction.

Source: Communication from the National Bank of Hungary.

Figure 6.1 Factors contributing to the change in the volume of aggregate demand

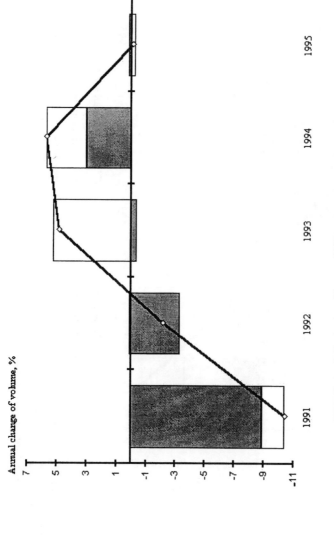

Annual change of volume, %

Note: See note to Figure 6.1.

Source: Communication from the National Bank of Hungary.

Figure 6.2 Factors contributing to the change in the volume of aggregate supply

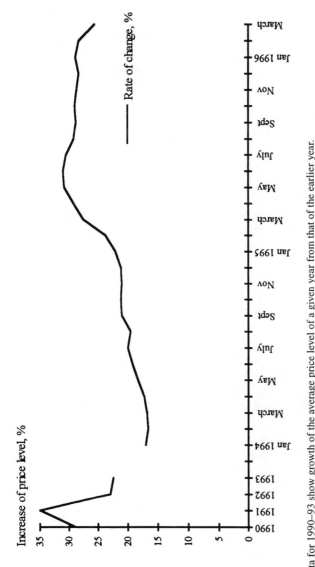

Note: Data for 1990–93 show growth of the average price level of a given year from that of the earlier year.
Data for 1994–96 show growth of the average price level of a given month from that of the month 12 months earlier.

Sources: 1991–93: Central Statistical Office (1995d), p. 286, 1994–95: National Bank of Hungary (1996b), p. 67, 1996: Central Statistical Office (1996b), p. 63.

Figure 6.3 Consumer price level.

The nominal wage rise far from equalled the rise in the price level, causing a drastic cut in real wages. Meanwhile several welfare benefits have been reduced or cut with the tightening of budget spending.

These changes will be discussed in the next section in more detail. Here it is only necessary to note how broad sections of the Hungarian public made major sacrifices in the approach to a healthier macroeconomic equilibrium. Many whose standard of living had already fallen saw it decline further, while social inequality has increased. The sense of security has weakened in much of the population, mainly, of course, among the direct financial losers by the programme. Disillusion and bitterness have taken hold.

3.   THE INSTRUMENTS OF THE PROGRAMME

The choice of instruments for ASP 95 was severely restricted by the fact that Hungary does not have a long history as a market economy. It is an economy that entered on a post-socialist transformation after several decades of social-ism. This difference of history is worth bearing in mind, even though Hunga-ry's situation and problems show close similarities with other countries at a similar level of economic development, including several Latin American countries, for instance.

The government and central bank have used instruments of several kinds simultaneously in applying the programme. The economic policy has been *heterodox*, with orthodox instruments of financial stabilization augmented by several unorthodox methods. One notable feature of ASP 95 is that it has *not* followed the dogmatic formula of restoring equilibrium simply by contrac-tion, that is, indiscriminate narrowing of aggregate demand, which would have brought a serious fall in production. The aim instead has been an adjustment that minimizes the albeit inevitable temporary slowdown in growth, and seeks to avoid an absolute fall in production. The approach to the desired macro proportions has been by way of reallocation of production and absorp-tion, not absolute contraction.[15]

A separate problem is that some of the instruments can only be used for a certain time. The most they can do is give an initial boost to the adjustment process; they cannot be relied on later. During the survey, I shall mention specifically which instruments can only be used temporarily.

---

[15] This idea was central to my economic-policy proposals, published in Hungary in the summer of 1994, before the definitive version of ASP 95 was devised. See Chapter 2.

3.1. Exchange-rate and Foreign-trade Policy

During the period before ASP 95, the government and central bank had devalued the forint (HFt) from time to time, but retained a fixed exchange rate between devaluations. There were two problems with this exchange-rate policy. One was that the real exchange rate of the forint was rising in spite of the nominal depreciation. This trend accelerated notably in certain periods, for example in 1991–2 (Figure 6.4, and see the studies by Halpern and Oblath).[16] The other problem was the unpredictability of the exchange-rate policy. No one knew beforehand when a devaluation would occur or how big it would be. Long overdue exchange-rate adjustments would be put off time and again. This made it hard for investors to make considered business calculations. Before the programme was announced, deflationary expectations had been mounting and speculative attacks against the forint emerging.

To overcome these two problems, ASP 95 included the following measures. As an initial step, the forint was devalued by 9 per cent. A *foreign-exchange regime with a pre-announced crawling peg* was introduced with immediate effect, under which the central bank announces for a longer period (6–12 months) in advance the pace at which it will devalue the forint.[17] This began with a monthly rate of 1.9 per cent, which was reduced gradually in the later stages. The monthly rate of devaluation for 1996 will be 1.2 per cent.

In setting the rate, monetary policy-makers attempt to retain more or less the real exchange rate produced by the initial devaluation, and prevent the real appreciation of the forint. The announced rate of nominal devaluation rests on a careful forecast of the rate difference between domestic and foreign inflation.[18] This entails gauging in advance on the expenditure side what nominal wage increase can be 'squeezed in' beneath the planned upper limit of inflation, given the likely trend in Hungarian productivity.

The pre-announced crawling peg needs to be coupled with an appropriate interest-rate policy. If the rate is not high enough, it becomes worth investors' while to start converting their forint holdings into foreign exchange on a mass scale and withdrawing them from Hungary. This would cause the exchange rate to collapse.

It is certainly an achievement that the announced exchange rate has been fully adhered to so far. The central bank has allowed itself a band of plus or minus 2.5 per cent around the announced rate. It would intervene if the exchange rate on the inter-bank currency market were to move out of this band. In the event, the market rate has never exceeded the intervention band.

[16] See Halpern (1996) and Oblath (1995).
[17] For the analysis of this exchange rate regime see Kopits (1995).
[18] Foreign inflation means here the average inflation for a basket of currencies that reflects the actual composition of Hungary's foreign trade.

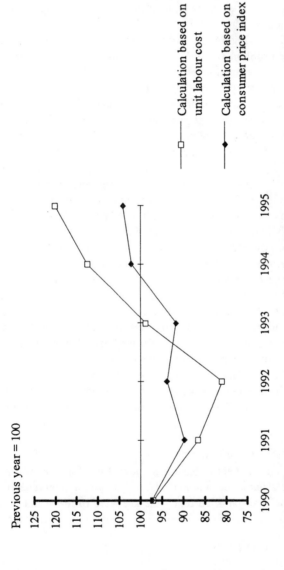

Note: An index larger than 100 means a real depreciation, and an index smaller than 100 a real appreciation compared with the previous year.

Source: Szentgyörgyvári and Baár (1996), p. 2.

Figure 6.4 Real exchange rate

Rates on the black (or rather grey) currency market in the street, catering for the general public and foreign visitors, do not deviate from the official rates either. In private savings, there is a trend away from savings in foreign exchange towards savings in forints. Starting on 1 January 1996 the Hungarian currency became convertible in current transactions.[19] This combination of circumstances has dampened the speculation in this sphere, and greatly increased confidence in the forint and the credibility of monetary policy.

The initial and subsequent continuous devaluations have caused a very drastic nominal depreciation of the forint. The exchange rate in November 1995 represented a nominal depreciation of 30.6 per cent over the rate 12 months earlier. The real effective exchange rate, as shown in Figure 6.4, changed much less, of course, since inflation accelerated. There are several accepted methods of measuring this. If inflation is measured by the industrial wholesale-price index, the real effective exchange rate decreased by 5.5 per cent over the above-mentioned period. Discounting seasonal effects and taking unit labour costs as a basis, the decrease was 17.1 per cent over the first ten months of 1995 (compared with the same period of 1994).[20] I will leave open here the problems of measurement methodology. Whatever the case, there was a nominal depreciation in excess of inflation, which substantially improved the competitiveness of Hungarian production in export markets.[21]

Apart from the devaluation and the new exchange-rate policy, ASP 95 tried other instruments designed to adjust foreign trade. An 8 per cent import surcharge was imposed, augmenting the effect of existing tariffs. The programme refrained from restricting imports by such administrative means as further quotas. However, it seemed expedient to curb temporarily (as is allowed by the international agreements) the runaway import demand with an import surcharge effective for a period of two years. This also yields substantial extra budget revenue.[22]

So to some extent, the programme is asymmetrical: it lays great emphasis on curbing import demand. However, this takes place in a differentiated way, because it seeks mainly to curb the import demand induced by consumption. The import surcharge is refunded to those who use the products imported for investment or for export production. This underlines still more that ASP 95 is designed to encourage investment and export-led growth.

[19] The convertibility of the Hungarian forint meets the criteria of 'current-account convertibility' in Article VIII of the IMF's 'Articles of Agreement'. Furthermore, it meets the OECD's convertibility requirements for certain capital transactions.

[20] National Bank of Hungary (1996a), p. 25.

[21] The study by Szentgyörgyvári and Baár (1996) provides an excellent survey of measurement of the real exchange rate and competitiveness, and the Hungarian situation and problems in this respect.

[22] Analyses showed that imports of certain products, such as private cars, had increased particularly. So extra consumer tax was imposed on these (alongside the import surcharge).

None the less, it must be admitted that the economic policy borders on protectionism in this respect. Special treatment of imports can only be justified by the threat of a balance-of-payments crisis. If the same course were pursued permanently, it would cause distortion of relative prices and slow down the improvement of efficiency. So later, when the results have been consolidated, the country will have to move towards reducing tariffs and opening up even more widely, for this is the road that leads to *lastingly* rapid growth.

There are various debates going on about the exchange-rate policy for the future. One issue concerns the connection between exchange-rate policy and policy designed to reduce inflation. Some people in Hungary, as in many other countries, advocate using real appreciation as an instrument for slowing down inflation.[23] This would be a big mistake, in my view. Inflation is a grave problem, but so long as it is kept under control and within a moderate range, it remains bearable. On the other hand, if real appreciation of the forint causes the trade and current-account balances to worsen, and confidence begins to erode again, the country will be back on the brink of a debt crisis. A tendency to real appreciation, alongside other factors, can be found among the culprits in all the countries where a payments and debt crisis has occurred.[24] This is confirmed by Table 6.3c, where every crisis episode was preceded by real appreciation. For Hungary, as for the other small open economies, export-led growth represents the true, permanent escape from the struggles of today. The competitiveness of the economy must be promoted by various instruments, of which more will be said later. However, this is certainly the aspect that the exchange-rate policy must promote in the first place.

3.2 Income Policy

In the framework of the adjustment, it was unavoidable to have a sharp reduction in consumption. The orthodox recipe is to achieve this by a thoroughly painful course of treatment. There is a serious fall in production, accompanied by a large increase in unemployment, which forces real wages down, through the mechanism of the labour market. This occurs after a long

[23] Under the present exchange-rate regime, this would amount to having a pre-announced rate of nominal depreciation much lower than the expected rate of inflation. The pre-announced exchange rate would act as a nominal anchor, pulling the rate of inflation down.

[24] See the literature quoted in note 7 in connection with the crises. There are also lessons for Hungary in the conclusions reached in the study by Dornbusch, Goldfajn and Valdés (1995), pp. 251–2: 'A policy of bringing down inflation by slowing the rate of depreciation below the rate of inflation ... is a common way of creating overvaluation. Because the real exchange rate is sticky downward, overvaluation is not easily undone by wage-price deflation and thus, ultimately, leads to collapse and devaluation ... The temptation to use the exchange rate to obtain early results on disinflation without much unemployment is all too obvious as a shortcut, but the results are often illusory. After the collapse, inflation will be higher than it was at the outset.'

delay, because of the rigidity of wages and the frictions in labour-market adjustment. Indeed a much larger unemployment increment is needed to achieve the wage level necessary in macroeconomic terms than would be the case if there were a mechanism free of friction and delay. Empirical writings on the 'wage curve'[25] suggest as a rule of thumb that unemployment must double to cause a 10 per cent fall in wages. It is not worth trying to decide how far this empirical regularity, based mainly on observations of regional differences within a particular country, would apply to Hungary today. However, the figure certainly demonstrates that without state intervention, only a very substantial rise in the already high unemployment rate of over 10 per cent would have led to the new proportions of consumption, investment and exports desirable in macroeconomic terms.

Instead, ASP 95 applied other, non-orthodox means of forcing down real wages, with the help of direct state intervention. Central wage controls ceased in Hungary in 1992. Year after year there are talks between the employees' and the employers' organizations and the government about pay, employment, and other current aspects of economic policy. Even if agreement is reached, it is not binding. Such talks duly took place early in 1995, but they dragged on fruitlessly. The announcement of ASP 95 fell like a thunderbolt. The employers gave reluctant support. The unions took various stances. The reactions in various trades at various times ranged from strong protests, strikes and street demonstrations to relatively resigned acquiescence. The Hungarian heterodox programme, unlike, for example, the Israeli stabilization, does not rest on a declared agreement reached with the unions.[26]

The government imposed unilateral limits on nominal pay rises in organizations funded by the budget (in public administration, the armed forces, education and health) and in firms still owned predominantly by the state. For brevity's sake, I shall not give details here of the differentiated nominal pay increases allowed in the state sector as interpreted in this broader sense; in general, the limit was 15 per cent nominal wage increase for 1995. Certainly this rise was substantially slower than the sudden increase in the level of consumer prices. The government did not interfere in private-sector pay. However, as the state and private sectors largely share a common pool of labour, private employers followed more or less the same wage policy as the state employers.

As Table 6.1 has shown, real wages fell by more than 12 per cent. This can also be taken to mean that the employed made a big sacrifice in real wages to maintain the existing employment level. There have been cases in labour-market history, on an enterprise or national scale, of employees voluntarily

[25] See, for example, Blanchflower and Oswald (1994).
[26] See Bruno (1993).

making such sacrifice out of solidarity. Under ASP 95, this sacrifice was compelled by two factors. One was state intervention, and the other the force of surprise. It is a well-known proposition of macroeconomics that the agents in the economy react differently to inflation depending on whether it is in line with expectations or unanticipated. They tailor wage demands to the former in advance, but they cannot adjust to the latter in time, since their scope for action is blocked, or at least impeded by existing wage contracts.[27] This effect, too, has certainly contributed to the very sudden fall in real income.

It can be stated that income-policy intervention, like exchange-rate policy, has been one of the keys to ASP 95's efficacy so far. However, it is doubtful how long these elements of income policy can be maintained. Certainly the state sector will decline in relative size, which in itself will narrow the scope for applying instruments similar to the 1995 intervention. The chance of increasing resistance to such an income policy cannot be ruled out either.

Nor is it just that the *scope* is narrowing. Thought should also be given to how *desirable* these instruments are. The criteria of a fair distribution of income speak against them. The incomes targeted have been the ones easiest to target, which affronts those who lose by the policy, and offends others' sense of justice as well.

3.3   Fiscal Policy

The budget deficit showed a tendency to increase in the period before ASP 95 (Table 6.4). There were fears that the country might enter a debt spiral. On the fiscal side, this would have meant the deficit would grow because of the budget's increasing interest burden, the interest rate would grow because of the crowding-out effect of the growing borrowing requirement of the budget, which would increase the interest burden further, and so on.[28]

ASP 95 has halted this tendency and begun to reverse it. The most important change is that the real value of expenditure in the primary budget has fallen significantly, while the real value of revenue has remained roughly the same. As a consequence, the primary budget deficit has passed into surplus.[29] This provides a source from which the great burden of debt on public finances can be reduced and the self-generating spiral of public debt can be broken.[30]

[27] On the effects of unanticipated inflation, see Sachs and Larrain (1993), pp. 349–52.
[28] The best account of the debt position in Hungarian public finance can be found in Borbély and Neményi (1994 and 1995).
[29] A thorough analysis of the fiscal policy of ASP 95 appears in the study by Oblath (1996), pp. 81–4 and 95–7.
[30] The index of gross debt of the general government over GDP remained practically unchanged, while the index of consolidated gross public debt over GDP has risen somewhat (see Table 6.4). A substantial reduction in both these indices would be desirable, so as to bring the country's macroeconomic situation closer to the norms required for EU membership.

Table 6.4 Fiscal balance and gross debt of the general government (% of GDP)

Indicators	1992	1993	1994	1995[a]
1. Primary GFS balance of the general government	2.1	−1.6	−2.7	1.7
2. Borrowing requirement of the general government				
SNA system[b]	−6.9	−5.5	−8.2	−6.6
GFS system	−6.0	−5.2	−7.6	−3.6
3. Gross debt of the general government	79.2	90.0	87.6	87.7
Consolidated gross public debt[c]	65.2	83.4	82.5	86.5
Domestic	12.1	23.2	23.5	24.5
Foreign	53.1	60.2	59.0	62.0
International reserves	15.7	21.9	20.2	32.9

Notes:
The general government alongside the central government includes the extra budgetary funds, social security and health insurance funds and local governments. The main differences between the System of National Accounts (SNA) and the General Financial Statistics (GFS) methods are as follows: under SNA, privatization income and repayment of state loans do not feature as revenue, so that the borrowing requirement is not lessened by the amount of them, as it is under the GFS system. The SNA system considers foreign borrowing as revenue, while the GFS system accounts it as financing.
[a] Preliminary data.
[b] Adjusted GFS balance (without privatization revenues and without lending minus repayments).
[c] The consolidated gross public debt includes the total debt (domestic and foreign) of the general government and the foreign debt of the National Bank of Hungary.

Source: National Bank of Hungary (1996c), and direct communication by the National Bank of Hungary.

The changes in the fiscal sphere have included some measures that reduce certain universal welfare entitlements or apply a means test to them, as follows:

1. Higher education has ceased to be free. Although the fees imposed cover only a fraction of tuition costs, they go some way to applying the principle that those who will enjoy a lifetime's higher income thanks to their degree should contribute to the educational investment. Regrettably, a system of loans for students has still not been instituted.
2. In line with the principle of need, the scope of entitlement to maternity benefits and family allowance has been reduced.

3.   Dental care has ceased to be generally and fully free of charge. The
     provision remains free for specified exceptional groups (such as children
     and young people, the elderly and the needy). The budget subsidy on
     pharmaceuticals has fallen and become more targeted.
4.   The period of active life has been lengthened by raising the general
     retirement age. (Hungary has been one of the countries where the retire-
     ment age is very low: 55 for women and 60 for men.)

Very few practical steps have been taken to reform the welfare sector.[31] It
was unfortunate that one or two of the measures were introduced too hastily,
without sufficient preparation.[32] Even so, there is symbolic significance in the
fact that such measures have been taken at all. The changes over the last three
decades had all been in the same direction, creating successive new entitlements year by year that added to the welfare commitments of the state. The
system of entitlements at any time was politically taboo. There was no
political force willing to tackle painful reforms.[33] It has now been shown that
change is possible, which opens the way to ideas for reform in this field as
well. A start has been made in devising and debating proposals for reforming
the welfare sector although, regrettably, the process is still only at the very
beginning.[34]

International experience shows that fiscal reforms are more sustainable if
they are based more on reducing expenditure than on increasing revenue.[35]
This applies all the more to Hungary, as a country with one of the highest
ratios of state spending to GDP in the world (Table 6.5). ASP 95 took this
radical approach. The decrease in the budget deficit in 1995 was achieved by
making spending cuts of HFt 3 for every additional HFt 1 of fiscal revenue.[36]

Most of the fiscal reform is still ahead, including concomitant reassess-
ment of the role of the state. Many functions that the state has hitherto
performed by bureaucratic means, at taxpayers' expense, must be transferred
– completely or partially – to the market, to for-profit and non-profit bodies,
and to the voluntary organizations of a civil society.

[31] The specific expenditure-reducing changes listed above had relatively little effect on the
fiscal situation in 1995. Their effect will really be felt in 1996, and still more in 1997.
[32] It was regrettable that some of the measures in their original form conflicted with the
principles of constitutionalism, and were therefore rejected by the Constitutional Court.
[33] See Section 3.3 in Chapter 5.
[34] See World Bank (1995a). Among those to comment on welfare-sector reform have been
Andorka, Kontradas and Tóth (1995), Augusztinovics (1993), Augusztinovics and Martos (1995),
Ferge (1995, 1996a and b), and myself (see Chapter 8). See also note 33 in Chapter 8.
[35] See Alesina and Perotti (1995) and Giavazzi and Pagano (1990 and 1996).
[36] Own calculation on the basis of data from the National Bank of Hungary (1996b), p. 110.

Table 6.5   Fiscal balance and gross debt of the general government (% of GDP)

Country	Year	Consolidated general government expenditure		
		Current	Capital	Total
Lithuania	1993	22.0	2.6	24.6
Kazakhstan	1993	–	–	23.5
Estonia	1993	30.2	2.0	32.2
Russia	1993	–	–	32.9
USA	1992	36.3	2.5	38.8
Romania	1992	37.0	4.4	41.4
United Kingdom	1991	39.7	4.1	43.8
France	1992	46.2	4.6	50.9
Czech Republic	1993	41.4	6.8	48.2
Canada	1991	48.3	2.2	50.5
Germany[a]	1992	45.7	4.9	50.6
Ukraine	1993	50.4	1.7	52.1
Austria	1992	46.8	5.5	52.3
Belgium	1992	50.7	3.1	53.8
Netherlands	1992	52.7	3.8	56.5
Norway	1990	53.2	3.5	56.7
Hungary	1994	55.1	6.7	61.8
Denmark[a]	1993	58.9	2.8	61.8
Sweden	1993	67.6	3.3	71.0

Note: [a] Data are provisional or preliminary.

Sources: Horváth (1996), p. 11. Primary sources: International Monetary Fund (1994a); for Lithuania and Estonia, International Monetary Fund (1994b); for Kazakhstan, International Monetary Fund (1994c); for Ukraine, International Monetary Fund (1994d); for Russia, International Monetary Fund (1994e); for Hungary, calculated on the basis of publications by the Ministry of Finance; source of GDP for Germany and Austria: World Bank (1995c).

3.4   Monetary Policy and Savings

The financial administration and the central bank, in opting for the exchange-rate regime described in Section 3.1, substantially reduced the room for manoeuvre in monetary policy. The chosen regime in effect sets a *fixed* exchange rate at a given time, or only allows the exchange rate to move within a narrow band around a fixed mean. Although the fixed exchange rate continuously changes over time, this does not alter the fact that the present system belongs to the fixed, not the flexible, floating category of regimes. Furthermore, it means that the central bank has no way of setting quantitative monetary targets for itself. It has to adapt to the conditions of money supply and demand.

Even so, some instruments remain: altering the compulsory reserve rates, changing the rate of interest paid on compulsory or voluntary deposits by commercial banks, open market transactions, and so on. Certainly it is worrying to think that the central bank, with its constitutional duty to combat inflation, has lost its leading role in this respect. The front-line battle concerns the budget deficit and the running away of incomes.

Although the monetary policy was tight, ASP 95 set out to reallocate lending, rather than reduce lending overall. Compared with the previous year, 1995 was one in which the budget received relatively fewer resources and the business sector relatively more. This redirection of lending is among the unorthodox features of the programme.

One of the most fortunate occurrences in the monetary sphere was somewhat unexpected. While economic policy reduced household income, household savings increased. Net lending by households rose from HFt 294 billion in 1994 to HFt 391 billion in 1995. Adjusted for inflation, the increase of savings was 3 per cent.[37] There were certainly several factors at work. For a while, real interest rates rose enough to encourage saving.[38] There may also have been an inducement to save in the growing general feeling that the future holds many uncertainties and people can no longer rely on help from a paternalist state. This has been brought home by several changes: from full employment and chronic labour shortage to mass unemployment; hardening of the earlier soft budget constraint and the associated constant threat to business survival; and the reduction in the universal commitments of the welfare state. The idea was put forward by Martin Feldstein[39] that the spread of state care will reduce private savings. Debate has continued in the West about how far this hypothesis can stand its ground. Now, the laboratory of post-socialist transition provides a new way of testing the hypothesis, with a process in the opposite direction. It is too soon to draw far-reaching conclusions from the Hungarian figures for 1995. Hungarian savings may still fluctuate a great deal in response to many other factors (above all interest rates and incomes). In any case it will certainly be instructive to follow the process by comparative studies across countries.

[37] Net lending by households equals gross money savings less increment in borrowing by households. (All three figures are flow variables.) The source of the figures is Ministry of Finance (1996b), Table 14.
[38] A contribution to the rise in total household savings expressed in forints was made by the fact that continuous depreciation of the forint increases the forint value of deposits held in foreign exchange.
[39] See Feldstein (1974).

It is of great importance to the internal and external equilibrium of the Hungarian economy that household saving rates should fluctuate as little as possible and total household savings, in real terms, grow reliably. If the household saving rate should fall again, one of the harmful effects would be on aggregate demand, and ultimately on the current account. There are several ways in which savings can be helped to grow.

First, it would be desirable to have as little fluctuation as possible in the real return on household savings, so that they remain lastingly positive. Figure 6.5 shows the failure to achieve such stability over many years. The trend was reversed after the first successes of ASP 95. Instead of capital flight (largely concealed), foreign capital began to flow into the country. Part of this is not intended as long-term real investment; some investors tend to buy short-term government securities and treasury bills only. These are extremely attractive investments, because the present exchange-rate regime almost eliminates the exchange-rate risk, and such Hungarian securities offer a sizeable, secure real return. This influx has already pushed the previously high rates of interest appreciably downwards. From the point of view of household savings, it would not be desirable for the interest level to fall too far.[40]

Second, reforms must continue to narrow the range of bureaucratic public services financed from taxation (or compulsory contributions levied, like taxes) and enhance the role of decentralized pension funds, health-insurance funds and building societies. As these reforms make themselves felt by reducing taxes and contributions, as well as by narrowing the range of free services and transfers, they will encourage private savings. This is also needed for the expansion of the decentralized capital market, where institutional investors can play a greater part.

3.5 Privatization

A new surge of privatization did not feature in the ASP 95 package. On the contrary, the financial administration emphasized several times that the economy's grave disequilibrium must be overcome even if there are no substantial revenues imminent from privatization. They rightly underlined that the

---

[40] Speculative short-term inflows of capital can cause other grave problems as well. The conversion of hard currency increases the inflationary pressure, and sterilized intervention (absorption of excess liquidity due to inflow of foreign capital) is extremely expensive. It is not possible to count on the resulting extra foreign-exchange reserves, which may evaporate as easily as they arrived. It is difficult to gauge what would be the ideal interest level and return on state securities. Even if this were known, the central bank could still only exert an indirect influence, after a long lag, on the narrow credit and capital markets, which continue to operate with a great deal of friction. On this, see Darvas (1996), Darvas and Simon (1996), Dornbusch, Goldfajn and Valdés (1995), and Sachs (1996).

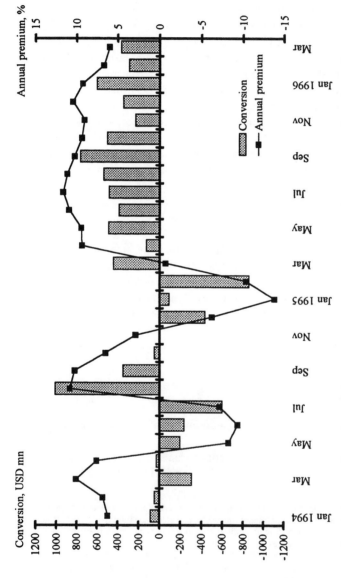

Note:
On the conversion graph, a negative sign represents a net conversion from Hungarian currency to hard foreign currency, and a positive sign a net conversion in hard foreign currency to Hungarian currency. On the premiums graph, the premiums are calculated on an annual basis. The premium is the excess on the return of the Hungarian government's three-month treasury bill over the nominal depreciation of the Hungarian currency, and the average interest rate of hard foreign currencies. (The basket of foreign currencies is determined according to the proportions of Hungarian foreign trade.) It is a proxy for the real return on government securities. For 1994 and 1995, the calculations are based on *ex post* actual data, while the figures for the first quarter of 1996 are *ex ante* estimates.

Source: Information provided by the National Bank of Hungary.

Figure 6.5   Premium on conversion

practical implementation of privatization must not be subordinated to short-term fiscal considerations.

Preparations for privatizing several key branches had been taking place for a long time. The legislation governing these was drawn up, and the legal and organizational infrastructure for regulating the natural monopolies prepared after much delay and procrastination. Once these tasks had been completed, the process speeded up suddenly. In the second half of 1995, within the space of a few months, the privatization of the energy sector and telecommunications made a great stride forward. Several large state-owned banks and a number of sizeable manufacturing companies were also privatized. The financial results of the accelerated privatization of 1995 (as well as those of the overall privatization process in earlier years) are shown in Table 6.6.

Table 6.6   Annual flow of foreign direct investment into Hungary, 1990–95 (US$ million)

Form of investment	1990	1991	1992	1993	1994	1995
Inward foreign capital in cash	311	1459	1471	2339	1147	4453
of which privatization income	8	329	519	1202	104	3024
Inward foreign capital in kind	589	155	170	142	173	117
Total inward flow of FDI	900	1614	1641	2481	1320	4570

Sources: Direct communication by the State Privatization and Property Management PLC (ÁPV Rt.), except for the figure for privatization revenue in 1995, which was communicated by the National Bank of Hungary.

Most of the buyers were large Western firms. The contracts made with them call for strong development of these key branches. To take one example, one of the most grievous manifestations of the shortage economy for decades was the telephone shortage, with several hundred thousand families waiting for years to have a phone in their homes. Since the beginning of privatization – from 1994 to the first quarter of 1996 – 650 000 new lines have been installed. The concession contract stipulates a mandatory annual increase of 15.5 per cent in the number of telephone lines, which so far has always been outstripped by the telecommunication company.[41] In a few years the telephone service will have changed from a sellers' to a buyers' market.

It is especially worth noting that this is not just a case of new foreign owners setting about development tasks under privatization agreements. Large international concerns that acquired property in Hungary earlier are making

[41] Information provided by the telecommunication company Matáv.

successive new investments, and these will contribute to modernizing the Hungarian economy.

This chapter does not set out to analyse the experiences with privatization in Hungary.[42] I shall confine myself to the macroeconomic side-effects. Foreign direct investment in 1995, including sums paid in connection with privatization, came to about US$ 4.6 billion (see Table 6.6). The scale of the sum can be gauged accurately from the fact that in 1994, the worst year of external disequilibrium, the deficit on the current account was US$ 3.9 billion. This fell in 1995 to US$ 2.5 billion, due to the factors already discussed (see Table 6.1).

There was a debate about how to utilize this windfall income. There were plenty of applicants, and great pressure was applied to use the money in a 'popular' way, in other words to consume it. Economic common sense prevailed at last, and it was decided to use the proceeds of privatizing the key branches to reduce Hungary's state debt. Given how large the debt burden is, the saving of interest in this way seems to be the safest and, when all is said and done, the most effective investment. Furthermore, a reduction in Hungary's indebtedness has numerous favourable external effects on the country's financial ratings and acts as a stimulus to investment.

4.　WHAT COMES NEXT?

To a large extent it will be the political, rather than the economic sphere that determines subsequent development. Will the government, its each and every member and its parliamentary majority, be prepared to persevere with the present economic policy? Will they not be tempted to change course, especially when they see the 1998 general elections approaching? What attitude will various groups in society take to the achievements and costs of adjustment and stabilization? What power relations will emerge between the programme's supporters and opponents? Indeed, most of the tasks entailed by it will extend beyond 1998. What will be the political composition of the next government and parliamentary majority, and what economic policy will it pursue? I have simply posed some questions here, to signify my appreciation of how important the answers are to assessing the future. Even so, I leave the task of answering such questions to other studies, confining myself here to economic and economic-policy forecasts and recommendations in the narrow sense.

---

[42] On this, see Laki (1993), Major and Mihályi (1994), Mihályi (1993, 1994 and 1995) and Voszka (1992, 1993 and 1994). See, furthermore, Section 4 in Chapter 5.

4.1 A Prolonged Process

ASP 95 was an example of 'shock therapy' on a small scale, and it brought a rapid improvement in certain macroeconomic indicators. International experience, however, shows that such results are fragile, and can easily slip from economic policy-makers' grasp.

Interactions of several kinds take place between the various problems in the economy. In some cases, easing one economic difficulty may help to reduce another. Let me give two instances of such a favourable interaction, one might say a 'virtuous circle'. As the budget deficit lessens, the fall in the government's aggregate demand for credit has a 'crowding-in' effect. This makes more funds available for private lending, which is conducive to the acceleration of growth. This in turn increases budget revenue, which further reduces the budget deficit. At the same time, the reduction in the state borrowing requirement reduces the demand for foreign credit, so improving the country's external debt position. The interest premium paid on the debt is reduced. This means it is worth going substantially further in reducing Hungary's budget deficit.

The other example of a virtuous circle is the climate of business opinion. In the space of a few months, ASP 95 increased confidence among entrepreneurs and investors, at home and abroad. One of Hungary's business research institutes has been putting the same questions every quarter about the business situation and prospects to top company managers since 1987. According to their report,[43] the situation in manufacturing was assessed more favourably in January 1996 than at any time in the previous decade. This is corroborated by the new surge of foreign investment, mentioned in connection with privatization. The confidence itself becomes a growth factor, and the continuing or, in the best case, accelerating growth in turn reinforces the optimism.

However, there also exist unfavourable interactions – 'vicious circles' – that must be taken into account. Let me give a few examples of these. Mention was made, in earlier parts of the chapter, of maintaining the real exchange rate which, at a given rate of inflation, requires nominal depreciation at the same pace. The depreciation becomes built into the inflationary expectations, which contributes to upholding the inertial inflation. It is extremely hard to improve the country's trading position, prevent a growth of indebtedness, and *concurrently* achieve disinflation. To take other examples, the forcing of growth by fiscal means may aggravate the budget deficit, and, conversely, attempts to reduce the budget deficit at any price, by large tax increases, for example, may cause recession. What is a remedy for one ill turns out to exacerbate another.

---

[43] See Kopint-Datorg (1996).

Experience in Latin American countries with similar problems shows that the struggle may even last for one or two decades. First one, then another economic tension intensifies, and the therapy applied for the ill of the moment causes a further problem to arise. Some countries have relapsed time and again into one of their original difficulties after successful partial stabilizations. Either production falls drastically, or the balance on the current account deteriorates, or inflation speeds up, or more than one problem arises. Chile, possibly the most successful Latin American country from the economic point of view, moved in 1978 from high inflation to the moderate rate of 20–40 per cent a year. It was another 17 years before the country finally reached single-digit inflation in 1995, but in the meantime, production continuously rose at an imposing rate of 4.8 per cent a year.[44] The chance of this happening sooner in Hungary cannot be excluded, but it cannot be relied upon either. It would be unfortunate to delude ourselves and others into thinking that a single great action like ASP 95 can suffice to right matters in two or three years.

One of the great dangers is complacency: 'The situation's a bit better now; there's no need to be as strict as before.' This is an enticing idea to any politician in government. There are already signs of it in Hungary. For instance, the total national wage bill jumped again at the beginning of 1996, imports began to resume their rise, and investment activity seemed to be slowing down. We have to be constantly prepared to combat the adverse phenomena immediately they appear.

The antecedents of ASP 95 are thought-provoking in this respect. Some researchers who studied the political economy of reforms[45] take the view that politicians are not prepared to take unpopular action until a crisis has actually *occurred*. The Hungarian ASP 95, as I emphasized earlier, is preventive in nature, which partly supports and partly refutes the hypothesis. It was the immediate threat, if not the crisis itself, that triggered the programme. The question is how imminent the crisis has to be before politicians can summon up the courage to act. Is it too much to expect that they could keep the economy in good repair simply by discernment of the economic situation, without a crisis looming or occurring?

I confess I am uncertain about the answer. Even consolidated, stable countries like the United States or France tend to protract and postpone long overdue fiscal reforms because their consequences would be unpopular.

---

[44] The sources of the data are International Monetary Fund (1995), pp. 122–3, 288–91, and for 1995: International Monetary Fund (1996), p. 65, and International Monetary Fund (1997) pp. 184–9.
[45] See, for instance, Drazen and Grilli (1993).

4.2 Selecting Priorities

Returning to Hungary's problems, one difficulty is to choose the correct economic-policy priorities and assign the right relative importance to the various parallel tasks. There has been much argument about this. In my view there is no universal rule, valid at all times in every country (or, more narrowly, every post-socialist country). If a country has rapid inflation, or even hyperinflation, the prime task must undoubtedly be to reduce it, at least to the annual rate of 30–40 per cent. There is enough evidence to show this is a prerequisite for healthy development.[46] What is less clear is how to choose the priorities when the inflation rate has come down to the moderate range.

In the moderate band of inflation, disinflation becomes very costly. In most cases it has not been achieved without a substantial rise in unemployment and a serious fall in production. So the lesser of two evils seems to be to allow the moderate inflation to continue. Care and strict control are needed to prevent it from running away. The emphasis, though, must shift to attaining the conditions for balanced, lasting growth. This includes reducing the budget deficit, cutting state expenditure, halting the increase in external indebtedness (and where necessary, improving the debt/GDP ratio), and promoting exports and investment. All these developments will contribute to the acceleration of growth, which should also be encouraged in other ways. As a by-product or side-effect of such measures, inflation may gradually slow down, so long as they are joined by the right price and income policy and monetary policy. In my view it would be unwise under such circumstances to impose an urgent and radical curb on inflation at the expense of all the other tasks.

The economies of the post-socialist countries may prove to be interesting experimental laboratories in this respect as well. The various governments have different points of departure and different economic policies. There are, and no doubt will remain, some countries where the financial administration uses real appreciation of the exchange rate to reduce the inflation rate. I would argue against doing this in Hungary. I continue to recommend caution, warning against real appreciation of the forint and the threat of a renewed deterioration in the balance of trade.[47]

4.3 A Reassuring Sign: Rising Productivity

Readers will gather that I feel the Hungarian economy is vulnerable in several respects. I have tried to point to the dangers, but there is one fundamentally important aspect of the Hungarian economy that fills me with

[46] See Bruno and Easterly (1995), Fischer, Sahay and Végh (1996) and Végh (1992).
[47] Darvas and Simon (1996) take a similar position.

confidence: the rise in labour productivity. Mention was made earlier of auspicious signs that the competitiveness of Hungarian exports is improving. This arises partly from the movement in the exchange rate, but even more important is the efficiency of the underlying real process. The trend in productivity is the key to growth (and for a small, open economy like Hungary's, export-led growth).

Table 6.7 compares productivity over time in several post-socialist countries.[48] Hungary shows the most favourable trend in this respect. There are several contributing factors. Although property relations were transformed more slowly than in countries that conducted so-called mass privatization (distributing fragmented property rights free of charge), Hungary's privatization process[49] was more inclined to generate genuine owners. Ownership has gone mainly to private persons or already operating businesses that can exercise real control over management and apply the profit motive. This has also helped to bring about a radical restructuring in many firms.

The budget constraint in Hungary has really hardened. This was promoted by legislation compatible with a market economy and conducive to financial discipline: the new Acts on bankruptcy, banking and accounting. Although some stipulations in the Bankruptcy Act, initially formulated in an extreme

Table 6.7 *Labour productivity in post-socialist countries: an international comparison*

Country	Average labour productivity (real GDP/employment, 1989 = 100)					
	1989	1990	1991	1992	1993	1994
Bulgaria	1.00	0.97	0.88	0.89	0.88	0.91
Czech Republic	1.00	0.97	0.88	0.89	0.88	0.91
Hungary	1.00	0.98	0.92	1.05	1.11	1.16
Poland	1.00	0.92	0.91	0.98	1.00	1.07
Romania	1.00	0.95	0.83	0.77	0.81	–
Russia	–	1.00	0.89	0.74	0.66	0.57
Slovakia	1.00	0.98	0.95	0.93	0.92	0.96

Source: Calculations from McHale (1996), Table 1, on the basis of the following sources: European Commission (1995), EBRD (1995), and various issues of the OECD publications, *Short-Term Economic Indicators* and *Transition Economies*.

[48] On the comparative productivity of post-socialist countries, see McHale (1996).
[49] See Section 4 in Chapter 5.

way, caused serious problems for a time, the mistakes were quickly remedied. The ultimate result is a process of natural selection that allows the truly fit, efficient and profitable businesses to survive.[50]

Connected to the above changes is the elimination of the phenomenon of 'unemployment on the job' that evolved under the socialist system. The larger part of this painful process – accompanied by human suffering, the tormented feeling of losing one's job – has already taken place in Hungary, while, as it seems, many other post-socialist countries try to put it off.

One common explanation for all the changes listed so far is the very high rate of foreign direct investment. Hungary has received about half the foreign capital investment entering Eastern Europe. Apart from its benefits in macro-financial terms, this has helped to introduce new products, technologies and management methods and tighten labour discipline and organization.

A steady rise in labour productivity is not enough by itself to produce lasting growth in the economy. There must also be a favourable development in several other areas, some of which have been detailed in this study. However, theory demonstrates, and the broad experience of international economic history confirms, that the rise in labour productivity is one of the most important conditions (perhaps *the* most important) for healthy, steady economic growth. It is among the factors that give cause for confidence in the future of the Hungarian economy, despite the many difficulties it faces.

---

[50] Regrettably, the tendencies are not unequivocal. Firms in grave financial difficulties are bailed out far less frequently than before, but some of the business sector's financial woes tend nowadays to take the form of 'non-performing bank loans', and in most cases the banks so far have been rescued from insolvency. (Even so, it must be admitted, they can rely less confidently on state assistance than they could in the past, following the liquidation of a few non-viable banks.) Nevertheless, it certainly cannot be said that Hungary has left the syndrome of a soft budget constraint behind.

7. The responsibility of the individual and society: an interview by Mihály Laki on social issues

What importance do you attach to the social question, in relation to the transition?

Enormous – it is one of the key issues of the transition. This has been clear to everyone from the outset. It must be said, of course, that the social question in many countries was upstaged by day-to-day politics during the first one to three years, although this was not the case in Hungary.

Could one say that the social question was resolved under socialism, or at least not a grave problem? How pronounced do you think social differences were under the socialist system? With this in mind, why do you think so many people look back fondly on that period?

Distinctions have to be drawn between countries here. The socialist system extended over 26 countries, ranging from China to Hungary, and their social welfare policies varied. So, instead of generalizing on this question, let me take the case of Hungary.

Hungary's welfare institutions in the Stalinist period operated only on an elementary level. There was unemployment. The aspects that now evoke nostalgia had not yet emerged at that time. A welfare system began to appear later, in the Kádár years, along with half-hearted reform of the economic mechanism. Each year, or every other year, important advances were made. Take the mid-1980s, for example. By then there was full employment, indeed a chronic shortage of labour, and the survival of firms was guaranteed by the soft budget constraint. This was accompanied not only by security of employment, but by security in the employee's specific job. So long as people abided by the unwritten rules and showed loyalty towards their place of work, they were entitled to a wide range of benefits, defined by law. These took the form of cash benefits, including retirement pensions, child-care allowances and sickness benefits. There was also a broad spectrum of entitlements associated with study or old age. Complementing these benefits there was a system of subsidized prices for goods and services, and subsidies for housing construction, all being part of the central system of income redistribution. These made up a social-welfare policy that exceeded that of all other socialist countries in its scope, performance and sheer comprehensiveness. So there are some grounds for the fond memories.

Why did this happen? Why was Hungary's socialist system taken on this course? I believe the origins go back to the trauma of 1956, the cathartic experience undergone by the ruling political élite when they were hunted and swept away by an enraged populace. So they felt they had to be on good terms with the people. As for full employment, it results from certain features of the socialist system, such as investment hunger, the expansion drive and the softness of the budget constraint. Full employment can even occur under repressive communist regimes that do not try particularly to be popular. The Hungarian leadership of the time compounded all this by thinking along the following lines after 1956: 'We do not want demonstrations or strikes. We shall prevent them first by tough reprisals, and then by reducing the level of public discontent.' There were several possible safety valves for pre-empting discontent, one of which was to build up a system of social entitlements and welfare assistance and support. This redistribution through the social-welfare system was coupled with a soft budget constraint. No region or enterprise could be allowed to enter a state of crisis, because the result would be an inability to carry out social functions, and local unemployment. The paternalism of the legal system and the soft budget constraint complemented one another. All this served the political interests of those in power. In other words, the welfare system was not born of a progressive struggle by the people, but of a political leadership keeping one step ahead. Those who urged the state to play such a role, the largely overlapping pressure groups advocating higher living standards and greater paternalism, did not have much trouble gaining their point. There was no need for people to go out and demonstrate.

The other main way of alleviating public discontent was to allow the expansion of a 'grey', second economy, in which those who wished to do so could make money. Jobs in the first economy guaranteed everyone paternalist care, and the income earned there was secure. Those who were shrewder and more resourceful could supplement this income in the second economy.

There were losers, naturally, but even they lost less than they would in a fully fledged market economy. The gains were unevenly divided among the winners, of course. In those days, we objected to the benefits that privileged cadres enjoyed, with their access to state holiday homes, official cars and decent housing. Now that the extremes of poverty and wealth are much further apart, Hungarians remember that the privileges of old were modest by comparison with those of the present day. Those who enjoyed the highest standard of living in those days were much closer to the average than the wealthiest 5 or 10 per cent are today. In this respect the Hungary of that period was more equal. No society can be strictly egalitarian, of course, but the distribution of incomes was certainly more even than it is now.

There is a feeling that some people gained a head start after 1989. They had capital in cash or kind, intellectual capital, and useful connections. Yet it was not their skills or achievements that gave them this position, but other qualities, such as loyalty to the old regime. This inequality, this head start for some people, has caused a lot of resentment, has it not?

Let us separate the positive component of the question – establishing whether the phenomenon exists – from its normative evaluation.

In every society, including societies in transition, there are advantages for people who have acquired and managed to retain assets at an earlier stage, who bring with them contacts they can exploit and, perhaps most importantly, who possess human capital in the form of intellectual skills. The advantage in the last case amounts to having a mind that is better-trained and operates more fluently, and to having accumulated more knowledge, covering everything from foreign languages to social graces. This is clearly an advantage when a new start is made.

So the judgement on this is strictly a moral one?

Let us stick to positive analysis for now. Whether people retain these advantages depends on whether there is expropriation of property and whether the leadership of the old regime is removed from the top positions. This is what the communist system did when it came to power. Existing assets were confiscated, existing personal connections were broken down, and the leadership under the previous political system was expelled from every important position in the administration, the economy, and the cultural sphere. The one pertinent question after such a transfer of power is who can be on good terms with the party secretary and the commissar. The old system of connections goes completely by the board. There is no way of removing the intellectual resources from the old élite, but they can be forced to work in places where they cannot make use of them.

The more peaceful the transition after the collapse of socialism, the less inclination remains to persecute individuals. The less talk there is of revenge, of using force to decide how individuals may use what they own, whether it takes the form of tangible assets or rests in their minds, the greater the practical advantages carried over from the previous system.

In 1991–92, I remember, there were individuals who had compromised themselves as devoted supporters of the Kádár regime, yet re-emerged as leading Hungarian representatives of a Western bank, or chief advisers to foreign companies interested in investing in Hungary. I asked a university colleague in the United States, who had specialized in business economics and was familiar with the mentality of the business world, how this could have happened. Were these institutions not aware of how these people had behaved and of the blots in their past career? At first my colleague could hardly understand what I meant. What business of theirs was an individual's political background? The person hired by the Western company was living and continued to live in Hungary, knew the country like the back of his hand, and had good connections. Indeed, he had learned the finer points of maintaining contacts with the West. Of course these were valuable traits that should be exploited. A peaceful transition makes sure the door is open for the sale of contacts and intellectual skills. A selection process takes place. The dim-witted cadres of old are eventually eliminated. The sharp-witted, professionally skilled cadres, who continue to have useful connections, manage to work their way into the new system. This is a key feature of the smooth, gradual, peaceful transformation that continues in Hungary's system.

But how can this be judged morally? According to my system of values, there is nothing ambivalent or self-contradictory about the situation. I think the bloodless, tolerant nature of Hungary's revolution – a 'revolution' because in historical terms I rate a change of political system as a revolution – has been to the country's general advantage. The drawback is that there was no radical restructuring, involving drastic demotion and artificial advancement of individuals on the basis of their past political behaviour. The majority of Hungarian society, I believe, felt the advantages, rather than the disadvantages of this. Although most Hungarians were irritated to see a parade of political chameleons, they did not demand a process of ruthless selection on the grounds of past political stance.

I personally would draw a distinction between advantages gained from personal connections and those gained by individuals during the changes because state assets were commandeered and transferred to the private sector.
Certainly those closer to the action in the past were more likely to have built up an advantageous starting capital, for example in their housing or other forms of assets. I have two observations to make here. First, it is by no means certain that a round of confiscations is the best way to begin the new era. That is a brutal step, and not a good start for a democracy that is just emerging. It is very hard, probably impossible, to conduct a comprehensive programme of confiscation in a lawful manner that takes all the mitigating and incriminating circumstances into account.

My second observation has more bearing on an analysis of the problem. Let us say that ten years hence, someone constructs a function to explain how income and assets were distributed at this time. The function will contain several explanatory variables, including some that show whether a citizen was a member of the élite, or close to the élite, before 1990, or legal heir to someone who belonged to the élite. I suspect that although these variables will have significant explanatory power, they will be relatively weak by comparison with certain other factors. The variables with greater explanatory power will be the ones that express who has done what since 1990: how lucky they have been, whether they squandered their starting capital, or whether they deftly and successfully adapted it to the new conditions.

I have no desire to offer a retrospective moral justification for former cadres retaining their fortunes through the transition. Ultimately there are two types of transition to choose from, neither of them wholly satisfying in moral terms. This country has suffered enough brutality in the twentieth century, with bloody upheavals aimed at bringing order and dealing out the cards all over again. This time Hungarian society has chosen the lesser of the two evils – a more tempered mode of change, with a transition that has allowed many people to retain their capital. Even in retrospect, I accept the choice.

On the other hand, those who came out of the socialist period as relative losers in some way want compensation of some sort, or at least some state or institutional assistance to ensure that they will not be disadvantaged all over again.
I agree with that principle. It constitutes a desire that can arise at any time, not just in a change of political system. People who in the end suffer great losses, due to some stroke of fate, rather than decisions they took for themselves, are entitled to special compensation from society – once certain conditions are met. This line of argument entails distinguishing between those who suffered discrimination under the former regime because of family background or political stance, and those who failed relatively to advance because their performance was weak, quite independently of politics. The former group, who suffered political persecution or discrimination, should not be confused, for example, with those who had a chance to study but did not take it. These are different issues. One thing to note is that education, the acquisition of intellectual capital, is an area in which the former system provided many opportunities.

So what if someone was just too lazy to study?
When you consider people then in their twenties, who were uneducated and generally poorly prepared in 1990 for the arrival of capitalism, there is another distinction to make: between someone who is one of eight children in a Gypsy family on the fringe of society, for instance, and someone living off his or her parents and the state, whose level of acquired education and skills were largely self-determined.

You would discriminate between those who lived precariously or even in a self-destructive manner by choice, and those who were handicapped by the system?

I agree with the spirit of the question, although I would put it in different terms. This is a philosophical issue, irrespective of the political system or historical circumstances. I consider individual responsibility fundamentally important. Everyone bears responsibility for his or her own life. No one can be excepted from that responsibility. Even prisoners in Auschwitz were responsible for what they did in the specific situation – and the Kádár system offered people a greater range of scope than the concentration camps did. So on a level of underlying moral criteria, I cannot accept that circumstances alone can absolve people from all aspects of personal responsibility. I do not apply the same standards to Pol Pot's Cambodia as I do to Kádár's Hungary. The Kádár system was a 'soft' dictatorship. It was paternalist, and it allowed the existence of a second economy, which extended the range of opportunities available. The amount of knowledge that Hungarians had individually acquired by the time the political system changed was more a matter of personal responsibility than was the case with Cambodians crippled by the Pol Pot regime and civil war. Hungarians had greater room for manoeuvre.

Nevertheless, I have no intention of denying that the Kádár regime had its victims, although there are degrees. I would not reproach an intelligent person for not having gone to university if the family had been deported to a rural area, which meant he or she was barred from attending. Even then, age and personal character could have a bearing. Many children of parents sent into internal exile managed to get to university after all, in the 'softer' decades that followed. Indeed, many members of the political and economic élite today had parents who were persecuted or discriminated against under the communist system, but managed to acquire a university education for themselves in the end.

In saying this, I am not belittling the importance of the social circumstances as a factor behind individual destinies. I am obliged by the dialectic of our conversation to state the other side of the problem as well. None the less, I want to avoid any appearance of denying the relevance of social circumstances, and the corresponding fact that the communist system in all its forms, including the Kádár regime, had an adverse, cramping effect on equality of opportunity.

Let us move on to the social-welfare system. Your main proposition about the 'premature welfare state' is that the socialist system developed a welfare system, including health care and education, that was beyond its means.
Behind the expression you mention lies the idea that the entirety of the entitlements enshrined in the law, including everything due, so to speak, to Hungarian citizens from the state, is disproportionate to the performance of the economy and exceeds its potential. The idea of a premature welfare state assumes there is an underlying connection between economic development –

economic strength – on the one hand, and the general standard of living on the other, including the level of state welfare provision. Hungary is singular in this respect. The level of state support is higher here than in any other former socialist country.

While this relationship between the economy's capacity and the achievable degree of state paternalism can be empirically observed, for economic capacity eventually puts a curb on paternalism, the opposite effect can also be discerned. Where state subsidies are lower, the growth of economic capacity is generally greater. This is easy to see. Paternalist care by the state calls for high social-security contributions and taxes, and this draws resources away from the investment that directly promotes growth.

That brings us again to a decision of a political and moral nature. I do not believe in attaining the fastest possible growth at any price. Twenty-four years ago, I wrote a book expressing my disapproval of forced growth, and proposing harmonic growth instead. But the conditions for 'harmony' can be disturbed on either side of the equation. When I look back now, taking into account the trends that have emerged over the decades, Hungary's problem was clearly not that it forced investment, but that it forced consumption, and the result was to retard its growth.

The trade-off between social tranquillity on the one hand and consumption and state paternalism on the other is worth noting. The more repressive Husák regime in Czechoslovakia left behind a considerably better macroeconomic situation than did the Kádár regime. With the help of the secret police, and by imprisoning Vaclav Havel and others, Husák secured the same tranquillity that Kádár gained by calming people down, instead of jailing the opposition, in those last decades of socialism. Kádár gave the public more in material terms, but at a cost of growing debt. Excessive government spending induced a chronic deficit and spurred inflation. We are now paying the price for that. If there were grumbles somewhere, the leadership's gut reaction was to throw a reward in that direction. If they heard there was griping in Borsod County, they did not simply send a state secretary down to make a speech; they gave the people there something tangible. If a firm was in trouble, credit or other assistance was quickly supplied, even if that meant a further deterioration in the budget and balance of payments. If a food shortage arose, the government immediately filled the gap with imports, again to the detriment of the trade balance and the balance of payments. This contrasts sharply with what Ceauşescu did in Romania. He went so far as to deny even electricity to his people, simply to assure a better balance of trade, so that he could repay the country's foreign debts almost to the last penny. The secret police were there to deal with the grumbling. This demonstrates graphically the difference of behaviour between the two communist regimes.

The bill now seems to have fallen due, and everyone thinks they should be asked to pay less of it than others. Everyone wants to minimize his or her losses. Are there any rules to follow in spreading the load or the shortfalls in profit?

As usual, there are two possible approaches. One is to make a positive analysis or observation, and the other to establish normative principles. With the first, there are two phenomena to be seen. One is a fundamental, strikingly unjust disparity in Hungary's economy in how the load is spread, between those who can evade taxes and those who cannot. According to the tax returns, the average annual income in 1994 of people registered as self-employed was 110 000 forints, which was, I believe, less than the minimum wage. This leads me to wonder why they stay in business; why they do not simply go out and get a job, where they would certainly earn more than that.

The other factor that contributes to the inequality is difference of ability between various strata and groups in society to articulate and assert their interests. This ability can be expressed on two levels. One is by extra-parliamentary means. A few hundred engine drivers or power-station workers are easy to organize, as their industries are concentrated. They control a type of production that is indispensable, and if withheld even for a few days, can bring the whole nation to a halt. As for taxi-drivers, they can communicate with each other by radio, which means they are capable of blockading and paralysing a city, as they did in Budapest in October 1990. Clearly such groups can assert their interests more forcefully by extra-parliamentary means than, for instance, manual labourers paid by the day, who could never paralyse a country by going on strike. The other level is parliamentary means. In a parliamentary democracy, great influence can be wielded by relatively homogeneous interest groups that represent large blocs of votes. Pensioners are a prime example, since one Hungarian voter in three is retired. They need not even take to the streets. The way they vote can largely determine the composition of parliament. The sheer weight of their votes is complemented by various other ways of applying pressure in a parliamentary democracy: delegations, representations to a local representative, and open or secret lobbying of politicians. So if one carefully considers the rules by which a parliamentary democracy operates, even Hungary's young democracy, with its semi-established market economy, the following forecast can be made. These two factors – the chance to avoid taxes and the ability to assert interests – are by far the most decisive forces determining how the burdens are divided among the different groups in society.

I must emphasize that, in making this forecast, I have not said what distribution of the burden I would prefer. This is a positive prognosis, not an assumption of a normative stance.

Let us stay with the positive approach. You say various groups, professions, and even individuals are in a good position to assert their interests, while others are in no such position. So some are going to win and some are going to lose.
There are two main ways in which a group or an individual can ensure that the real division of income departs from the putative one, if the game were played simply according to market rules. One is to dodge obligations to the state, and the other is to put pressure on the state to intervene on their side in the market distribution.

These two types of behaviour exist everywhere, but would you say they had more relevance than usual during the post-socialist transition?
The level of tax evasion is notably high. This can be traced back to modes of behaviour that became prevalent under the Kádár regime. Such behaviour is not considered morally reprehensible by the public. On the contrary, it is thought to be natural that almost every Hungarian citizen should evade taxes in one way or another. Certainly the degree of this tax evasion is related to the transition period. With the second method, using parliamentary and extra-parliamentary means to apply pressure, I see no notable difference. This occurs in all parliamentary democracies, more or less in equal measure.

Who do better, those who wangle their way out of taxes or those who shout loudest? Let us narrow the question down for the moment, and take tax evasion first.
That way of putting it paints too black a picture. I think ultimately there are two main ways of making exceptional profits. The proportions of the two methods vary among individuals and groups. In many cases they both appear at once. There are those who make real market profits, and there are those who make their profits, or increase their profits to an exceptional extent, by avoiding taxes. Let us take a closer look at both methods.

I would not like to confine the category of legitimate market profits to those earned by a hard-working cobbler, say, who hammers away from dawn to dusk, so that many would agree his earnings are a well-deserved reward. The market functions in such a way that the more chaotic and opaque the situation becomes, the more money can be made by those who plug the gaps between supply and demand. The market rewards resourceful, clever and tough individuals. They may become millionaires, while the hard-working cobbler earns only a modest livelihood.

Do you not draw a distinction between profiteering and hard-working capitalists?
Profiteers are rightful participants in a market economy, whose role is to match supply and demand. Those who have only a slight understanding of the

market economy and are biased in this respect may use the pejorative term 'speculation' for this, but such activity is vital to a balance between supply and demand.

Those who reap their profits in the market, rather than tapping it or wheedling it out of the state, include all sorts of businesses. There are numerous successful import–export companies. There are expanding industries like informatics or building construction. Some of these businesses meet demands that the previous, arbitrarily distorted supply could not, and, understandably, they are profitable. High incomes are earned in occupations for which the foreseeable trends of technical development predict an especially encouraging future. Big profits accrue at all these points in the economy during the transition period, and I think this is as it should be.

The other group derives its exceptional profits from avoiding taxation. Here there are two variants again. There are loopholes in the tax regulations. These every Hungarian citizen has the right to exploit. No one doing so can be accused of tax fraud. It is up to the legislators and the tax authorities to plug the loopholes.

In many cases, of course, exploiting loopholes in the law is accompanied by fraud. There are situations in which resourceful, legal use of the market conditions of supply and demand, exploitation of legal loopholes, and plain tax fraud coincide. The three become bound up together, and may end up by multiplying earnings. None the less, distinctions must be preserved when moral judgements are made. The best solution would be to prevent such tax avoidance altogether. This will never happen, but it would be good if it could be restricted to an ever smaller sphere.

I would like at this point to draw attention to an essential distinction that often becomes obscured in discussion. It is one thing to ask whether all the large profits made are legitimate in market terms (as opposed to the illegitimate extra profits made by tax evasion). It is another to ask whether the same proportion of these high, but legitimate gains, should be retained by those who made them as that retained by those who earn less. In other words, should all legitimate market earnings be taxed at the same rate, or should there be progressive taxation? That leads on to the problem of sharing the public burden of taxation fairly, above all its ethical aspects. (I ignore here other tax-related issues such as the incentive effects of taxes.) So I repeat, do we want those who earn more, legally, by their demonstrable performance in the market and by good fortune, to bear a greater share of the tax burden not only in volume terms, proportionate to their higher incomes, but through progressive rates of tax? Do we want to place a heavier burden on those who have legitimately made more money, in order to provide more for those who are in need, for a variety of reasons? This leads to the question of state redistribution based on the principle of social solidarity.

We have now turned to the normative requirements of income distribution, redistribution, taxation and state subsidies. How should economists such as you and me advise those who may listen to what we say? Redistribution involves economic and technical principles, on the one hand, and ethical principles on the other, and it makes sense to take these separately. The desirable system of redistribution cannot be concluded from just one set; this would lead to false conclusions.

You have often written about the state as an inefficient distributor. But I cannot see any other candidate, at least in the medium term, capable of overcoming these anomalies. The tax collector is always the state.
The idea of a society without a state is just a Utopia. We must look at every actor in society realistically. I have no illusions, for instance, about entrepreneurs or enterprises motivated by profit, or about individual, ordinary citizens – yet they can all be assigned key roles in normative thinking. I have no illusions about the state, either. I think the state is a flimsy institution. None the less, I would give it a large number of functions. There is no other option. However, auxiliary mechanisms must be built in to compensate for the flimsiness of the state, at least in part. It would be going too far to call the state 'a bad thing'. It is simply that its functions are performed by fallible people, subject to all kinds of influences.

This leads to an important practical conclusion. I would like there to be as few functions as possible where the state has no competitors, where it wields an absolute monopoly. The situation immediately improves if the state has to compete. To take an example, most countries have state-owned postal services. The best situation is to have private postal services alongside the state's.

The same applies to state education ...
Yes, and non-state education. Let state health care be paralleled by non-state health care, state funeral services by non-state funeral services, and so on, from the cradle to the grave. This, by the way, is a strong economic argument for reducing the scope of the state. Taxes must not be raised to a level that precludes non-state provision of certain functions and entrenches the monopoly of the state, ruling out the possibility of any competition. If the sum extracted from the total income of society to finance state health care and education is so high that there is no scope left for non-state institutions and no chance of citizens paying for their services, the level of taxation imposed has secured a state monopoly.

Even if it has to compete, the state will still play an important role in redistribution. What principles do you think the state should follow as it redistributes resources?

On the revenue side, I favour the approach I have already mentioned: progressive taxation. Here in Hungary, we are over the first rush of introducing the market economy and private ownership. It is now time to apply the principle that those with the means should contribute a greater share than those without. That means accepting progressive taxation, with the stipulation that the system should not be too progressive and act as a counter-incentive. The progressive nature of the tax system must not reach a degree that discourages performance. For if that happens, total revenue will fall, and those whom redistribution is mainly designed to help will get less in absolute terms in the long term.

So entrepreneurs should not be tempted to take a break for eight months of the year, because four months' earnings have brought them to the threshold of an unacceptable rate of tax.

There was a time in Sweden when the marginal tax rate was 90 per cent. A doctor who received a fee of a 100 crowns from a patient kept only 10 of them. The doctor would feel it was just not worth staying on at work in the afternoon under the circumstances, and go fishing instead. Excessive taxation must be avoided, and the progressive principle must not be taken to extremes. Perhaps some of the legislators who drew up that Swedish tax system were motivated by sheer envy when they went beyond all reasonable bounds.

This brings us back to the experience under socialism. One reason why socialism did not thrive in the long term was its dysfunctional distribution system. An aspect of socialism that was seen as an advantage to some extent – the levelling down it performed – brought with it a huge drawback that outweighed the advantages in the long run. Socialism collapsed partly because of its failure to develop a system of proper incentives. The levelling process had a masking effect. Socialism proved unable to distinguish properly between good and bad performance. For example, a pension system that makes no great distinction between a superstar and an assistant book-keeper needs re-examining. By the time they reached the end of their lives, the system of state 'care' would have entirely obscured the difference between the exceptional performance of the one and the relatively minor contribution of the other. I am one of those who refrain from ascribing intrinsic value to equality as such.

Only to more equal opportunities?

I do not want to begin compiling a complete set of postulates for social justice at this point. Those who depend on society's help for certain reasons should get it. The other important principle is for society to be arranged so that the situation of the needy improves over time. They should not be left out of social development; they should have their portion as well. This is what I feel is just. According to my moral principles, it is not right to be satisfied simply because those at the top have been pushed down to the level of those in the middle. There is a strong difference between a kind of malicious glee, a 'make the rich pay' attitude fuelled, let us admit, by envy, and the exalted principle of fair distribution of the tax burden. In the latter case, the increased taxation of those at the top is not an end, but a means, providing the resources needed to help those below. Socialism has bequeathed to Hungarian society a curious mentality that we often joke about, but also notice on a serious level. Many people feel they would rather be poorly off themselves than see others really well off. That remains the principle for broad sections of the Hungarian population to this day. What a good thing it would be to replace it with a sober acceptance: there are some who earn a hundred times more than even those who enjoy a relatively good income. In short, the concern should not be that some people have a great deal of money, but that others have very little indeed.

Here we can move on to those at the bottom. The real questions to ask are how they came to be there, and how they can be raised upwards. The main problem with raising them is the impetus. We need to attain a degree of social development that allows those at the bottom to improve their lives as well. This is the most important factor, I think, and it presumes lasting economic growth over a period of ten to 20 years.

I do not mean to deny the importance of redistribution, but the prime question is always the quantity of goods to be distributed and the rate at which they increase. The question of how they are distributed or redistributed at a given time is only secondary.

How can the sphere of the needy be defined?
There are well-known quantitative measures of poverty – how much people earn, and so on. As a first, rather rough approach, people need help from the rest of society if they are so poor, if their income and property are so small, that they cannot provide a minimum subsistence for themselves and their dependants. The specific indices and threshold values to apply for practical purposes can be drawn up for each country.

I think some further, auxiliary criteria need to be applied when deciding who is entitled to social assistance. I would propose two such criteria. One is that we cannot ignore the reason why someone has ended up unable to secure themselves or their dependants even a bare subsistence. How much was their situation influenced by the career they chose from the options open to them, by the performance they gave, and by how much they were prepared to save?

We cannot omit to analyse how the situation of need arose. Let us assume it is possible to decide what role in the present situation has been played by the claimants' decisions in the past. Did their choices cause them to become dependent on assistance from society, or at least contribute to this, or do outside circumstances provide a complete explanation? Was it because of an accident or unavoidable illness, a natural or political upheaval, or some other bolt from the blue?

The second criterion is equally, or perhaps more important. How can the claimants extricate themselves from their present situation of need? How big a part could they themselves play in escaping from the situation, and to what extent would they depend on help from others to do so?

Why are these two complementary criteria so important? I did not mention the first with any punitive intent. If someone really has ended up in a mess due to his or her own decisions, I would rather this very flimsy state of ours refrained from taking on the role of a dispenser of justice. None the less I regard the distinction as necessary, because it has an educational value. The notion of education I refer to here is not confined to childhood. It is relevant to the various decisions taken when choosing a career and in the course of that career. This brings us back to something mentioned at the beginning of the conversation, in an entirely different context. If people cannot be morally exempted from responsibility for their fate, they cannot be exempted from the consequences of their decisions, either. It would give rise to apathy, cynicism and irresponsibility if they were. People would come to feel it did not matter whether they took their decisions lightly, or whether they weighed the consequences of them carefully. One problem with socialism in this respect was that people's rewards depended only partly on their contributions. People must consider seriously what they do. The mentality of passive acceptance, implanted in us by socialism, must cease.

You attach great importance to personal responsibility.
Individuals must accept the consequences of their decisions. If society is charitable, it can alleviate the consequences, but it need not compensate for them entirely. Individuals should think ahead. They are autonomous beings, and the state does not decide on their behalf. For example, if they decide they do not want to continue studying, because they would rather earn money sooner, that is fine. They will earn money sooner, there will be no years of university during which they earn nothing, but they should accept the consequences of this decision. The outlay entailed in obtaining a university degree would be recovered during the course of a better-paid career, but they will have no access to this. Incomes should not be levelled to a point where the highly qualified and the relatively poorly qualified earn almost the same. A university education is a sacrifice to some extent. Those who wish to start earning early avoid five, or even eight or ten years in which they cannot earn a respectable income. So they should not wait until they are 50 to complain that they did not go to university. They have a point to make only if it can be

shown that they had no opportunity to study further. I am coming back time and again to the same point. Did people have the chance to decide? The question that must be asked repeatedly is whether their future was in their own hands. I have intentionally used an example that involves an important decision with major consequences, not just a single decision with limited consequences.

The other question is how to climb out of a situation of need, and it is of great importance. Here again, the mentality I would like to see implanted in society after the change of system would differ sharply from the one embedded by socialism. Essentially, the initial premise should be that individuals beset by troubles, or arriving in a difficult or adverse situation in another way, should try to make up for the loss themselves, finding their way out of the trouble by using their own resources. They should try to accommodate themselves to the circumstances. In other words, their main task is not to go whining to society, or put on pressure until they receive some sort of assistance, but to pull themselves together and take action. That is the key.

A familiar counter-argument would be that individuals acquire, from their families and from their immediate or wider environment, a specific model – a mentality – of how to conduct their lives. One kind of inherited disadvantage is to have had acceptance of poverty presented as an example in one's formative years. Poverty is not just a lack of money, not just material distress, but a lack of motivation.

There is a great deal of truth in that. Neither in this respect nor in any other do I wish to proclaim the principle of individual responsibility in an extreme form. I emphasized this at the start of our conversation.

As for an inclination towards passive acceptance, it could be that with some people it is partly or wholly inherited – genetic. Then many people may be strongly influenced by the acquiescent, passive attitude shown in their environment. However, the same applies to most of the characteristics and traits that strike us as wrong, and for which we criticize our fellow men. So far as I know, the positive behavioural sciences have not lit upon a universal formula for determining the degree to which some form of discountenanced behaviour is genetic, the degree to which it results from childhood experience and later environment, and the degree to which it depends on the individual *per se*. I am convinced that behaviour is an autonomous, discretionary component in virtually all cases, and that society will function dynamically if it builds primarily upon this idea, cultivating and promoting it. If society goes too far in offering a helping hand to those who would be willing to act for themselves, it only suppresses potential impetus. God helps those who help themselves. Those who help themselves should be helped still more to get ahead. The first to be left by the wayside should not be those who are doing something for themselves. On the contrary, they are the ones who should be given a still greater stimulus. I am not afraid to say that even for those who apparently cannot help themselves – through serious physical or mental disability, for example – the only assistance that ensures their human dignity is assistance that provides them with an opportunity to work so far as they are able. Most of those disabled in this way do not wish to sit idle and be provided for. They would rather be given the chance to work. I am always touched by the special games held annually in the United States for people in wheelchairs. The event improves their sense of dignity. Those who need one must be helped to acquire a wheelchair, but they should not be encouraged to wait in inert expectation of all manner of further support. I think of this as a specific example and a metaphor for being in need of social assistance. Support is one thing, but paternalism as a substitute for individual action is quite another.

Here let me make a corrective observation. I have been speaking so far of pairs of situations as if they were mutually exclusive: individuals end up in a state of need either as a result of their own decisions or as a result of external circumstances, and they are able to change their situation either themselves or with outside assistance. In reality such cases are a mixture of both, in an infinite number of combinations. Naturally, there is often a sharp division in practice between a situation in which a person largely emerges from difficulty by his or her own strength, but with a bit of help, and one where the person depends fundamentally on help, but it is still worth providing an incentive, so that the claimant can contribute to the process by his or her own exertions. Activity must be rewarded.

We can now turn to a few problems of how to implement this in practice. To repeat, I would not suggest establishing a huge bureaucracy to serve as a moral tribunal for examining people's actions, judging each case down to the last detail according to these criteria. An effort must be made to draw up general rules that apply these criteria with a high degree of probability. In addition, a corrective mechanism must be developed to handle the mistakes that can slip into the practical process even if the ground rules are fairly sound. It is necessary, for example, to provide chances for some kind of appeal. Considering the general principles, someone might be entitled to a certain type of social assistance, but is excluded from receiving it by the legal rules or by the mechanism for enforcing them. There must be a way of leaving some scope for exceptions in cases like these.

The principles discussed so far can be applied with a fair degree of success, I think. Take the example of social insurance. I am not talking about setting specific figures for today's sick pay or pensions in Hungary, but of a new social-insurance system that would be developed gradually. It is reasonable to say to a 20-year-old today,

You should accept the fact that you will need savings to deal with the varying circumstances of life. You could fall ill, lose your job, or be affected by some disaster, and you will grow old. You are the one mainly responsible for saving. You may save by joining a pension plan and paying into it all your life, or you may save by investing your money, and the savings are yours. One way or other, you must save all your life. You must not spend all your income. Instead you must keep to a strategy that tells you when you may spend, and when you may not, based on how you plan to save for the various contingencies in life.

Where does the state come into this? Let us stay with pension insurance. The state should support the establishment of institutions that provide for institutional savings and accumulation of reserves. This purpose can be served by various non-profit insurance organizations and funds, as well as profit-oriented insurance companies. Both are needed. The state should grant tax concessions or deferment of tax payments on certain kinds of saving. For pensions, for example, it should allow people to deduct their pension contributions from their taxable income, within rational, reasonably generous limits. I think the principle of tax deferment is appropriate here. One should not be required to pay taxes on such payments, but there should be no exemption for the services themselves. Pensions received should be taxable, for instance. Tax deferment and other allowances would serve as enormous incentives. A high proportion of the public would be willing to lay aside a significant part of their income once they knew it was imperative to do so, that they would need the money later, and provided this could be deducted from their taxable income. Yet another important condition is that the state should ensure that the payments are largely protected against misappropriation. The role of the state must be to create the framework and the supervisory institutions for a decentralized insurance system, and offer state guarantees within certain limits and under certain conditions. Thus the state ensures that swindlers do not make off with the public's savings and that savings are not eroded by inflation. If a swindler should make off with the money, the state should take it upon itself to compensate the public. Thus the role of the state in this regard can be summed up as establishing civilized, reassuring, institutional forms of non-state voluntary insurance.

The state has a further task. It should provide at least minimum assistance to those who have failed to accumulate adequate savings, whether by misfortune, or simply by their mistakes. No one would wish those who have failed to build up savings for their old age, for whatever reason, to spend their final years in penury. At least a minimum pension must be paid according to the solidarity principle, at taxpayers' expense, even to those who have committed a succession of irresponsible acts, who have taken their lives and careers down risky paths, or who have suffered from plain bad luck. However, I certainly do not suggest that the state in such circumstances should pay more than a minimum, humanely determined level of pension at taxpayers' expense, given that such assistance in effect takes money from those prepared to reduce present consumption in order to accumulate savings.

I have illustrated the basic ideas through the example of pensions. The state plays a dual role. It throws life-belts, at the taxpayers' expense, to those who have ended up in disastrous circumstances through their own mistakes or by misfortune, and it sees that those who wish to look after themselves do not make the effort in vain. This is a big responsibility.

Special emphasis should be placed on the state's duty to guard against inflation, a very heavy responsibility. Say the rate of inflation suddenly shoots up. It would be unpardonable to allow those growing old to find themselves in a tragic situation where they think, 'We have been saving for years, and now inflation has swept away our pensions.' People must be protected against this by law. After all, the state is responsible for monetary stability. If the fiscal policy of the government in power generates hyperinflation, it should not be allowed to wash its hands of the capital value of pension funds it has wiped out.

But that is just what it has done, and could well do again.
Fortunately this has not happened to such an extreme extent. Inflation in Hungary has not gone beyond the moderate bounds. However, the 1980s certainly saw a marked fall in the real value of pensions set earlier. The body of rules at present offers some measure of protection against inflation. I cannot emphasize strongly enough that the reform of the pension system that lies before us – which, I think, must go further in the direction of decentralization – must strengthen inflation-proofing, not weaken it. That is a rather complicated issue, of course, and we cannot go into the technicalities here.

Having outlined the ultimately desirable state of affairs, I suppose we can turn to the problems of the transition period.
Let us stay with pensions. Various opportunities must be offered to various age groups. The older the group, the more account must be taken of the fact that they can do less for themselves, and in extreme cases nothing at all, to build up their own financial resources. They are the most dependent on state pensions, or in Hungary the 'semi-state' pensions offered by the country's social-security system.

This applies to those who are now 60 years old, say.
Perhaps you have put the threshold a bit low. After all, 60-year-olds today, sound in mind and body and still able to work, cannot be said to be incapable of doing anything for themselves.

They are fairly limited.
I cannot accept that people aged 60 or 62 should stop all activity. Yes, they have the right to remain inactive from the time they reach the official retirement age, but they should not then be in the same situation, thanks to some levelling principle, as those who do not retire on reaching retirement age. They must enjoy tangible benefits from having postponed their retirement.

The extreme case consists of older people who clearly cannot do anything to earn income. From this extreme down to 20-year-olds with complete freedom of choice, there are infinite intermediate, transitional cases. In drafting the new regulations, an attempt must be made to set the proportions of state pensions, decentralized pensions and income tax – as humanely and sympathetically as possible – to ensure they collectively accord as far as possible with the moral principles I have advanced in this conversation. Of course, as I have stressed already, there will always be individual cases that do not match the general schemes, even if the rules work quite well. So there must be scope for adjustment in such cases.

I know this is difficult. Decades of totalitarian power and paternalist protection have left a deep impression on people's mentality and behaviour. Hungarians need to become used to making their own decisions in fields where the state or the party secretary always decided for them. This enhanced freedom of choice needs to be felt over an extended period of time before people gain confidence and control their destinies with an increased sense of responsibility, in line with the precepts of such freedom. Nor will the reformed system run without friction. What I wished to underline in this conversation is that we should not throw ourselves at once into a morass of practical detail, which is what often happens in debate these days. Such debates take place without principles to guide them. If there is any reasoning in them, it consists for the most part in saying that the state coffers are empty, and so spending has to be cut. Then there is the other side of the coin, with everything subordinated to being socially 'sensitive'. My approach tries to offer criteria, principles to help in choosing possible reforms. The criteria and moral postulates I have advanced may be disputed, but it would be good to debate them and other principles, and not just some practical detail or other.

Why have non-cash methods of payment not become widespread in Hungary? I suppose one reason is that people have not become used to the idea. Then there is the question of why so few people buy shares as opposed to gold, and why many still keep their money under the mattress. It is because they have not learnt the art of optimal investment. My question, then, is whether the situation will not be the same when it comes to creating new insurance schemes, savings accounts and alternative pension schemes. The more astute, cultivated and otherwise successful people will exploit the more refined and sophisticated opportunities, and create for their own benefit institutions that suit their purposes. Meanwhile, the non-competitive people who are slower to learn will be left on the state's hands. So the process you wish to advance institutionally – reducing and limiting the role of the state – will impose new duties on the state.

I trust it has been clear from what I have said so far that the state naturally has a variety of important roles, while other actors also bear major responsibilities. However, I would add another observation. In numerous developed economies, a significant portion of insurance institutions are connected to employers. At one time it used to be said in Hungary that the railways provided a good livelihood, because they had their own pension fund. Before the Second World War, I used to live in a block of flats owned by the pension fund of a big coal-mining concern. Big employers like Hungarian State Railways and the Post Office, and certain trade associations or inter-trade associations, had their own pension funds and health-insurance funds. These too would be decentralized, non-state institutions. The edge gained by such employers in the labour market would be that they could offer staff membership of the pension and health funds, and that meant they could attract and keep the best labour force. It is characteristic of the labour market in a market economy that many competitive employers pay more than equilibrium wages, with the aim of offering a strong incentive; workers need to fear losing a good job. This phenomenon even has a theory attached to it, that of an efficiency wage. Part of an efficiency wage is non-pecuniary advantage, taking the form of good welfare provision. It is as if we in Hungary were just rediscovering hot water. Company-based welfare institutions, which many wanted to abolish during the switch to private ownership, exist in many big corporations in a number of developed capitalist economies.

I think socialism learnt about those from capitalism.
At present, though, welfare institutions are being eliminated on a mass scale, but it will soon be discovered that even a firm's holiday home can be commercially useful to it. Certainly corporations and trade associations will come to regard it as in their best interests to organize pension and health-insurance funds. Moreover, employers already have to pay a proportion of their employees' sick pay. So they too have an incentive to enter insurance programmes that take full or partial responsibility for sick pay. The legal framework already exists, more or less. There is legislation making it possible to establish such funds. Non-profit institutions have appeared on the scene, and they are multiplying fast. In my opinion, this sector will firmly establish itself in Hungary within a few years.

The process also has a key macroeconomic aspect. It was a characteristic of socialism that the state collected taxes, but voluntary savings were astoundingly low. Compulsory taxes were used to finance investment through the state budget. So the main source of investment finance was compulsory taxation, not voluntary savings. In mature market economies, on the other hand, voluntary savings are the source for most investment. As a rule, this decentralized form of financing does not take place as direct investment by the savers themselves. They tie up some of their money in a bank, for an extended term, and the bank in turn provides long-term credit to investors. Savers may also take out insurance policies with pension and health-insurance funds, or deposit money in a unit trust. So the big institutional investors arrive, and finance a quarter to a half of all investment in some developed market economies.

This would give an entirely new structure to savings. Voluntary savings can increase to the extent that taxes are reduced. Private savings cannot be boosted significantly while taxes continue to absorb a large portion of society's total savings. There are two kinds of savings and investment process competing: paternalist savings based on compulsory taxes, and decentralized savings of a voluntary nature.

Unfortunately, this rivalry has come to the fore precisely at a time of sizeable budget deficit, so that the reform process cannot begin with a conspicuous tax reduction. The first savings that appear on the expenditure side of the balance sheet are used to reduce the deficit, not taxes. A perceptible drop in state revenues can be considered once the deficit has come down to an acceptable level. The reforms in the role of the state would meet with more understanding and goodwill from the public if it could be said unequivocally from the start that the less the state need pay, the less the taxpayers need pay. Then a gap would open, allowing voluntary savings to increase immediately. This is regrettably not the case at present because of the deficit, and it poses an exceptional difficulty during the switch-over. Perhaps we shall get over this phase eventually.

People fear they are losing forever a vested right, a vested advantage, if the state withdraws from financing certain kinds of social-welfare benefit. They want some guarantee or promise that this is only a temporary withdrawal, so that some time or other they will recover their lost advantage. How do you see the chance of recovering an entitlement once it has been lost?
I would prefer to find that, from now on, not one of the economic measures taken in the interests of stability and equilibrium was temporary. To avoid any misunderstanding, I should add that we are now talking about reducing entitlements financed out of the budget, as codified earlier by law, and not about reducing real wages. Real wages invariably fluctuate. Let us hope that the drop in the real value of wages in 1995 is indeed temporary. I sincerely hope they will rise again as the situation improves. Real wages rise and fall

regardless of the economic system, under socialism and capitalism alike. But your question, if I understood it correctly, was not directed at this, but at entitlements codified in law.

Not a single entitlement should be removed with the promise, 'We are taking it away now because we are in trouble, but we shall return it once the situation has improved.' The entitlements taken away should all be those we are convinced should not have been given in the first place, those which were introduced under an excessively paternalist, ultra-étatist system, and which one can say, with a clear conscience, it would be healthy to abolish. It is desirable both ethically and economically for the emerging welfare systems to be multi-sectoral. This presumes a role for the state, even a state-owned sector providing certain services, but one that does not have a monopoly and does not dominate the entire welfare system. This is the spirit in which we must proceed, in a single direction, rather than vacillating by dealing out new entitlements as we take away old.

So what you are saying is that we should not argue as follows against those who defend entitlements unconditionally: 'Your idea is quite sound, but the country is undergoing hard times, and you must give up the entitlements temporarily. Stay calm, and as soon as the opportunity presents itself, your idea can be acted on once again.'
True. Let me illustrate this with something decided by the Constitutional Court – maternity benefit.[1] I concur with the judgement of the Constitutional Court that those who decided to have children with the expectation of maternity benefit cannot be confronted with a *fait accompli* – withdrawal of an existing entitlement. On the other hand, informing the public in advance that the old system of maternity benefit will cease after a year is in accordance both with the Constitution and with my moral principles. Families making family planning decisions must bear in mind that they can now expect only a limited range of entitlements. Starting from this point, we should no longer make changes in these entitlements. Instead, this should become the permanent, calculable legal situation, valid in the long term.

Here I wish to go beyond this particular question. I have already touched on the Constitutional Court ruling, and would add another comment. As I showed by the example I used, I concur with one of the principles implied by the Constitutional Court: people should not be confronted with a *fait accompli* without being granted an adequate period for adjustment. In this limited, specific sense a vested right cannot be withdrawn. There is also a populist

[1] The Constitutional Court rejected various elements of the government's economic austerity package following its parliamentary approval in March 1995, including cutbacks in entitlement programmes such as maternity benefit, partly on the grounds that the government had not allowed for a sufficient period of adjustment.

interpretation of just what the protection of vested rights entails, which views the process by which welfare entitlements emerge as a sort of ratchet that can turn in one direction, but not in the opposite one. Additions may be made to entitlements, but taking any away is out of the question. What has been given can never be withdrawn. This would mean that if any society or any government (including the communist regime), at any time, brings in a welfare entitlement, this action can never be undone. Such an interpretation of protecting vested rights would tie the hands of all future parliaments and governments. If the ratio of state expenditure in Hungary is about 60 per cent of GDP and the corresponding West European figure is about 45 per cent, there is no way of moving from 60 to 45 per cent other than by taking certain responsibilities away from the state. The ratchet principle, the populist interpretation of vested rights, cannot be accepted, and even the Constitutional Court emphasized that this was not how it intended its warning to be taken. The Court does not oppose the withdrawal of earlier entitlements so long as this is preceded by an adequate adjustment period. Indeed, the unconditional defence of entitlements cannot be upheld either legally or morally, and it cannot be deduced from any general moral or economic principle. To apply it would take social progress up a one-way street where only giving was allowed, and taking away prohibited. Legislators should think carefully before giving, and they should consider carefully before taking things away, but the need for sound preparation should not paralyse the reform process. We must proceed at a steady pace – prudently, humanely, and tactfully – in reforming welfare institutions, and in determining the role the state is to play in them.

8.   The citizen and the state: reform of the welfare system[1]

This chapter covers a subject that is especially relevant not only to my own country, Hungary, and other countries of the post-socialist region, but also to Western European countries, including Austria. I shall leave the task of analysing the situation in Austria to my colleagues. However, I the discussion of the Hungarian reform can be taken as an illustrative example to support a more general message.

1.   THE VALUE ATTACHED TO SECURITY: WHAT IS EXPECTED OF THE STATE?

I begin with a polemic. Zsuzsa Ferge, an outstanding researcher into welfare systems who has spent decades fighting for development of Hungary's welfare institutions, wrote an article entitled 'Freedom and Security'.[2] She backed up her statements with a public opinion poll that set out to clarify how much importance the Hungarian public attaches to various social phenomena. The ultimate purpose of the questions was to reveal the value preferences shown by citizens. Hungarians, it emerged, attach almost maximum values to financial security, job security and security of health care, which score strikingly more than the various rights of freedom.

Another public-opinion survey phrased the title for the table of findings in a characteristic way: 'It is the government's duty to ...', followed by the various tasks it ought to fulfil. Some 94–98 per cent of respondents considered the government's prime responsibility was to provide jobs and health care.[3]

---

[1] In 1996, as in earlier years, the International Institute for Applied Systems Analysis (IIASA) in Laxenburg, Austria, held a lecture series in honour of the Nobel Prize-winning economist Tjalling C. Koopmans, one of its founders. The common subject of the series was 'From Central Planning to Market Economies'. The first in the 1996 lecture series was delivered by the Swedish Professor Anders Åslund, research fellow of the Carnegie Institute in Washington, and the second by Leszek Balcerowicz, the Polish former finance minister who implemented his country's 'shock therapy'. The author delivered the third lecture, the text of which is given here.

[2] See Ferge (1994). In her more recent researches, she augments her earlier statements about Hungary with some international comparisons.

[3] See Róbert (1995).

Several other investigations have yielded similar results. This approach has some Hobbesian overtones. Hobbes argued that the individual's fears induce him to promote over himself a 'sovereign', the state, which provides him with security. He not only accepts, but demands the Leviathan of the state, that charitable and indispensable monster.

Hobbes, though, gave a sharply delineated, narrower interpretation to security. The individual's chance of mere survival and his property must be defended from other individuals who might steal from or kill him, or plunge society into civil war.[4] This line of argument justifies the *classic* role of the state by the rational self-interest of the individual.

The interpretation of security adopted in the researches mentioned earlier goes far beyond these bounds. Security has come to include protection from such uncertain factors as the financial stresses of unemployment, sickness or old age. So how does the public really envisage the state's role in this area of security?

The truth is that respondents were never asked *how much tax they would be ready to pay* if the state were to perform these security tasks. The vast majority of the public fails even to realize the connection. They feel that the *state* pays, full stop. The rest is no business of theirs. The Hungarian public shows an almost total lack of *tax awareness*. This belief by taxpayers that the tax levied on them is less than its actual extent, known in economic writing as the 'fiscal illusion', has reached extreme proportions in Hungary and the whole post-socialist region.[5]

Let us make a calculation, to see the extent of the taxation, taking the case of an average Hungarian employee under the rules applying in 1995.[6] Let the starting-point be the *total compensation of an employee*. This, as we shall see in a moment, includes the various taxes and social-security contributions that both the employer and the employee have to pay into the central funds. Let us deduct these one by one from a notional Ft 100 of total compensation.

First deduction. Compulsory contribution by the *employer* to the social-security scheme, and compulsory payments into the Solidarity Fund, the Wage Guarantee Fund and the Vocational Training Fund.

Remainder after the first deduction: Ft 66.70.

Second deduction. Compulsory contribution by the *employee* to the social-security scheme, and a compulsory payment into the Solidarity Fund.

---

[4] The task of the sovereign (whether king or parliament), according to Hobbes, is to care for the Safety of the People, a phrase which Hobbes himself underlines (Hobbes, 1981 [1651], p. 376). He goes on to explain how he construes the concept of safety. It covers preservation not only of the individual's life, but of the property he has acquired by lawful industry – the objects that satisfy his wants without injury to others.

[5] On the fiscal illusion, see Buchanan (1967) and Oates (1988). An excellent survey of the literature is provided in a study by Csontos (1995).

[6] Piroska Horváth and Mária Kovács helped in assembling the data for the calculation.

Remainder after the second deduction: Ft 59.00.

Third deduction. The *employee* pays personal income tax, of which the expected average amount has been considered here.[7]

Remainder after the third deduction: Ft 44.40.

Fourth deduction. The employee saves some of his or her income and spends the rest on consumption.[8] When consumer goods are bought, the price of these includes various taxes and other tax-like levies by the state. The main item is value-added tax (VAT), in addition to which there are consumption taxes and import duties levied on certain consumer items. A deduction must be made from the total of these to account for the state contributions to consumption, in the form of subsidies on pharmaceuticals, medical aids and public transport, for instance.[9] Summing up the positive and negative items, we estimated how much tax would be paid on Ft 44.40 of available income spent on consumption.

Remainder after the fourth deduction: Ft 38.50.

This, therefore, is the *net wage* remaining after the deduction of taxes directly proportionate to wages and consumption. The real 'purchasing power' of Ft 100 of total compensation for employment is Ft 38.50.[10]

This proportion of tax is among the highest in the world, possibly the highest of all. It is higher than in Sweden, the epitome of a welfare state, or in any other post-socialist country.

Public spending can be divided notionally into two parts. One part covers the classic tasks of the state: public administration, the armed forces, the police, the judiciary and foreign affairs. The other concerns the 'welfare' functions of the state. Interpreted in the broadest sense, these include, for example, education, health care, the pension system, and all forms of benefit and subsidy awarded on various grounds, so long as these are funded by the state or the various centralized funds. Let us suppose that the utilization of the taxes and the other sums levied like taxes is divided equally between the two kinds of task.[11]

---

[7] The calculation rests on actual figures for the first half of 1995 and on forecasts of tax yield for the second half of the year. The ratio of personal income tax to full income from employment will have been somewhat higher in 1995 than the figures show for 1994. Actual sums of personal income tax paid are dispersed widely round the average, of course.

[8] An average savings rate of 7.9 per cent has been assumed.

[9] We have estimated the tax content of consumption on the basis of the 1993 input–output tables drawn up by the Central Statistical Office. More recent information was not available. Again, an average value has had to be used. The actual consumption of individuals and the attendant taxation will be dispersed around the average.

[10] The four deductions have not covered all the taxation. All inputs used in the production of consumer goods have a certain tax content. The maker of the consumer good is also a taxpayer (of company tax, for instance). Those familiar with Leontief's input–output analysis will easily comprehend what is meant by the *total* tax content of Ft 100 of product. It can be proved that the 61.5 per cent tax demonstrated in the calculation is less than the total tax paid on compensation for employment.

[11] Initial calculations yielded such an equal division as a rough approximation. We would like to improve the accuracy of this calculation in the future.

Let us now perform a mental experiment. Let us assume that half the tax gathered is retained to finance the classic activities of the state, but the other half is restored to the employee. Instead of Ft 38.50, he or she immediately has a purchasing power of Ft 69.25, or Ft 70, let us say, for simplicity's sake. The employee's real earnings have been raised at a stroke by about 80 per cent! However, he or she and all the other members of society have been left quite on their own. The state is not going to look after them any longer.[12] So he or she has to rethink matters. Who will look after him or her and the other citizens in times of sickness or unemployment, parenthood or old age, and so on? There is not a penny in the state coffers for such purposes. The money has all stayed in the employees' pocket.[13] Now that they have to decide where this money goes, a range of questions can be asked:[14]

1. How much of the income available to you do you want to consume, and how much do you want to set aside as savings for hard times?
2. Look at the uncertainty factors in life: sickness, unemployment, old age and so on. You have to build up a security reserve. How will you apportion this?

    a. How much will you set aside yourself (in cash, bank deposits, securities or other forms of saving)?
    b. How much will you spend on various forms of insurance, assuming here that reliable companies exist, offering various sickness, pension and unemployment policies under legally regulated terms?[15]

The present line of argument discounts the fact that expenditure should be reduced by improving the efficiency of state activity, in both the classic and the welfare spheres.

[12] I have heightened the logic of the supposition intentionally. This redistribution, undertaken in an imaginary, hypothetical world, clearly cannot be performed in this extreme way in the real world. Apart from anything else, the state has statutory duties, which it cannot abandon instantly and unilaterally. However, a clear, thorough examination of the problem becomes easier if we start from zero, so to speak.

[13] To return to the line of thinking begun in the previous footnote, I would like the subjects of the supposed experiment *not* to start from the *status quo* – not to derive their responses from the income and expenditure of the present-day pension system and health-insurance scheme, but to begin thinking about the system from the beginning. Let the subjects sense the presence in their pocket of the money that will then be taken from it to pay for pensions, hospital costs, schools, maternity benefits and other welfare spending.

[14] To avoid any misunderstanding, I am not drafting here a putative public opinion questionnaire, stating what the 'technique' of questioning should be, or saying how the questions should be phrased to make the responses susceptible to interpretation and processing. I am trying to outline what are the questions on which Hungarian citizens' opinions, preferences and value choices need to be known. Let us start with ourselves, clarifying our own value choices on such questions.

[15] The ignorance of Hungarian society is apparent from the fact that people can usually envisage only two alternative ways of financing the costs of the welfare sector. One is to pay for the services oneself, out of one's own pocket. The other is for the state to pay, so that people receive them free. This omits a third, fundamentally important option, in which an individual pays a regular, modest sum as an insurance premium, and the insurance company sharing the risks will pay for some or all of the service.

    c. How much tax should the state gather from you for the purpose of performing certain such insurance tasks on your behalf?

3. How much do you want to give the needy? These are the options:

    a. You can decide for yourself whom you consider needy and whom you want to help. You pay the support yourself.

    b. You yourself choose the charitable institutions to which to give money, with which they can help the needy.

    c. The money to help the needy is gathered from you by the state as a tax, and used by the state for this purpose.

The list of questions is by no means a full one. It seems to suffice, however, to convey what a *tax-conscious* line of inquiry entails. The question each one of us has to address fully is this: who should handle *my* money? Should I do so myself, or should the state take it out of my pocket, collect it from me by the force of state authority, and use it according to its own rules?

Not long ago, several colleagues and I organized a broad survey of public opinion. Our purpose was to discover how 'tax-aware' Hungarian society is, and when it is given requisite information on the link between taxes and welfare provisions, what preferences it shows concerning reform of the welfare sector. I shall confine myself here to a single observation.[16]

Among the questions put to a sample of about a thousand Hungarian respondents were these. What burdens are placed on the average taxpayer by the provision of free higher education, by free hospital care, by the high state subsidy on medicines, and by the financing of the present pension system? Let us call it (with great latitude) a 'roughly correct' response to estimate these four items within a margin of error of plus or minus 25 per cent. It turned out, for instance, that only a fifth of the respondents gave a correct response for the tax burden associated with free hospital care. The majority did not venture a reply, or grossly underestimated the tax burden, while a sizeable minority grossly overestimated the tax burden.

Having been told the correct figures for tax costs, only a third of respondents wanted to retain the present centralized, bureaucratic system of state health care. The rest expressed preferences for various composites of a state role with market forms.

I shall make a couple more references to the survey in this chapter. It represents, of course, a modest first step towards exploring the public's tax awareness and preferences. Hungarian society's views on these matters are still not known thoroughly enough, but even this first more accurate survey

[16] The survey was conducted under the auspices of the Social Research Informatics Centre (TÁRKI). Publication of the results began in the study by Csontos, Kornai and Tóth (1996), which will be followed by further publications.

shows that a considerable part of society does not want to preserve the present *status quo* in the welfare sector.

This, above all else, is why a reform of the welfare system is required.

2.   THE GUIDING PRINCIPLES OF REFORM

I am an economist. My consideration of the principles of welfare reform starts out, however, not from economic principles, but from a critique of the role of the state. The benchmark here is not a desired or tolerable level of budget deficit, or even the needs of comprehensive macroeconomic stabiliz-ation. What needs elucidating is the desirable apportionment of decision-making powers between the state and its citizens. For this the experiment imagined in the previous section was designed to provide inspiration. What is to be the autonomous province of the individual? At what point should this province be limited for the good of others?

Let me set forth some *guiding principles*. These are not 'inferences' from observed experience, but postulates or desiderata, advanced in this context simply to reflect closely my own value judgements. For I see it as essential, when drawing up a considered plan of reform, to examine the question from a strictly normative point of view as well.

This chapter, however, only goes halfway even in considering the norma-tive criteria. I do not deal with the normative demands of rational, efficient management, that is, with normative analysis of the reform's economic ef-fects. I have intentionally shifted the emphasis of this discussion towards the ethical and political philosophical side of the problem.

Even if the normative examination had been fuller, it would not have sufficed in itself. There is also a need for careful study of the programme's potential – of whether it is politically and socially acceptable, and economi-cally and organizationally feasible. This chapter omits such considerations altogether, which means that it cannot be seen as a proposal for reform, simply an expression of a few normative ideas on the reform.

Principle no. 1: Human Dignity. Let the decision-making province of the individual expand in the field of welfare services, and that of the state contract. Let the sovereignty and autonomy of the individual increase, but individual responsibility increase concurrently. Everyone, come what may, is responsible for his or her own life. Basically, we must all take care of ourselves.[17]

---

[17] At this introductory, summarizing level of the discussion, I leave open the question of how the individual relates to his or her nuclear family, and of how the decision-making provinces and responsibilities are shared among members of the family. Principle no. 1 might indeed be rephrased to include the word 'family' in parentheses after the word 'individual'. Similar additions might be made appropriately elsewhere in the chapter as well.

The facts mentioned in the first section of this chapter lead me to conclude that there should be a substantial increase in the decision-making province of the individual as compared with its present scope. The autonomy of the individual needs strengthening against the sprawling Leviathan of the state. Eventually we should reach a position where there is a concurrent fall in the state's welfare spending and in the taxes it levies. This will ensure that people do not feel the reforms *are robbing them of their rights*. They must sense the opposite: they must feel that they are regaining one of their basic human rights – the right of individual choice.[18]

Principle no. 2: Solidarity. Those who are suffering, in trouble or disadvantaged must be helped. The principle of compassionate solidarity is prompted by Judaeo-Christian religious ethics, the morality of the labour movement and left-wing political convictions. It may also derive from plain human goodness, fellow-feeling and altruism, without a specific ideological or intellectual tradition behind it.

A rider or comment can be added to the second principle: Let there be social justice in the apportionment of burdens and benefits. The criterion or an easily identifiable measure for this is a steady improvement in the situation of the groups in society that are at the greatest disadvantage.[19]

The first two criteria are meta-rational, ethical requirements.[20] There is no way of 'proving' they are justified. They have come to the fore because they are fundamentally important, whereas the remaining three principles offer more in the nature of practical guidance for the implementation, in the light of the first two principles.

Principle no. 3: Transparency. Designation of the state's role and responsibilities should come to the fore in political debate. Pressure must be put on politicians, parties and movements, and not least the politically active intelligentsia, to show their colours on these sensitive issues.

To my mind it is quite inadmissible for a politician to promise greater (or unchanged) social spending, coupled with lower taxation for society as a whole. It is cheap populism to do so. Let that politician declare his/her true intentions. Let him/her state that he/she wants greater social spending, and

[18] It can be seen from an economic point of view that it will become possible to make such a parallel change only when the budget deficit has been reduced to an acceptable level. Until that happens, reduction of expenditure will serve primarily to reduce the deficit.

[19] This is akin to Rawls's criterion of justice (see Rawls, 1971) or, more precisely, a dynamic version of this criterion. I call it dynamic because it places in the foreground the *improvement,* over time, in the situation of those worst off in society.

[20] I do not imagine that these two principles, along with the three still to come, constitute a full system of ethical postulates. There can be no question of that. Yet, to my mind, the sum of these guidelines seems sufficient for an initial, outline normative consideration of how to reform the welfare system.

thus greater taxes imposed on society, or promise to set about reducing taxes, without concealing the fact that social spending will be cut as well.

The dilemma discussed in the first section – the citizen's choice in the extent and purpose of taxation – takes the form, under a parliamentary democracy, of a choice between parties and individual candidates. This choice, however, can only give expression to individual preferences if politicians honestly state their intentions on the question of state spending and taxation.

I would like to say a special word about the ambivalence so commonly shown by members of the intelligentsia interested or involved in politics. They watch the performances of politicians on television or radio, they follow their doings in the papers, and they repeatedly sigh about how common are stupidity and dishonesty in politics. Alternatively, they complain about bureaucracy, lack of professionalism and corruption. Yet having grumbled about these things one day, they demand state services and subsidies the next. But, to be sure, the state is run by politicians and the state apparatus! Clearly, there are present – even in important positions – in that political sphere and that state apparatus the very politicians and bureaucrats about whom they have spoken previously in such disparaging and indignant tones. I believe that such inconsistency is unworthy of the intelligentsia. I do not suppose I am alone in feeling that we have had enough empty, inconsistent rhetoric, and avoidance of the real dilemmas. Let the members of the intelligentsia have the courage and intellectual honesty to decide what sphere they wish to entrust to the state – not a notional state of exclusively expert and honest representatives and officials, but to today's real, flesh-and-blood politicians and public servants.[21]

Principle no. 4: Competition. The state's monopoly, the excessive bureaucratic centralization and the stifling of competition in the welfare sector must end. All the main attributes of the old system survive lustily in the welfare sector. The dominant role of state ownership has survived. So have central planning, the command method of coordination and the shortage economy. The social situations and behaviour norms so typical of a socialist planned economy have likewise remained: comprehensive bureaucratic hierarchies, eternal bargaining over state allocations, and the defencelessness of the individual (as patient or customer). The absence of competition leaves too little incentive to improve the quality of services or to be economical.

Even the terminology is revealing. Economists' jargon in Hungarian reserves the term 'competitive sphere' for the branches where items like bricks

---

[21] In the public-opinion poll mentioned earlier, only 21 per cent of respondents want to retain the present centralized, state–corporatist system of pensions unchanged. The vast majority would rather see a greater degree of decentralization, through a 'mixed' or 'market' system combining state and non-state institutions, and compulsory and voluntary forms of insurance.

and braces are made and sold. Education, health-care and pension schemes, on the other hand, are 'saved' from the rough and tumble of competition, and still permitted to shelter behind a monopoly.

It would require a separate chapter to examine why the centralized, socialist planned economy has survived in the welfare sphere. Here I shall underline just one factor: the personal interests of those in *power positions* in this sector. The ministerial, local-government and social-security bureaucracies running the welfare sector, the union leaders active in the sector and their allies in the political sphere form together a highly influential group. Its members are tied together by many strands, and there is interaction between the functions – between ministerial, social-security, union and parliamentary posts. If decentralization and privatization were to speed up in this sector as well, some positions of power would disappear or weaken. Although some staff have the expertise to enable them to find good jobs elsewhere, there would certainly be a new selection process and reorganization of positions, which many people fear.

Principle no. 4 includes the following requirements:

a. Better legal and economic conditions must be offered so that non-state organizations can emerge and develop in the sector, offering welfare services alongside the state-owned organizations. There should be room for a range of ownership forms: non-profit and profit-making organizations, individual and corporate private ownership, ownership by foundations, church ownership, and so on.
b. All monopolies of single organizations must be replaced by competition between parallel providers of services.
c. The excessive centralization must be reduced and give way to the fullest possible decentralization.

This chapter runs a strong risk of being branded with epithets such as 'Chicago', 'neo-liberal' and '*laissez faire*', with pejorative intent. Although it is clear from what has already been said, I would like to emphasize again that the five principles advanced here, including the fourth, do *not* prescribe unlimited competition. The operating conditions for organizations in most divisions of the welfare sector, above all in education, health care and insurance, need regulation and supervision by law. There should be a licence required even for the entry of a business, and subsequent supervision by a specialized state inspectorate to ensure that the law is kept. Citizens availing themselves of the service must be protected from the provider, whether it is in state or non-state ownership. Finally, the state as ultimate guarantor must settle the bill in cases where a non-state organization goes bankrupt, and cannot meet its obligations to citizens. The legislation must clearly define the scope of the guarantees, the financial resources for which must be covered in every budget.[22] A simple list of tasks makes it plain that I do not advocate that the state withdraw, leaving the welfare sector in the lurch. All I recommend is that the role of the state be substantially reduced, and, what is more important still, redefined. To regulate by law, supervise, and give an ultimate guarantee is less than, and above all *different* from, being a ubiquitous monopoly provider.

Principle no. 5: Adjustment time. Time must be allowed for the adaptation. Clear, transparent and explicit laws are required. These should be drafted as soon as possible. It is a great shame that so much time has already been lost. If the previous or present government had set about the task earlier, we would have advanced further by now. But however much delay there has been, there is no cause for haste in drafting the legislation. The new Acts on health, pensions, financing education and so on must be robust enough to withstand the passing of time and governments, since individuals will have to adjust their strategies in life and their individual savings and insurance decisions to the long-term commitments these Acts imply. It would be very harmful if some of the new Acts needed repeated amendments; this would undermine their authority.

The programme of reform must allow for the time it takes for new institutions and organizations to form. It is impossible to establish the non-state division of the welfare sector by state decree. Nor does it need to be planned artificially in advance. The most viable organizations and forms of ownership will emerge in time, by a process of natural evolution. Under no circumstances should a situation be created in which citizens fall between two stools. The centralized state or semi-state, corporatist organizations that operate, however well or badly, cannot wind up *before* decentralized, non-state organizations have emerged to assume their tasks, and won the confidence and voluntary consent of individuals to do so. Competition should do the main work of supplanting the old organizations, not bureaucratic, arbitrary bans or hasty liquidations.

The new laws and the state's implementation of them must allow people enough time for adaptation, without prolonging the process further than necessary. When carrying out the reform, realistic and human account must be taken of the fact that individuals first have to become acquainted with the new conditions. Having done so, they still need time to rearrange their lives and family finances. The laws, and still more the administrative orders imple-

---

[22] Suppose that a citizen has expected a non-state insurer to pay for a costly item of medical care, but the insurer goes bankrupt. In this case the costs must be paid by a reinsurance institution, but, in the last resort, if the costs cannot be covered within the insurance industry, the state must pay the bill as ultimate guarantor.

menting them, must try to distinguish between the various groups in society, in terms of their capacity to adapt.[23]

3. AN EXAMPLE: REFORM OF THE PENSION SYSTEM

The general practice in Hungary is for those advancing reform proposals to come up straight away with detailed plans of action. Only from these is it possible to unravel what principles lie behind the proposal, assuming it accords with some system of values at all. I am taking the opposite course here. I have stated the principles first, and now I shall try to apply these to a specific task of reform – the transformation of the pension system. I should mention in advance that I can only draw an outline within the scope of this chapter.

I draw a distinction between three age groups. The first is *the young*. Here I am thinking of those who have yet to enter paid employment, which means they have not started to pay pension contributions.

It must be made possible for these people to open *individual pension accounts*, to be held in pension funds. The pension fund will invest the regular contributions in the capital market, and add the gains from this to the account. By the time today's young people retire, several decades' contributions, yield and compound yield will have accumulated in the account. The insured person will then receive this sum as a pension.[24]

This is a 'fully-funded' scheme, in which the pension is met from accumulated savings, as opposed to a 'pay-as-you-go' scheme, whereby the contributions levied and paid by the active population in a given year are divided among the existing pensioners. There is a difference in financing technique between the two schemes, but also a sharp economic and ethical difference. The pay-as-you-go system suggests dependence: the economically active population in a given year 'keep' the economically inactive. The fully-funded individual account scheme suggests thrift: the individual enjoys the fruits of his or her own savings and investments.

Let us leave open the question of how the payment of pension contributions should be shared between employer and employee.[25] Whatever the case,

---

[23] Young people and old have different capacities to adapt to a new pensions Act, for instance. The same applies to the healthy and the chronically sick in relation to a new health-care Act, or, with the financing of education, to those already studying and those who have yet to apply, and so on.

[24] There may be a further choice open to the insured at this point: to take a lump-sum payment, or request its conversion into an annuity.

[25] So long as conditions of perfect competition prevail in the labour market, it is quite immaterial whether the employer or the employee pays the social-security and other social contributions and payroll taxes. They will reduce the employee's net wage either way. If the competition is imperfect, however, the shares paid are not wholly immaterial. Some of the actual cost

the sum that has accumulated by the time of retirement is the fruits of the individual's lifetime performance. Its size will depend primarily on how much he or she has earned in a lifetime and how much of this has been saved in the form of pension insurance.[26] The formation of an individual pension-savings account perfectly fulfils the first principle. The sum built up in the account and the pension paid on that basis do *not* depend fundamentally on what the parliamentary majority decides for momentary political reasons during the insured's retirement, say in 2040, or what indexation or other pension adjustment legislators are prepared to make.[27] The insurer and the insured conclude a private commercial contract, not a political agreement; there is a clear proportionality between the inward and outward payments.

The law will have to prescribe *compulsory* minimum pension insurance.[28] Above that, everyone will be able to decide for themselves whether to take out further, voluntary insurance policies.

If some people are unable to pay their own compulsory contribution, the state should pay it for them. This is a step that accords with the second principle, social solidarity, made by the state at the expense of the other taxpayers. It should not be taken lightly, but confined to cases where people are demonstrably unable to pay. Where that is the case, however, such a step must certainly be taken. The administration must first find out who has not paid the compulsory pension contribution. Where the reason is negligence, payment must be enforced by law. Where the reason is inability, however, for lack of information or funds, the state must step in.

While this provides a minimum pension for all, there must be no levelling of pensions above the minimum either. Everyone has the right to decide

(though not the whole) may reduce the entrepreneur's profits, instead of the net wage, or the entrepreneur may be able to pass some of the cost on to the consumer, in the form of higher prices (see Musgrave and Musgrave, 1980 [1973] pp. 504–10).

[26] It also depends, of course, on the performance of the handling pension fund in the capital market – whether it has invested the money effectively and wisely, and in general how the capital market of the country concerned, and ultimately its economy, have performed during the insured's working life. To that extent he or she is 'in the same boat' as other savers and investors.

[27] We cannot, of course, hope that those living and spending their income in 2040 will be entirely free of the momentary influence of parliament. The purchasing power of the money will be affected by the rate of inflation and other economic processes not immune from the influence of state factors.

[28] My defence of the obligation to insure would not be on paternalistic grounds, that is, not out of a desire to further the prosperity of unwilling individuals by state compulsion.

If Citizen *X*, who always had the chance to pay pension insurance throughout his active life, never did so, he might suffer serious poverty in old age, reaching the brink of starvation and homelessness. A civilized, humane society would not allow this to happen (see Principle no. 2); he would receive relief at taxpayers' expense. The interests of future taxpayers therefore require that Citizen *X* be compelled to pay a pension contribution sufficient to absolve society from relieving him in his old age. So the compulsory minimum insurance requirement is not for the sake of 'forced happiness', but a preventive measure to protect other taxpayers.

whether to live their active lives like an industrious ant or like a profligate grasshopper.[29] Once the final stage in life has been reached, however, there should be no egalitarian adjustments between their old-age income by an omnipotent state. The ant has a right to the kind of old age she has saved for over her lifetime.

Pension insurance should not be a state monopoly. Competition in this field of insurance must be allowed, indeed encouraged, in line with the fourth principle. This will raise the choice of alternative insurance policies, reduce the management costs of insurance and, what is more important still, allow decentralized investment of accumulated pension-insurance deposits. This allows one of the most important, indeed indispensable actors of the modern capital market to develop: pension funds as institutional investors. They control a sizeable proportion of the investments in the capital markets of advanced market economies. If all the pension savings remain concentrated in the hands of the state, this gives the state too great a role in investment.

Although the state monopoly over pensions must be broken up, the state retains some important tasks (apart from its obligations towards older generations, which will be discussed in a moment). The province, responsibilities and duties of the pension funds will have to be regulated by law. The task of providing insurance that entails running individual pension accounts will need to be subject to state licence, and certain elements of a prudent and careful investment policy for pension funds be prescribed.[30] A system of reinsurance must be built up and, as a last resort, the state must guarantee that people's pension investments are not lost even if funds are misused by the institution.

The pension savings of individuals should receive preferential treatment under tax law. There should be ways of deferring tax payments up to certain limits. The income later received as a pension, on the other hand, should not receive any concessions.

The second age group is *pensioners*. We cannot refer here to the first principle. Those who are already on a pension have no way of taking an autonomous decision about their pension savings. Society, in my view, has an obligation to provide them with a decent pension.

---

[29] One of the questions in the survey of public opinion mentioned earlier was, 'How are you preparing for your old age?' An astonishingly large proportion, 49 per cent, said they had not thought about it yet. Up to now they had thought this was a matter for the state, not them, to consider. The finding shows how strongly the old norms still feature in people's mentality. The first basic principle, that everyone is responsible for his or her own life, has yet to strike root in the minds of a very significant proportion of society.

[30] Initially, for instance, it will be compulsory to invest a high proportion of the savings in safe state securities. Only as the pension fund strengthens and builds up solid reserves can it be allowed to broaden its portfolio to cover riskier forms of investment.

Let us face the facts: the position of pensioners is ambivalent. They feel they have worked for a lifetime, and have paid their pension contributions. They are not being 'kept' by society, since they simply must receive back their savings in the form of a pension. However, if we take a closer, individual look at the relation between lifetime earnings and contributions paid on the one hand, and the real value of the pension received since retirement on the other, the correlation turns out to be weak. A great effect on the nominal and real value of a pension has been exerted by the time the pensioner retires. Let us assume that *A* and *B* have had exactly the same flow of earnings and pension contributions, but there is a difference in time between the two. Because *A* started and finished his working life earlier than *B*, there may be a substantial difference in their pensions. The system of calculating pensions has changed several times in the last decade, while inflation has speeded up and slowed down, and the methods of indexing pensions have varied as well. Meanwhile the pension system has been patched up and tinkered with, with strong levelling effects.

Because of all these factors, the pension received is not an annuity received under an insurance policy, and the pension contribution cannot be called an insurance premium. The transaction has nothing to do, either in an economic or legal sense, with what one might call an 'insurance transaction'. To call a spade a spade, the so-called pension-insurance contribution is nothing other than a *tax*, a proportionate payroll tax. Today's pensions are paid out of taxpayers' money. The ostensibly self-financing system of pension 'insurance' is the largest institution with a soft budget constraint in the country: the government is legally bound to cover any deficit. As is customary where there is a soft budget constraint, the amount of financial benefit paid is the subject of pressure-group activity, political criteria and bargaining. The actual amount of pensions at any time is decided in the political arena, in contravention of the first principle.

I wrote just now that a decent pension should be paid. Let us acknowledge that we can only resort to the second principle here. 'Decency' is an ethical, not an economic category. There is no question of a private contract between the insurance institution and the insured, with benefits proportionate to premiums. The size of the pensions paid today is quite arbitrary in a commercial sense. We can only fall back on the goodwill and decency of society and its respect and sympathy for the older generation, and of course on the fact that pensioners form a vast bloc of votes, which any political party seeking to win an election will think twice about offending.

The third age group is *the intermediate generation*. Here I am thinking of those who have been paying pension contributions, but have yet to reach retirement. The most important principle that I advocate in their case is the right of free choice. They have two main opportunities open to them.

1. To stay in the present state insurance system.
2. To transfer to the decentralized system of individual pension savings.

If they choose the latter, they must be allowed to take with them the accumulated value of the contributions they have already paid. The economic content of the transfer is plain.[31] In return for the contributions, the state undertook payment obligations that fall due on retirement. A numerical value can clearly be put on this 'pension debt' of the state under the present laws. The state's promissory note, made out accordingly, can then be placed in the new pension fund. Special long-term state bonds could serve as such a 'promissory note', and be tradable on the secondary security markets.

I cannot say what proportion of employees would remain in the old system and what proportion would choose the new. The essential aspect is the chance to choose – the knowledge that, in line with the first principle, the individual is not confined to a single pension track laid by the state. Moreover, even if relatively few people chose to opt out, the possibility of doing so would apply competitive pressure to the hitherto monopoly state system. This accords with the requirements of the fourth principle.

Here I would like to return to the case of young people. Let us suppose a decentralized system of pension funds has already emerged. There is no reason to stop the successor to the present monopoly pension and social-insurance system carrying on as one of the competitors. Young people with more faith in a state institution than a non-state one may choose the former to manage their pension accounts.

The fifth principle also needs to be applied in developing the new pension system. The legislation must be carefully prepared, with time allowed for the system of decentralized, non-state insurers to develop, along with a reliable system of state supervision. Time must be allowed for people to grasp the new opportunities and brief themselves thoroughly before choosing the alternative that promises to be best for them.

Those familiar with pension systems abroad will know that this proposal does not match any foreign example accurately. There is a similarity with the system in the United States, but it differs from this in some essential respects. Many features have been taken from the Chilean scheme, which has pioneered a new path in the development of pension systems, while use has been made of Australian experience and New Zealand proposals, but the system suggested here is not identical with any of these.[32] Nor would it be right

---

[31] Here I am merely putting forward a general principle. Practical implementation of it raises many important economic, technical, financial and legal problems that I cannot cover here.

[32] On the Chilean pension reform, see Camacho (1992), Corsetti and Schmidt-Hebbel (1995) and Gillion and Bonilla (1992). On New Zealand's reform proposals, see Douglas (1993). The volume compiled by the World Bank (1994) gives an excellent general view of the alternatives

simply to replicate some foreign system, because close attention must be paid to Hungary's specific conditions.[33]

4. SOME CONCLUDING REMARKS

This outline for the pension system serves simply as an example. I might have chosen another illustration – reform of the financing of higher education, for example, or reorganization of the health service. The purpose of this chapter is not to popularize a specific pension reform.

The 'message' of the chapter is connected with the third principle: that those who contribute to discussion of the welfare system, and still more those who will decide on the legislation and regulations concerning it, should declare their true colours.

The reason why I refer to one or other of the five principles repeatedly while presenting the proposal for pension reform is to demonstrate a firm link between principles and practice. There is no need to 'dodge' principles to arrive at a pragmatic, practical approach, or, conversely, to become bogged down in empty rhetoric about principles without converting them into the small change of a practical proposal.

I am aware that many Hungarians do not share the system of values I adhere to and have explained briefly in this chapter. They espouse another one. Since the welfare system must be transformed for the good of the whole Hungarian population, and in a way that persists for a long time, the aim must be to base the reform on as broad a consensus as possible. There must inevitably be mutual concessions, away from some or other 'pure' system of values or consistent body of principles. This, however, makes it all the more important to know the *basis* from which we are making the concession. To be well prepared to take part in the debate, we must clarify in our minds the system of values we espouse in relation to the welfare sector, and the practical position we adopt accordingly.

for pension reform and the reforms carried out in several countries (including Australia and a number of Latin American states), along with a rich body of calculations.

[33] There has been little widespread public debate so far in books and periodicals on the alternatives for pension reform in Hungary. I would mention particularly the works of Augusztinovics (1992 and 1993), Augusztinovics and Martos (1995), Bod (1992) and Martos (1994), and also the World Bank study of Hungary (1995d), pp. 31–46 and 97–130. The last contains many elements of the reform outlined in this article, although my proposal takes decentralization further.

References

Ágh, A. (1995), 'A magyar politika jövője' (The future of Hungarian politics), *Mozgó Világ*, **21** (2), 17–28.

Aghion, Philippe and Olivier J. Blanchard (1993), *On the Speed of Transition in Central Europe*, Working Paper, no. 6, London: European Bank for Reconstruction and Development.

Alesina, Alberto and Roberto Perotti (1995), 'Reducing Budget Deficits', prepared for the conference 'Growing Government Debt – International Experiences', Stockholm, 12 June, mimeo.

Alt, James E. and Kenneth A. Shepsle (eds) (1990), *Perspectives on Positive Political Economy*, Cambridge: Cambridge University Press.

Andorka, R. (1994), 'Elégedetlenség, elidegenedés, anómia' (Discontent, alienation and anomie), in István György Tóth (ed.), *Társadalmi átalakulás: 1992–94. Jelentés a Magyar Háztartás Panel III. hullámának eredményeiről* (Social Transformation 1992–94. Report on Results of Phase III of the Hungarian Household Panel), Műhelytanulmányok series no. 5, Budapest: BKE, KSH and TÁRKI, pp. 83–90.

Andorka, R., A. Kondratas and I.Gy. Tóth (1995), 'A jóléti rendszer jellemzői és reformjának lehetőségei' (Characteristics of the welfare system and ways of reforming it), *Közgazdasági Szemle*, **42** (1), 1–29.

Antal, L. (1994), 'Az örökség. A gazdaság helyzete és a feladatok' (The legacy. The situation of the economy and the tasks), *Társadalmi Szemle*, **49** (10), 12–21.

Arthur, W.B. (1984), 'Competing Technologies and Economic Prediction', *Options*, journal of the IIASA, Laxenburg, April, pp. 10–13.

Árvay, János and András Vértes (1994), *A magánszektor és a rejtett gazdaság súlya Magyarországon, 1980–92. Összefoglaló* (The Share of the Private Sector and Hidden Economy in Hungary, 1980–92. Summary), Budapest: Gazdaságkutató Rt.

Ash, T.N. and P.G. Hare (1994), 'Privatisation in the Russian Federation: Changing Enterprise Behaviour in the Transition Period', *Cambridge Journal of Economics*, **18** (4), 619–34.

Augusztinovics, M. (1992), 'A nyugdíjrendszer válsága' (Crisis in the pension system), *Közgazdasági Szemle*, **39** (7/8), 624–41.

Augusztinovics, M. (1993), 'Egy értelmes nyugdíjrendszer' (An intelligent pension system), *Közgazdasági Szemle*, **40** (5), 415–31.

Augusztinovics, M. and B. Martos (1995), 'Számítások és következtetések nyugdíjreformra' (Calculations and deductions for a pension reform), *Közgazdasági Szemle*, **42** (11), 993–1023.

Balassa, Á. (1994), 'Van-e válság, és ha igen, miféle?' (Is there a crisis, and if so, of what kind?), *Népszabadság*, 29 October, pp. 17 and 21.

Balassa, Ákos (1993), 'Makrogazdasági folyamatok, 1986–1992' (Macroeconomic processes, 1986–92), manuscript, Budapest: Magyar Nemzeti Bank.

Banco de Mexico (1996), *Indicadores Económicos*, November.

Barro, R.J. (1974), 'Are Government Bonds Net Wealth?', *Journal of Political Economy*, **82** (6), 1095–117.

Barro, R.J. and H.I. Grossman (1971), 'A General Disequilibrium Model of Income and Employment', *American Economic Review*, **61** (1), 82–93.

Bauer, Tamás (1981), *Tervgazdaság, beruházás, ciklusok* (Planned economy, investment, cycles), Budapest: Közgazdasági és Jogi Könyvkiadó.

Baumol, William J., John C. Panzar and Robert D. Willig (1982), *Contestable Markets and the Theory of Industry Structure*, New York: Harcourt Brace Jovanovich.

Békesi, L. (1993), 'A feladat öt szöglete. Farkas Zoltán interjúja Békesi Lászlóval' (The five angles of the task. Interview with László Békesi by Zoltán Farkas), *Társadalmi Szemle*, **48** (3), 3–13.

Békesi, L. (1994), 'A társadalom még nincs tisztában a gazdasági helyzettel. Karsai Gábor interjúja Békesi Lászlóval' (Society is still unclear about the economic situation. Interview with László Békesi by Gábor Karsai), *Figyelő*, 14 July, pp. 13–15.

Békesi, L. (1995), 'Mást választhatunk, de „jobbat" aligha' (We can choose something else, but hardly something better), *Népszabadság*, 8 July, pp. 17–18.

Benassy, J.-P. (1993), 'Non-Clearing Markets: Microeconomic Concepts and Macroeconomic Applications', *Journal of Economic Literature*, **31** (2), 732–61.

Berg, A. (1994), 'Supply and Demand Factors in the Output Decline in East and Central Europe', *Empirica*, **21** (1), 3–36.

Berg, A. and J. Sachs (1992), 'Structural Adjustment and International Trade in Eastern Europe: The Case of Poland', *Economic Policy*, **7** (14), 117–73.

Blanchard, Olivier. J. and Stanley Fischer (1989), *Lectures on Macroeconomics*, Cambridge, Mass.: MIT Press.

Blanchflower, David G. and Andrew J. Oswald (1994), *The Wage Curve*, Cambridge, Mass. and London: MIT Press.

Bod, P. (1992), 'Mennyibe kerül egy társadalombiztosítási nyugdíjrendszer működtetése. I. Biztosítástechnikai alapfogalmak. II. A finanszírozási típusokról' (What does it cost to operate a social insurance pension system? I. The basic insurance concepts. II. On the types of financing), *Közgazdasági Szemle*, **39** (2), 123–45 and (3), 244–61.

Bokros, L. (1995a), 'A leendő pénzügyminiszter huszonöt pontja. Bokros Lajos szakmai cselekvési programjának alapvonalai' (The 25 points of the finance minister elect. Main outlines of Lajos Bokros's action programme), *Népszabadság*, 17 February, p. 15.

Bokros, L. (1995b), 'Az államháztartásról, a stabilizációról. Dr. Bokros Lajos pénzügyminiszter tájékoztatója' (On the state budget and stabilization. Exposition by Dr. Lajos Bokros, finance minister), *Pénzügyi Szemle*, **40** (4), 259–62.

Bokros, L. (1996), 'Növekedés és/vagy egyensúly – avagy az 1995. március 12-én meghirdetett stabilizáció tanulságai' (Growth and/or stabilization – lessons from the stabilization programme announced on 12 March 1995), *Népszabadság*, 11 March, p. 8.

Borbély, L.A. and J. Neményi (1994), 'Az államadósság növekedésének összetevői 1990–1992-ben' (The factors behind the growth in the state debt, 1990–92), *Közgazdasági Szemle*, **41** (2), 110–26.

Borbély, László András and Judit Neményi (1995), 'Eladósodás, a külső és belső államadósság alakulása az átmenet gazdaságában (1990–1993)' (Indebtedness and the development of external and internal state debt in the transition economy, 1990–93), in Tamás Mellár (ed.), *Rendszerváltás és stabilizáció. A piacgazdasági átmenet első évei* (Change of System and Stabilization. The First Years of Market Economic Transition), Budapest: Magyar Trendkutató Központ, pp. 123–66.

Bornstein, M. (1994), 'Russia's Mass Privatisation Programme', *Communist Economies and Economic Transformation*, **6** (4), 419–57.

Bossányi, K. (1995), 'Aki kapja, marja' (Up for grabs), *Népszabadság*, 7 October, pp. 17 and 21.

Boycko, Maxim, Andrei Shleifer and Robert Vishny (1995), *Privatizing Russia*, Cambridge, Mass.: MIT Press.

Bozóki, A. (1994), 'Vázlat három populizmusról: Egyesült Államok, Argentína és Magyarország' (Outline of three types of populism: The United States, Argentina and Hungary), *Politikatudományi Szemle*, 1994, **3** (3), 33–68.

Bozóki, A. and É. Kovács (1991), 'A politikai pártok megnyilvánulásai a sajtóban a taxisblokád idején' (The political parties' statements in the press during the taxi drivers' blockade), *Szociológiai Szemle*, no. 1, pp. 109–26.

Bozóki, A. and M. Sükösd (1992), 'Civil társadalom és populizmus a kelet-európai demokratikus átmenetekben' (Civil society and populism in the democratic transitions of Eastern Europe), *Mozgó Világ*, **18** (8), 100–112.

Brabant, J. M. van (1990), 'Socialist Economics: The Disequilibrium School and the Shortage Economy', *Journal of Economic Perspectives*, Spring, **4** (2), 157–75.

Brabant, J.M. van (1993), 'Lessons from the Wholesale Transformation in the East', *Comparative Economic Studies*, Winter, **35** (4), 73–102.

Brom, K. and M. Orenstein (1994), 'The Privatised Sector in the Czech Republic: Government and Bank Control in a Transitional Economy', *Europe–Asia Studies*, **46** (6), 893–928.

Bruno, Michael (1993), *Crisis, Stabilization, and Economic Reform: Therapy by Consensus*, New York: Oxford University Press.

Bruno, Michael and William Easterly (1995), *Inflation Crises and Long-Run Growth*, NBER Working Paper series, no. 5209, Cambridge: National Bureau of Economic Research, Harvard University, August.

Bruszt, L. (1992), 'Transformative Politics: Social Costs and Social Peace in East Central Europe', *East European Politics and Societies*, Winter, **6** (1), 55–72.

Bruszt, L. (1994a), 'Reforming Alliances: Labour, Management, and State Bureaucracy in Hungary's Economic Transition', *Acta Oeconomica*, **46** (3/4), 313–32.

Bruszt, László (1994b), 'Az Antall-kormány és a gazdasági érdekképviseletek' (The Antall government and the representatives of business interests), in Csaba Gombár, Elemér Hankiss, László Lengyel and Györgyi Várnai (eds), *Kormány a mérlegen, 1990–94* (Assessing the Government, 1990–94), Budapest: Korridor Politikai Kutatások Központja, pp. 208–30.

Buchanan, James M. (1967), *Public Finance in Democratic Process: Fiscal Institutions and the Individual Choice*, Chapel Hill: University of North Carolina Press.

Buckley, Róbert, Zsuzsa Dániel and Margret Thalwitz (1993), 'The Welfare Cost and Transparency of Housing Policies in Socialist Economies: The Hungarian Experience', manuscript, Washington DC: World Bank.

Bunce, Valerie and Mária Csanádi (1992), 'The Systematic Analysis of a Non-System. Post-Communism in Eastern Europe', in György Szoboszlai (ed.), *Flying Blind: Emerging Democracies in East-Central Europe*, Budapest: Magyar Politikatudományi Társaság. Évkönyv, pp. 177–203.

Burke, Edmund (1982) [1790], *Reflections on the Revolution in France*, London: Penguin.

Burkett, J. P. (1988), 'Slack, Shortage and Discouraged Consumers in Eastern Europe: Estimates Based on Smoothing by Aggregation', *Review of Economic Studies*, **55** (3), 493–505.

Calvo, G. and F. Coricelli (1993), 'Output Collapse in Eastern Europe', *IMF Staff Papers*, **40** (1), 32–52.

Camacho, L.A. (1992), 'Financing Social Security in Latin America: New Perspectives in the Light of Current Economic Developments', *Interna-*

tional Social Security Review, **45** (3), 19–38.

Central Statistical Office (1971), *Statisztikai évkönyv 1970* (Statistical Yearbook 1970), Budapest: Központi Statisztikai Hivatal.

Central Statistical Office (1974), *Statisztikai évkönyv 1973* (Statistical Yearbook 1973), Budapest: Központi Statisztikai Hivatal.

Central Statistical Office (1976), *Statisztikai évkönyv 1975* (Statistical Yearbook 1975), Budapest: Központi Statisztikai Hivatal.

Central Statistical Office (1981), *Statisztikai évkönyv 1980* (Statistical Yearbook 1980), Budapest: Központi Statisztikai Hivatal.

Central Statistical Office (1986), *Statisztikai évkönyv 1985* (Statistical Yearbook 1985), Budapest: Központi Statisztikai Hivatal.

Central Statistical Office (1989), *Tudományos kutatás és kísérleti fejlesztés 1988* (Scientific Research and Experimental Development 1988), Budapest: Központi Statisztikai Hivatal.

Central Statistical Office (1991), *Hungarian Statistical Yearbook 1990*, Budapest: Központi Statisztikai Hivatal.

Central Statistical Office (1994a), *Magyar statisztikai zsebkönyv 1993* (Hungarian Statistical Pocket Book 1993), Budapest: Központi Statisztikai Hivatal.

Central Statistical Office (1994b), *Lakásstatisztikai évkönyv 1993* (Yearbook of Housing Statistics 1993), Budapest: Központi Statisztikai Hivatal.

Central Statistical Office (1994c), *Tudományos kutatás és kísérleti fejlesztés 1993* (Scientific Research and Experimental Development 1993), Budapest: Központi Statisztikai Hivatal.

Central Statistical Office (1994d), *Statisztikai Havi Közlemények* (Monthly Statistical Bulletins), no. 1.

Central Statistical Office (1994e), *Statisztikai Havi Közlemények* (Monthly Statistical Bulletins), no. 12.

Central Statistical Office (1994f), *Magyar statisztikai évkönyv 1993* (Hungarian Statistical Yearbook 1993), Budapest: Központi Statisztikai Hivatal.

Central Statistical Office (1995a), *Magyar statisztikai zsebkönyv 1994* (Hungarian Statistical Pocket Book 1994), Budapest: Központi Statisztikai Hivatal.

Central Statistical Office (1995b), *Tájékoztató* (Bulletin), 1st quarter.

Central Statistical Office (1995c), *A nemzetgazdaság munkaerőmérlege* (The Labour Balance of the National Economy), 1 January, Budapest: Központi Statisztikai Hivatal.

Central Statistical Office (1995d), *Magyar statisztikai évkönyv 1994* (Hungarian Statistical Yearbook 1994), Budapest: Központi Statisztikai Hivatal.

Central Statistical Office (1996a), *Főbb munkaügyi folyamatok. Negyedéves jelentés* (Main Labour-Market Processes. Quarterly Report), Budapest: Központi Statisztikai Hivatal.

Central Statistical Office (1996b), *Statisztikai Havi Közlemények* (Monthly Statistical Bulletins), no. 4.

Central Statistical Office (1996c), *Statisztikai Havi Közlemények* (Monthly Statistical Bulletins), no. 5.

Central Statistical Office (1996d), *KSH Statisztikai Hírek* (CSO Statistical News), 2 April.

Central Statistical Office (1996e), *A KSH jelenti* (The CSO Reports), no. 1.

Central Statistical Office (1996f), *Magyar statisztikai évkönyv 1995* (Hungarian Statistical Yearbook 1995), Budapest: Központi Statisztikai Hivatal.

Central Statistical Office (1996g), *Magyar statisztikai zsebkönyv 1995* (Hungarian Statistical Pocket Book 1995), Budapest: Központi Statisztikai Hivatal.

Chamberlin, Edward H. (1962) [1933], *The Theory of Monopolistic Competition*, Cambridge, Mass.: Harvard University Press.

Chikán, Attila (1984), *A vállalati készletezési politika* (Enterprise Inventory Policy), Budapest: Közgazdasági és Jogi Könyvkiadó.

Chikán, A. (1994), 'Joint Micro and Macro Effects on Inventories in the Transition Economies', *International Journal of Production Economics*, **37** (June), 11–14.

Collier, David (ed.) (1979), *The New Authoritarianism in Latin America*, Princeton: Princeton University Press.

Cooper, Richard N. (1992), *Economic Stabilization and Debt in Developing Countries*, Cambridge, Mass. and London: MIT Press.

Corsetti, Giancarlo and Klaus Schmidt-Hebbel (1995), *Pension Reform and Growth*, Policy Research Working Paper no. 1471, Washington DC: World Bank, June.

Crane, Keith (1996), 'The Effectiveness of Hungarian Privatization Policies', paper presented at the conference 'Dilemmas of Transition: the Hungarian Experience', 27–9 September 1996, University of Toronto, mimeo, Washington DC: PlanEcon.

Csaba, L. (1995), 'Gazdaságstratégia helyett konjunktúra-politika' (Trade-cycle policy instead of economic strategy), *Külgazdaság*, **39** (3), 36–46.

Csontos, L. (1995), 'Fiskális illúziók, döntéselmélet és az államháztartási rendszer reformja' (Fiscal illusions, decision theory, and reform of the public finance system), *Közgazdasági Szemle*, **42** (12), 1118–35.

Csontos, László, János Kornai and István György Tóth (1996), 'Adótudatosság, fiskális illúziók és a jóléti rendszer reformja: egy empirikus vizsgálat első eredményei' (Tax awareness, fiscal illusions and reform of the welfare system: first results of an empirical study), in Rudolf Andorka, Tamás Kolosi and György Vukovics (eds), *Társadalmi riport 1996* (Social Report 1996), Budapest: TÁRKI, pp. 238–71.

Dániel, Zs. (1989), 'Housing Demand in a Shortage Economy: Results of a Hungarian Survey', *Acta Oeconomica*, **41** (1/2), 157–80.

Darvas, Zsolt (1996), *Exchange Rate Premia and the Credibility of the Crawling Target Zone in Hungary*, Discussion Paper series no. 1307, London: Centre for Economic Research, January.

Darvas, Zsolt and András Simon (1996), 'Tőke beáramlás, árfolyam-és pénzpolitika' (Capital Inflow, Exchange Rate and Monetary Policy), mimeo, Budapest: Magyar Nemzeti Bank, February.

Davis, Christopher and Wojciech W. Charemza (eds) (1989), *Models of Disequilibrium and Shortage in Centrally Planned Economies*, London: Chapman and Hall.

Dewatripont, M. and G. Roland (1992), 'The Virtues of Gradualism and Legitimacy in the Transition to a Market Economy', *The Economic Journal*, **102** (411), 291–300.

Dixit, A.K. and J.E. Stiglitz (1977), 'Monopolistic Competition and Optimum Product Diversity', *American Economic Review*, **67** (3), 297–308.

Dlouhý, V. and J. Mládek (1994), 'Privatization and Corporate Control in the Czech Republic', *Economic Policy*, Supplement, December (19), 156–70.

Domar, Evsey (1989), 'The Blind Men and the Elephant: An Essay on Isms', in *Capitalism, Socialism, and Serfdom*, Cambridge: Cambridge University Press, pp. 29–46.

Dornbusch, R. and S. Edwards (1990), 'The Macroeconomics of Populism in Latin America', *Journal of Development Economics*, **32** (2), 247–77.

Dornbusch, R. and S. Fischer (1993), 'Moderate Inflation', *The World Bank Economic Review*, **7** (1), 1–44.

Dornbusch, R., I. Goldfajn and R.O. Valdés (1995), 'Currency Crises and Collapses', *Brookings Papers on Economic Activity*, no. 2, pp. 219–93.

Dornbusch, R. and A. Werner (1994), 'Mexico: Stabilization, Reform and No Growth', *Brookings Papers on Economic Activity*, no. 1, pp. 253–315.

Douglas, Roger (1993), *Unfinished Business*, Glenfield: Random House New Zealand Ltd.

Drazen, A. and V. Grilli (1993), 'The Benefit of Crises for Economic Reforms', *American Economic Review*, **83** (3), 598–607.

EBRD (1995), *Transition Report*, London: European Bank for Reconstruction and Development.

Ehrlich, Éva (1984), *Japan, a Case of Catching Up*, Budapest: Akadémiai Kiadó.

Elliott, J.E. and A.F. Dowlah (1993), 'Transition Crises in the Post-Soviet Era', *Journal of Economic Issues*, **27** (2), 527–35.

Erdős, T. (1994), 'A tartós gazdasági növekedés realitásai és akadályai' (The realities of lasting economic growth and obstacles to it), *Közgazdasági Szemle*, **41** (6), 463–77.

European Commission (1995), *Employment Observatory: Central and Eastern Europe*, no. 7.

Evans, Peter (1979), *Dependent Development: The Alliance of Multinational, State, and Local Capital in Brazil*, Princeton: Princeton University Press.

Fazekas, Károly and János Köllő (1985), 'Fluctuations of Labour Shortage and State Intervention after 1968', in Péter Galasi and György Sziráczki (eds), *Labour Market and Second Economy in Hungary*, Frankfurt and New York: Campus Verlag.

Federal Ministry of Finance (Prague) (1992), 'Coupon Privatization: An Information Handbook', *Eastern European Economics*, **30** (4), 5–38.

Fehér, Ferenc, Ágnes Heller and György Márkus (1983), *Dictatorship over Needs*, Oxford: Basil Blackwell, and New York: St Martin's Press.

Feldstein, M. (1974), 'Social Security, Induced Retirement, and Aggregate Capital Accumulation', *Journal of Political Economy*, **82** (5), 905–26.

Ferge, Zs. (1994), 'Szabadság és biztonság' (Freedom and security), *Esély*, no. 5, pp. 2–24.

Ferge, Zs. (1995), 'A magyar segélyezési rendszer reformja, 1' (Reform of the Hungarian System of Cash Benefits, 1), *Esély*, no. 6, pp. 43–62 .

Ferge, Zs. (1996a), 'A magyar segélyezési rendszer reformja, 2' (Reform of the Hungarian System of Cash Benefits, 2), *Esély*, no. 1, pp. 25–42.

Ferge, Zs. (1996b), 'A szociálpolitika esélyei' (The prospects of social policy), *Vigilia*, **61** (7), 528–35.

Fischer, S. (1987), 'The Israeli Stabilization Program, 1985–1986', *The American Economic Review*, **77** (2), 275–8.

Fischer, S., R. Sahay and C.A. Végh (1996), 'Stabilization and Growth in Transition Economies: The Early Experience', *Journal of Economic Perspectives*, **10** (2), 45–66.

Funke, N. (1993), 'Timing and Sequencing of Reforms: Competing Views and the Role of Credibility', *Kyklos*, **46** (3), 337–62.

Gábor, R.I. (1979), 'The Second (Secondary) Economy. Earning Activity and Regrouping of Income outside the Socially Organized Production and Distribution', *Acta Oeconomica*, **22** (3/4), 291–311.

Gábor, R. István (1985), 'The Major Domains of the Second Economy', in Péter Galasi and György Sziráczky (eds), *Labour Market and Second Economy in Hungary*, Frankfurt and New York: Campus Verlag, pp. 133–78.

Gács, J. (1991a), 'A liberó második éve' (The second year of liberalization), *Figyelő*, 3 January, p. 9.

Gács, János (1991b), 'Liberalization of the Hungarian Foreign Trade, 1968–1990', in András Köves and Pál Marer (eds), *Foreign Economic Liberalization: Transformations in Socialist and Market Economies*, Boulder, San Francisco and Oxford: Westview Press.

Gács, János (1994), 'Trade Liberalization in the CSFR, Hungary, and Poland: Rush and Reconsideration', in János Gács and Georg Winckler (eds), *International Trade and Restructuring in Eastern Europe*, Laxenburg: IIASA and Physica-Verlag, pp. 123–51.

Gazsó, F. and I. Stumpf (1995), 'Pártok és szavazóbázisok két választás után' (Parties and constituencies after two elections), *Társadalmi Szemle*, **50** (6), 3–17.

Giavazzi, F. and M. Pagano (1990), 'Can Severe Fiscal Contractions be Expansionary? Tales of Two Small European Countries', *NBER Macroeconomics Annual*, pp. 75–116.

Giavazzi, F. and M. Pagano (1996), 'Non-Keynesian Effects of Fiscal Policy Changes: International Evidence and the Swedish Experience', *Swedish Economic Policy Review*, May, forthcoming.

Gillion, C. and A. Bonilla (1992), 'Analysis of a National Private Pension Scheme: The Case of Chile', *International Labour Review*, **131** (2), 171–95.

Goldfeld, S.M. and R.E. Quandt (1990a), 'Rationing, Defective Inputs and Bayesian Updates under Central Planning', *Economics of Planning*, **23** (3), 161–73.

Goldfeld, Stephen M. and Richard E. Quandt (1990b), 'Output Targets, Input Rationing and Inventories', in Richard E. Quandt and Dusan Triska (eds), *Optimal Decisions in Market and Planned Economies*, Boulder: Westview Press, pp. 67–81.

Gombár, Csaba (1995), 'Száz nap, vagy amit akartok' (One hundred days or what you will), in Csaba Gombár, Elemér Hankiss, László Lengyel and Györgyi Várnai (eds), *Kérdőjelek: a magyar kormány, 1994–95* (Question Marks: the Hungarian Government, 1994–95), Budapest: Korridor Politikai Kutatások Központja, pp. 235–59.

Gomulka, S. (1985), 'Kornai's Soft Budget Constraint and the Shortage Phenomenon: A Criticism and Restatement', *Economics of Planning*, **19** (1), 1–11.

Greskovits, Béla (1993a), *Dominant Economy, Subordinated Politics. The Absence of Economic Populism in the Transition of East Central Europe*, Working Paper series, no. 1, Budapest: Central European University.

Greskovits, Béla (1993b), 'The "Loneliness" of the Economic Policy Maker. An Approach Based on Reviewing the Literature on the Politics of Economic Transition in LDCs, and East Central Europe', paper presented at the Polish Academy of Sciences workshop 'Institutionalizing Social Transformations', Radziejowice, manuscript.

Greskovits, Béla (1994), 'A tiltakozás és türelem politikai gazdaságtanáról. Latin-Amerika és Közép-Kelet-Európa átalakulásának tapasztalatai alapján' (The political economy of protest and patience, based on the experience of

Latin America and Central Eastern Europe), manuscript, Budapest: Közép-Európai Egyetem.

Greskovits, B. (1995), 'Demokrácia – szegény országban' (Democracy—in a poor country), *Társadalmi Szemle*, **50** (5), 3–23.

Grosfeld, Irena (1989), 'Disequilibrium Models of Investment', in Christopher Davis and Wojciech W. Charemza (eds): *Models of Disequilibrium and Shortage in Centrally Planned Economies*, London: Chapman and Hall, pp. 361–74.

Haggard, Stephan (1990), *Pathways from the Periphery. The Politics of Growth in the Newly Industrializing Countries*, Ithaca and London: Cornell University Press.

Haggard, Stephan and Robert R. Kaufman (1989), 'Economic Adjustment in New Democracies', in Joan M. Nelson and contributors, *Fragile Coalitions: The Politics of Economic Adjustment*, New Brunswick and Oxford: Transaction Books, pp. 57–78.

Haggard, Stephan and Robert R. Kaufman (1992a), 'The Political Economy of Inflation and Stabilization in Middle-Income Countries', in (eds), *The Politics of Economic Adjustment*, Princeton: Princeton University Press, pp. 271–315.

Haggard, Stephan and Robert R. Kaufman (1992b), 'Economic Adjustment and the Prospects for Democracy', in (eds), *The Politics of Economic Adjustment*, Princeton: Princeton University Press, pp. 319–50.

Halpern, László (1996), *Real Exchange Rates and Exchange Rate Policy in Hungary*, Discussion Paper series, no. 1366, London: Centre for Economic Policy Research, March.

Hare, Paul (1989), 'The Economics of Shortage in the Centrally Planned Economies', in Christopher Davis and Wojciech W. Charemza (eds), *Models of Disequilibrium and Shortage in Centrally Planned Economies*, London: Chapman and Hall, pp. 49–81.

Hart, O. D. (1982), 'A Model of Imperfect Competition with Keynesian Features', *Quarterly Journal of Economics*, **47** (1), 109–38.

Hart, Oliver D. (1985), 'Imperfect Competition in General Equilibrium: An Overview of Recent Work', in Kenneth J. Arrow and Seppo Honkapohja (eds), *Frontiers of Economics*, Oxford: Basil Blackwell, pp. 100–169.

Hausner, Jerzy (1992), *Populist Threat in Transformation of Socialist Society*, Economic and Social Policy series, no. 29, Warsaw: F. Ebert Foundation in Poland, December.

Hayek, Friedrich A. (ed.) (1935), *Collectivist Economic Planning*, London: Routledge and Kegan Paul.

Hillion, Pierre and David S. Young (1995), 'The Czechoslovak Privatization Auction: An Empirical Investigation', manuscript, INSEAD, May.

Hobbes, Thomas (1981) [1651], *Leviathan*, Harmondsworth: Penguin Books.

Holzmann, Róbert, János Gács and Georg Winckler (eds) (1995), *Output Decline in Eastern Europe: Unavoidable, External Influence or Homemade?* International Studies in Economics and Econometrics series, no. 34, Dordrecht, Boston and London: Kluwer Academic Publishers.

Horváth, Piroska (1996), 'Vizsgálatok az állami redisztribúció tanulmányozásához' (Examinations towards a study of state redistribution), mimeo, Budapest.

Hungarian Government (1994), *A Magyar Köztársaság Kormányának privatizációs stratégiája* (The Government of the Republic of Hungary's Privatization Strategy), Budapest: Magyar Köztársaság Kormánya, 11 November.

International Monetary Fund (1994a), *International Financial Statistics Yearbook 1994*, Washington DC: International Monetary Fund.

International Monetary Fund (1994b), *IMF Economic Review*, no. 7.

International Monetary Fund (1994c), *IMF Economic Review*, no. 16.

International Monetary Fund (1994d), *IMF Economic Review*, no. 17.

International Monetary Fund (1994e), *IMF Economic Review*, no. 18.

International Monetary Fund (1995), *International Financial Statistics Yearbook 1995*, Washington DC: IMF.

International Monetary Fund (1996), *International Financial Statistics*, April.

International Monetary Fund (1997), *International Financial Statistics*, February.

Kapitány, Zs. (1989), 'Kereslet és kínálat a 80-as évek autópiacán' (Demand and supply on the car market of the 1980s), *Közgazdasági Szemle*, **36** (6), 592–611.

Kapitány, Zsuzsa (1993), 'Elosztási mechanizmusok és vevői viselkedés Kelet-Európa autópiacain' (Allocation mechanisms and consumer behaviour on the car markets in Eastern Europe), manuscript, Budapest: MTA Közgazdaságtudományi Intézet.

Kapitány, Zs., J. Kornai and J. Szabó (1982), 'Reproduction of the Shortage on the Hungarian Car Market', *Soviet Studies*, **36** (2), 236–56.

Kaufman, Robert R. and Barbara Stallings (1991), 'The Political Economy of Latin American Populism', in Rüdiger Dornbusch and Sebastian Edwards (eds), *The Macroeconomics of Populism in Latin America*, Chicago and London: University of Chicago Press, pp. 15–34.

Kende, Péter (1994), 'Politikai kultúra, civil társadalom és elit az 1988 utáni Magyarországon' (Political culture, civil society and the élite in Hungary after 1988), in *Miért nincs rend Kelet-Közép Európában?* (Why Is There No Order in East Central Europe?), Budapest: Osiris and Századvég, pp. 244–357.

Kéri, L. (1994), 'Mari néni, a száz nap, meg az egyszerű nép' (Aunt Mary, the hundred days, and the ordinary people), *Népszabadság*, 24 October, p. 13.

Kindleberger, Charles P. (1978), *Manias, Panics, and Crashes: A History of Financial Crisis*, New York: Basic Books.

Kis, J. (1994), 'Veszélyből esély – Kis J. a koalícióról' (Prospect out of peril – J. Kis on the coalition), *168 óra*, 14 June, p. 7.

Kocsis, Gy. (1995), 'Mégis, kinek a bőrére?' (Even so, who's paying?), *Heti Világgazaság*, 28 October, p. 100.

Kolodko, G.W. (1993), *From Output Collapse to Sustainable Growth in Transition Economies. The Fiscal Implications*, Working Papers no. 35, Warsaw: Institute of Finance.

Kolodko, G.W. and W.W. McMahon (1987), 'Stagflation and Shortageflation: A Comparative Approach', *Kyklos*, **40** (2), 176–97.

Kopint-Datorg (1994), *Ipari konjunktúrateszt eredmények* (Test Results for Industrial Activity), 4th quarter, Budapest: Kopint-Datorg.

Kopint-Datorg (1996), *Konjunktúrateszt-eredmények a feldolgozóiparban, az építőiparban és a kiskereskedelemben, 1995. IV. negyedév* (Activity Test Results in Manufacturing, Construction and the Retail Trade, 1995, 4th Quarter), Budapest: Kopint-Datorg.

Kopits, G. (1994), 'Midway in the Transition', *Acta Oeconomica*, **46** (3/4), 267–92.

Kopits, G. (1995), 'Hungary's Preannounced Crawling Peg', *Acta Oeconomica*, **47** (3/4), 267–86.

Kornai, János (1959) [1957], *Overcentralization in Economic Administration*, Oxford: Oxford University Press.

Kornai, János (1971), *Anti-Equilibrium*, Amsterdam: North-Holland.

Kornai, János (1972), *Rush versus Harmonic Growth*, Amsterdam: North-Holland.

Kornai, J. (1979), 'Resource-Constrained versus Demand-Constrained Systems', *Econometrica*, **47** (4), 801–19.

Kornai, János (1980), *Economics of Shortage*, Amsterdam: North-Holland.

Kornai, J. (1986), 'The Hungarian Reform Process: Visions, Hopes and Reality', *Journal of Economic Literature*, **24** (4), 1687–737.

Kornai, János (1990) [1989], *The Road to a Free Economy. Shifting from a Socialist System: The Example of Hungary*, New York and London: W.W. Norton.

Kornai, J. (1992a), 'The Principles of Privatization in Eastern Europe', *De Economist*, **140** (2), 153–76.

Kornai, J. (1992b), 'The Postsocialist Transition and the State: Reflections in the Light of Hungarian Fiscal Problems', *American Economic Review*, Papers and Proceedings, **82** (2), 1–21.

Kornai, J. (1992c), 'Visszaesés, veszteglés vagy fellendülés' (Recession, stagnation or recovery), *Magyar Hírlap*, 14 December, pp. 12–13.

Kornai, János (1992d), *The Socialist System: The Political Economy of Com-*

munism, Princeton: Princeton University Press and Oxford: Oxford University Press.

Kornai, J. (1993a), 'The Evolution of Financial Discipline under the Postsocialist System', *Kyklos*, **46** (3), 315–36.

Kornai, J. (1993b), 'Transformational Recession: A General Phenomenon Examined through the Example of Hungary's Development', *Économie Appliquée*, **46** (2), 181–227.

Kornai, J. and J.W. Weibull (1978), 'The Normal State of the Market in a Shortage Economy: A Queue Model', *Scandinavian Journal of Economics*, **80** (4), 375–98.

Kornai, J. and J.W. Weibull (1983), 'Paternalism, Buyers' and Sellers' Market', *Mathematical Social Sciences*, **7** (2) 153–69.

Körösényi, András (1995), 'Kényszerkoalíció vagy természetes szövetség?' (Forced coalition or natural alliance?), in Csaba Gombár, Elemér Hankiss, László Lengyel and Györgyi Várnai (eds), *Kérdőjelek: a magyar kormány, 1994–95* (Question Marks: The Hungarian Government, 1994–95), Budapest: Korridor Politikai Kutatások Központja, pp. 260–80.

Köves, A. (1995a), 'Egy alternatív gazdaságpolitika szükségessége és lehetősége' (The need and scope for an alternative economic policy), *Külgazdaság*, **39** (6), 4–17.

Köves, A. (1995b), 'Gazdaságpolitikai dilemmák és lehetőségek a Bokros-csomag után' (Economic policy dilemmas and potentials after the Bokros package), *Külgazdaság*, **39** (11), 4–18.

Köves, A., K. Lányi, G. Oblath, *et al.* (1993), 'Az exportorientált gazdaságpolitika feltételei és eszközei 1993-ban' (The conditions and means for export-oriented economic policy), *Külgazdaság*, **37** (5), 4–22.

Kowalik, Tadeusz (1992), 'Can Poland Afford a Swedish Model? Social Contract as the Basis for Systemic Transformation', paper presented at the conference 'Post-Socialism: Problems and Prospects', Ambleside, Cumbria, 3–6 July, manuscript.

Krugman, P. R. (1979), 'Increasing Returns, Monopolistic Competition, and International Trade', *Journal of International Economics*, **9** (4), 469–79.

Krugman, Paul (1991), 'Financial Crises in the International Economy' in Martin Feldstein (ed.), *The Risk of Economic Crisis*, Chicago and London: University of Chicago Press, pp. 85–128.

Krugman, Paul (1994), *Peddling Prosperity. Economic Sense and Nonsense in the Age of Diminished Expectations*, New York and London: W. W. Norton.

Kuenne, Robert E. (1967), 'Quality Space, Interproduct Competition, and General Equilibrium Theory', in Robert E. Kuenne (ed.), *Monopolistic Competition Theory: Studies in Impact*, New York: Wiley.

Kurtán, Sándor, Péter Sándor and László Vass (eds) (1991), *Magyarország politikai évkönyve 1991* (Political Yearbook of Hungary 1991), Budapest: Ökonómia Alapítvány and Economix Rt.

Labour Research Institute (1994), *Munkaerőpiaci helyzetjelentés. A munkaerőpiac keresletét és kínálatát alakító folyamatok* (Report on the Labour-Market Situation: The Processes Shaping Supply and Demand on the Labour Market), Budapest: Munkaügyi Kutatóintézet, April.

Lackó, M. (1975), 'Consumer Savings and the Supply Situation', *Acta Oeconomica*, **15** (3/4), 365–84.

Lackó, M. (1989), 'A beruházási hitelpiac feszültségeinek újratermelődése Magyarországon' (The reproduction of tension on the investment credit market in Hungary), *Közgazdasági Szemle*, November, **36** (11), 1323–41.

Lackó, Mária (1995), *Hungarian Hidden Economy in International Comparison – Estimation Method Based on Household Electricity Consumption and Currency Ratio*, paper presented at the conference 'Hungary: Towards a Market Economy', Budapest, 20–21 October 1995, Discussion Paper series no. 25, Budapest: Institute of Economics.

Laki, M. (1993), 'Chances for the Acceleration of Transition: The Case of Hungarian Privatization', *East European Politics and Societies*, Fall, **7** (3), 440–51.

Laky, T. (1984), 'Mítoszok és valóság: Kisvállalkozások Magyarországon' (Myth and reality: small enterprises in Hungary), *Valóság*, **27** (1), 1–17.

Laky, T. (1995), 'A magángazdaság kialakulása és a foglalkoztatottság' (Development of the private economy and employment), *Közgazdasági Szemle*, **42** (7/8), 685–709.

Lányi, K. (1994–95), 'Alkalmazkodás és gazdasági visszaesés Magyarországon és más országokban. I. Tények és magyarázatok. II. Gazdaságpolitika és szelekció' (Adjustment and economic recession in Hungary and other countries. I. Facts and explanations. II. Economic policy and selection), *Társadalmi Szemle*, **49** (12), 13–25 and **50** (1), 3–19.

Larrain, Felipe B. and Marcelo Selowsky (eds) (1991), *The Public Sector and the Latin American Crisis*, San Francisco: ICS Press, International Center for Economic Growth.

Laski, Kazimierz, Amit Bhaduri, Friedrich Levcik *et al.* (1993), 'Transition from the Command to the Market System: What Went Wrong and What to Do Now', manuscript, Vienna: Vienna Institute for Comparative Economic Studies.

Lázár, G. (1993), 'Jólét vagy szabadság? Közvélemény-kutatások a rendszerváltásról' (Welfare or freedom? Public opinion surveys on the change of system), *Mozgó Világ*, **19** (8), 38–51.

Lengyel, György (1994), 'Vélemények a gazdaságról' (Opinions on the economy), in István György Tóth (ed.), *Társadalmi átalakulás: 1992–94.*

Jelentés a Magyar Háztartás Panel III. hullámának eredményeiről (Social Transformation 1992–94. Report on Results of Phase III of the Hungarian Household Panel), Műhelytanulmányok series no. 5, Budapest: BKE, KSH and TÁRKI, pp. 83–90 and 91–9.

Lengyel, László (1995), 'Egérfogó' (Mousetrap), in Csaba Gombár, Elemér Hankiss, László Lengyel and Györgyi Várnai (eds), *Kérdőjelek: a magyar kormány, 1994–95* (Question Marks: the Hungarian Government, 1994–95), Budapest: Korridor Politikai Kutatások Központja, pp. 13–49.

Lindbeck, Assar (1990), *The Swedish Experience*, paper presented at the OECD Conference on the Transition to Market Economies in Central and Eastern Europe, Paris, 28–30 November, Seminar Paper no. 482, Stockholm: Institute for International Economic Studies, December.

Lindbeck, Assar, Per Molander, Torsten Persson *et al.* (1994), *Turning Sweden Around*, Cambridge, Mass. and London: MIT Press.

Lipton, D. and J. Sachs (1990), 'Creating a Market Economy in Eastern Europe: The Case of Poland', *Brookings Papers on Economic Activity*, no. 1, pp. 75–145.

Little, I.M.D., Richard N. Cooper, W. Max Corden and Sarath Rajapatirana (1993), *Boom, Crisis and Adjustment. The Macroeconomic Experience of Developing Countries*, Oxford: Oxford University Press (for World Bank).

Major, I. and P. Mihályi (1994), 'Privatizáció – hogyan tovább?' (Privatization – how to go further), *Közgazdasági Szemle*, **41** (3), 214–28.

Malinvaud, Edmond (1977), *The Theory of Unemployment Reconsidered*, Oxford: Basil Blackwell.

Marshall, Alfred (1961) [1890], *Principles of Economics*, London: Macmillan.

Martos, Béla (1983), 'Gazdasági szabályozási struktúrák és működésük. A nem walrasi eset' (Economic control structures and their functioning. The non-Walrasian case), manuscript, Budapest: MTA Közgazdaságtudományi Intézet.

Martos, B. (1994), 'A nyugdíjak egyenlőtlensége és dekompozíciója' (The disparity and decomposition of pensions), *Közgazdasági Szemle*, **41** (1), 26–48.

McHale, John (1996), 'Equilibrium Employment Rates and Transformational Slumps', mimeo, Cambridge, Mass.: Harvard University, March.

Mexican Ministry of Finance (SHCP) (1995), *Informe sobre la Situación Económica, las Finanzas Públicas y la Deuda Pública*, 4th quarter, Mexico City.

Mexican Ministry of Finance (SHCP) (1996), *Informe sobre la Situación Económica, las Finanzas Públicas y la Deuda Pública*, 4th quarter, Mexico City.

Mihályi, P. (1993), 'Plunder – Squander – Plunder. The Strange Demise of State Ownership', *The Hungarian Quarterly*, **34** (Summer), 62–75.

Mihályi, Péter (1994), 'Privatization in Hungary: An Overview', in Yilmaz Akyüz, Detlef J. Kotte, András Köves and László Szamuely (eds), *Privatization in the Transition Process. Recent Experiences in Eastern Europe*, Geneva: UNCTAD and Budapest: Kopint-Datorg, pp. 363–85.

Mihályi, Péter (1995), 'Privatisation in Hungary: Now Comes the "Hard Core"', paper presented at Fifth World Congress for Central and East European Studies, Warsaw, 6–11 August, mimeo.

Ministry of Finance (1996a), *A gazdaság helyzete 1995–96 fordulóján* (The Economic Situation at the Turn of 1995–96), Budapest: Pénzügyminisztérium, February.

Ministry of Finance (1996b), *Tájékoztató az 1995. évi és az 1996. év eleji gazdasági folyamatokról* (Report on the Economic Processes in 1995 and Early 1996), Budapest, Pénzügyminisztérium, March.

Mizsei, K. (1992), 'Privatisation in Eastern Europe: A Comparative Study of Poland and Hungary', *Soviet Studies*, **44** (2), 283–96.

Muraközy, László (1993), 'Az átmenet költségvetése Magyarországon, 1986–1992' (The transition budget in Hungary, 1986–92), manuscript, Debrecen: Kossuth Lajos Tudományegyetem.

Murphy, Emma (1993), 'Israel', in Tim Niblock and Emma Murphy (eds), *Economic and Political Liberalization in the Middle East*, London and New York: British Academic Press.

Murrell, Peter (1990), 'An Evolutionary Perspective on Reform of the Eastern European Economies', manuscript, College Park: University of Maryland.

Murrell, P. (1992), 'Evolutionary and Radical Approaches to Economic Reform', *Economics of Planning*, **25** (1), 79–95.

Murrell, P. and Y. Wang (1993), 'When Privatization Should Be Delayed: The Effect of Communist Legacies on Organizational and Institutional Reforms', *Journal of Comparative Economics*, **17** (2), 385–406.

Musgrave, Richard A. and Musgrave, Peggy B. (1980) [1973], *Public Finance in Theory and Practice*, 3rd edn, New York: McGraw-Hill.

Nagy, A. (1994a), 'Transition and Institutional Change', *Structural Change and Economic Dynamics*, **5** (2), 315–27.

Nagy, A. (1994b), 'Import Liberalization in Hungary', *Acta Oeconomica*, **46** (1/2), 1–26.

National Bank of Hungary (1994), *Annual Report 1993*, Budapest: Magyar Nemzeti Bank.

National Bank of Hungary (1995a), *Annual Report 1994*, Budapest: Magyar Nemzeti Bank.

National Bank of Hungary (1995b), *Monthly Report*, no. 3.

National Bank of Hungary (1996a), *Az 1995. évi gazdasági és pénzügyi folyamatokról* (The Economic and Monetary Processes in 1995), Budapest: Magyar Nemzeti Bank, February.

National Bank of Hungary (1996b), *Havi Jelentés* (Monthly Report), no. 2.

National Bank of Hungary (1996c), *Előterjesztés és jelentés az 1996. évi rendes közgyűlésnek a Magyar Nemzeti Bank 1995. évi üzlettervéről* (Presentation and Report to the 1996 Annual General Assembly on the 1995 Business Plan of the National Bank of Hungary), Budapest: Magyar Nemzeti Bank, April.

Nelson, Joan (1988), 'The Political Economy of Stabilization: Commitment, Capacity and Public Response', in Robert H. Bates (ed.), *Toward a Political Economy of Development: A Rational Choice Perspective*, Berkeley: University of California Press, pp. 80–130.

Nelson, L.D. and I.Y. Kuzes (1994), 'Evaluating the Russian Voucher Privatization Program', *Comparative Economic Studies*, **36** (1), 55–67.

Nelson, Richard R. and Sidney G. Winter (1982), *An Evolutionary Theory of Economic Change*, Cambridge, Mass.: Harvard University Press.

Nuti, D.M. (1986), 'Hidden and Repressed Inflation in Soviet-Type Economies: Definitions, Measurements and Stabilization', *Contributions to Political Economy*, **5** (March), 37–82.

Oates, Wallace E. (1988), 'On the Nature and Measurement of Fiscal Illusion: A Survey', in Geoffrey Brennan, Bhajan S. Grewal and Peter Grenewegen (eds), *Taxation and Fiscal Federalism: Essays in Honour of Russell Matthews*, Sydney: Australian National University Press, pp. 65–82.

Oblath, G. (1991), 'A magyarországi importliberalizálás korlátai, sikerei és kérdőjelei' (The limits, successes and queries of import liberalization in Hungary), *Külgazdaság*, **35** (5), 4–13.

Oblath, G. (1995), 'A költségvetési deficit makrogazdasági hatásai Magyarországon' (The macroeconomic effects of the budget deficit in Hungary), *Külgazdaság*, **39** (7/8), 22–33.

Oblath, Gábor (1996), 'Makrogazdasági folyamatok' (Macroeconomic processes), in *Konjunktúrajelentés. A világgazdaság és a magyar gazdaság helyzete és kilátásai 1996 tavaszán* (Business Activity Report. The Situation and Prospects of the World Economy and the Hungarian Economy), Budapest: Kopint-Datorg, no. 1, pp. 79–118.

Oblath, G. and Á. Valentinyi (1993), 'Seignorage és inflációs adó – néhány makroökonómiai összefüggés magyarországi alkalmazása. I. A pénzteremtésből eredő állami bevétel és az államadósság. II. Az államháztartás, a jegybank és az államadósság dinamikája' (Seignorage and inflationary tax – application to Hungary of some macroeconomic relations. I. State revenue from money creation and public debt. II. The budget, the bank of issue and the dynamics of public debt), *Közgazdasági Szemle*, **40** (10), 825–947 and **40** (11), 939–74.

OECD (1996), *OECD Economic Outlook*, December.

OECD (1997), *Economic Indicators*, January.

Offe, C. (1991), 'Capitalism by Democratic Design? Democratic Theory Facing the Triple Transition in East Central Europe', *Social Research*, **58** (4), 864–902.

Phelps, Edmund S. (1994), *Structural Slumps. The Modern Equilibrium Theory of Unemployment, Interest, and Assets*, Cambridge, Mass.: Harvard University Press.

Portes, R. (1994), 'Transformation Traps', *The Economic Journal*, **104** (426), 1178–89.

Portes, R., R.E. Quandt, D. Winter and S. Yeo (1987), 'Macroeconomic Planning and Disequilibrium: Estimates for Poland, 1955–1980', *Econometrica*, **55** (1), 19–41.

Portes, R. and D. Winter (1980), 'Disequilibrium Estimates for Consumption Goods Markets in Centrally Planned Economies', *Review of Economic Studies*, **47** (1), 137–59.

Przeworski, Adam (1991), *Democracy and the Market: Political and Economic Reforms in Eastern Europe and Latin America. Studies in Rationality and Social Change*, Cambridge: Cambridge University Press.

Przeworski, Adam (1993), 'Economic Reforms, Public Opinion, and Political Institutions: Poland in the Eastern European Perspective', in Luiz Carlos Bresser Pereira, José María Maravall and Adam Przeworski (eds), *Economic Reforms in New Democracies: A Social-Democratic Approach*, Cambridge: Cambridge University Press, pp. 132–98.

Rawls, John (1971), *A Theory of Justice*, Cambridge, Mass.: Harvard University Press.

Razin, Assaf and Efraim Sadka (1993), *The Economy of Modern Israel: Malaise and Promise*, Chicago and London: University of Chicago Press.

Róbert, Péter (1995), *A szociálpolitikával kapcsolatos attitűdök alakulása* (The Trend in Attitudes towards Social Policy), study for the research project 'The Effects of the Public Finance Reform on the Distribution of Household Income', Budapest: TÁRKI.

Robinson, Joan (1933), *The Economics of Imperfect Competition*, London: Macmillan.

Rockenbauer, Zoltán (1991), 'Társadalmi ünnepek, tüntetések és sztrájkok az 1990-es esztendőben' (National holidays, demonstrations and strikes in 1990), in Sándor Kurtán, Péter Sándor and László Vass (eds), *Magyarország politikai évkönyve 1991* (Political Yearbook of Hungary 1991), Budapest: Ökonómia Alapítvány and Economix Rt, pp. 213–9.

Roland, G. (1994a), 'The Role of Political Constraints in Transition Strategies', *Economics of Transition*, **2** (1), 27–41.

Roland, G. (1994b), 'On the Speed and Sequencing of Privatisation and Restructuring', *The Economic Journal*, **104** (426), 1158–68.

Rosati, Dariusz K. (1993), 'Poland: Glass Half Empty', in Richard Portes (ed.), *Economic Transformation in Central Europe. A Progress Report*, London: Centre for Economic Policy Research, pp. 211–73.

Rosati, D.K. (1994), 'Output Decline during Transition from Plan to Market: A Reconsideration', *Economics of Transition*, **2** (4), 419–41.

Rose, Richard and Christian Haerpfer (1993), *Adapting to Transformation in Eastern Europe: New Democracies Barometer – II*, Studies in Public Policy series no. 212, Glasgow: University of Strathclyde.

Rutland, P. (1994), 'Privatisation in Russia: One Step Forward, Two Steps Back?', *Europe-Asia Studies*, **46** (7), 1109–31.

Sachs, Jeffrey D. (ed.) (1989), *Developing Country Debt and Economic Performance*, Chicago: University of Chicago Press and National Bureau of Economic Research.

Sachs, J.D. (1990), 'What Is to Be Done?', *The Economist*, 13 January, pp. 19–24.

Sachs, Jeffrey D. (1993), *Poland's Jump to the Market Economy*, Cambridge and London: MIT Press.

Sachs, Jeffrey D. (1994), 'Life in the Economic Emergency Room', in John Williamson (ed.), *The Political Economy of Policy Reform*, Washington DC: Institute for International Economics, pp. 503–23.

Sachs, Jeffrey D. (1996), 'Economic Transition and the Exchange Rate Regime', mimeo, Cambridge: Harvard Institute for International Development, Harvard University.

Sachs, Jeffrey D. and Felipe B. Larrain (1993), *Macroeconomics in the Global Economy*, New York: Harvester Wheatsheaf.

Sachs, Jeffrey D., Aaron Tornell and Andres Velasco (1995), *The Collapse of the Mexican Peso: What Have We Learned?*, Discussion Paper no. 1724, Cambridge: Harvard Institute of Economic Research, Harvard University, May.

Saunders, Christopher T. (ed.) (1995), *Eastern Europe in Crisis and the Way Out*, Houndmills and London: Vienna Institute for Comparative Studies and Macmillan.

Schumpeter, Joseph A. (1976) [1942], *Capitalism, Socialism and Democracy*, New York: Harper and Row.

Scitovsky, T. (1985), 'Pricetakers' Plenty: A Neglected Benefit of Capitalism', *Kyklos*, **38** (4), 517–36.

Seleny, Anna (1993), 'The Long Transformation: Hungarian Socialism, 1949–89', manuscript, Cambridge, Mass.: Department of Political Science, MIT.

Sen, A. (1995), 'Rationality and Social Choice', *American Economic Review*, **85** (1), 1–24.

Shleifer, A. and Vishny, R. (1992), 'Pervasive Shortages under Socialism', *RAND Journal of Economics*, **23** (2), 237–46.

Siklaky, I. (1989), 'Perújrafelvétel az állami tulajdon ügyében' (Retrial in the case of the state ownership), *Magyar Nemzet*, 11 July, p. 5.

Simon, A. (1988), 'A hiány makroökonómiájáról. A hiány fogalma' (On the macroeconomics of shortage. The concept of shortage), *Közgazdasági Szemle*, **35** (1), 1–17.

Simon, A. (1989), 'Piac, adagolás, kiutalás' (Market, rationing, allocation), *Közgazdasági Szemle*, **36** (12), 1445–67.

Simonovits, András (1992), *Cycles and Stagnation in Socialist Economies: A Mathematical Analysis*, Oxford: Basil Blackwell.

Slider, D. (1994), 'Privatization in Russia's Regions', *Post-Soviet Affairs*, **10** (4), 367–96.

Smith, Adam (1898) [1776], *An Inquiry into the Nature and Causes of the Wealth of Nations*, London: George Routledge and Son, Limited.

Soós, Károly Attila (1986), *Terv, kampány, pénz* (Plan, Campaign, Money), Budapest: Közgazdasági és Jogi Könyvkiadó.

Stark, D. (1990), 'Privatization in Hungary: From Plan to Market or From Plan to Clan?', *East European Politics and Societies*, **4** (3), 351–92.

Stark, David (1994), *Recombinant Property in East European Capitalism*, Public Lecture series 8, Budapest: Collegium Budapest, Institute for Advanced Study, December.

Stark, David and László Bruszt (1995), 'Network Properties of Assets and Liabilities: Patterns of Inter-Enterprise Ownership in the Postsocialist Transformation', paper presented at the workshop on 'Dynamics of Industrial Transformation: East Central European and East Asian Comparisons', Budapest: Budapest University of Economics, May.

Sükösd, M. (1995), '1995: az identitás gondjai' (1995: The problems of identity), *Mozgó Világ*, **21** (2), 29–33.

Sunkel, Oswaldo (ed.) (1993), *Development from Within. Toward a Neostructuralist Approach for Latin America*, Boulder and London: Lynne Rienner Publishers.

Surányi, Gy. (1995a), 'A gazdaság örökölt struktúrái gúzsba kötik az országot. Válaszol Surányi György, a Nemzeti Bank elnöke' (The inherited economic structures shackle the country. György Surányi, President of the National Bank, replies), *Heti Világgazdaság*, 29 April, pp. 47–8.

Surányi, Gy. (1995b), 'Önmagunkkal kell megállapodásra jutni. Beszélgetés árakról, bérekről, kamatokról Surányi Györggyel, az MNB elnökével. Bossányi Katalin interjúja' (We have to come to terms with ourselves. Conversation about prices, wages and interest rates with György Surányi,

President of the National Bank. Interview by Katalin Bossányi), *Népszabadság*, 30 December, pp. 1 and 10.

Surányi, Gy. (1996), 'Jobban igen, másként nem. Szombati MH-extra Surányi Györggyel, a Magyar Nemzeti Bank elnökével. Pintér Dezső riportja' (It can be done better, but not in other ways. A Saturday supplement interview with György Surányi, President of the Hungarian National Bank. Report by Dezső Pintér), *Magyar Hírlap*, 6 January, p. 9.

Szabó, I. (1994), 'Minden a mézeshetekben dől el' (Everything depends on the honeymoon), interview by Gy. Varga, *Figyelő*, 26 May, pp. 16–17.

Szabó, I. (1995), report in *168 óra*, 7 March, p. 15.

Szabó, J. (1985), 'Kínálati rugalmatlanság, elszaladó kereslet, készletek és hiány' (Inelasticity of supply, runaway demand, stocks and shortage), *Közgazdasági Szemle*, **32** (3), 305–19.

Szakolczai, Attila (1994), 'A forradalmat követő megtorlás során kivégzettekről' (Those executed during the reprisals after the revolution), in János Bak, *et al.* (eds), *Évkönyv III, 1956* (Yearbook III, 1956), Budapest: 1956-os Intézet, pp. 237–56.

Szalai, E. (1994), 'Az elitek metamorfózisa' (Metamorphosis of the élites), *Magyar Hírlap*, 24 September, p. 8.

Szelényi, Iván (1994), *Circulation of Elites in Post-Communist Transitions*, Working Paper series 3, Chicago: University of Michigan, Advanced Study Center, International Institute, August.

Szentgyörgyvári, Artúr and Ilona Baár (1996), 'A magyar nemzetgazdaság nemzetközi versenyképessége 1995-ben, kitekintés 1996-ra és 1997-re' (The international competitiveness of the Hungarian economy in 1995, and the outlook for 1996 and 1997), mimeo, Budapest: Magyar Nemzeti Bank, April.

Tóth, I.Gy. (1994), 'A jóléti rendszer az átmenet időszakában' (The welfare system in the transition period), *Közgazdasági Szemle*, **49** (3), 313–40.

Tyrie, A. (1995), 'Statistical Review. Recent Macroeconomic Developments', *Economics of Transition*, **3** (1), 129–48.

United Nations (1992), *Industrial Statistical Yearbook 1989. Volume 1. General Industrial Statistics*, New York: United Nations.

United Nations Economic Commission for Europe (1993), *Economic Bulletin for Europe 1992*, vol. 44, New York: UN ECE.

United Nations Economic Commission for Europe (1994a), *Economic Survey of Europe in 1993–94*, New York and Geneva: UN ECE.

United Nations Economic Commission for Europe (1994b), *Economic Bulletin for Europe 1994*, vol. 46, New York and Geneva: UN ECE.

United Nations Economic Commission for Europe (1995), *Economic Survey of Europe in 1994–95*, New York and Geneva: UN ECE.

Vanicsek, M. (1995), 'A privatizált társaságok hatékonysága' (The efficiency of privatized companies), *Figyelő*, 26 January, pp. VI–VII.

Várhegyi, Éva (1993), 'A monetáris politika jellege és hatása 1987–1992 között' (The nature and influence of monetary policy between 1987 and 1992), manuscript, Budapest: Pénzügykutató Rt., October.

Végh, C.A. (1992), 'Stopping High Inflation', *IMF Staff Papers*, **39** (3), 626–95.

Vintrová, R. (1993), 'The General Recession and the Structural Adaptation Crisis', *Eastern European Economics*, **31** (3), 78–94.

Voszka, É. (1992), 'Not Even the Contrary is True: The Transfigurations of Centralization and Decentralization', *Acta Oeconomica*, **44** (1/2), 77–94.

Voszka, É. (1993), 'Variations on the Theme of Self-Privatization', *Acta Oeconomica*, **45** (3/4), 310–18.

Voszka, Éva (1994), *Centralization, Renationalization, Redistribution: The Role of the Government in Changing the Ownership Structure in Hungary, 1989–93*, Discussion Paper series 916, London: Centre for Economic Policy Research, February.

Waterbury, John (1989), 'The Political Management of Economic Adjustment and Reform', in Joan M. Nelson and contributors, *Fragile Coalitions: The Politics of Economic Adjustment*, New Brunswick and Oxford: Transaction Books, pp. 39–56.

Weibull, J.W. (1984), 'A Stock–Flow Approach to General Equilibrium with Trade Frictions', *Applied Mathematics and Computation*, **14** (1), 63–76.

Weitzman, Martin L. (1989), 'On Buyers' and Sellers' Markets under Capitalism and Socialism', manuscript, Cambridge, Mass.: Harvard Institute of Economic Research, Harvard University.

Williamson, John (ed.) (1990), *Latin American Adjustment. How Much Has Happened?*, Washington DC: Institute for International Economics.

World Bank (1994), *Averting the Old Age Crisis. Policies to Protect the Old and Promote Growth*, Oxford: Oxford University Press.

World Bank (1995a), *Hungary: Structural Reforms for Sustainable Growth. First Draft*, Document of the World Bank, Country Operations Division, Central Europe Department, Report no. 13577-HU, Washington DC: World Bank, 10 February.

World Bank (1995b), *Hungary: Structural Reforms for Sustainable Growth*, Document of the World Bank, Country Operations Division, Central Europe Department, Report no. 13577-HU, Washington DC: World Bank, 12 June.

World Bank (1995c), *World Tables 1995*, Washington DC: World Bank.

World Bank (1995d), *Magyarország. Szerkezetváltás és tartós növekedés* (Hungary: Structural Change and Lasting Growth), Washington DC: World Bank, November.

World Economy Research Institute (1994), *Poland: International Economic Report 1993–94*, Warsaw: WERI, Warsaw School of Economics.

Zukowski, R. (1993), 'Stabilization and Recession in a Transitional Economy: The Case of Poland', *World Development*, **21** (7), 1163–78.

Appendix: List of studies and details of their first English publication

'Eliminating the Shortage Economy. A general Analysis and Examination of the Developments in Hungary', *Economics of Transition*, 1995, **3** (1), 13–37 and **3** (2), 149–68. Reproduced by permission of Oxford University Press.

'Lasting Growth as the Top Priority: Tensions and Government Economic Policy in Hungary', *Acta Oeconomica*, 1995, **47** (1), 1–38.

'A Steep Road. A Conversation with János Kornai' (An interview by László Zsolt Szabó), *The Hungarian Quarterly*, 1995, **36** (Summer), 11–20.

'The Dilemmas of Hungarian Economic Policy', *Acta Oeconomica*, 1996, in Béla K. Király and András Bozóki (eds), *Lawful Revolution in Hungary, 1989–94*, Boulder: Social Science Monographs, Highland Lakes: Atlantic Research and Publications and New York: Columbia University Press, 1995, pp. 323–49.

'Paying the Bill for Goulash Communism: Hungarian Development and Macro Stabilization in a Political Economy Perspective', *Social Research*, Winter 1996, **63** (4), 943–1040.

'Adjustment without Recession. A Case Study of Hungarian Stabilization', presented at the OECD–CCET Colloquium 'Economic Transformation and Development of Central and Eastern Europe: What Lessons from the 1990s?', 29–30 May 1996, Paris. © OECD, 1997, *Lessons from the Economic Transition – Central and Eastern Europe*, edited by Salvatore Zecchini, pp. 123–51. Reproduced by permission of the OECD and Kluwer Academic Publishers.

'The Social Issue in the Era of Transition. János Kornai in Conversation with Mihály Laki', *The Hungarian Quarterly*, 1996, **37** (Spring), 58–71.

'The Citizen and the State: Reform of the Welfare System', paper presented as the 3rd Tjalling C. Koopmans Lecture of International Institute for Applied System Analysis (IIASA, Laxenburg, Austria), June 1996. First published in this volume.

Name index

Subject index